Gender Perspectives in Law

Volume 3

The series 'Gender Perspectives in Law' discusses all-encompassing gender-competent legal questions. Having a gender-competent approach is required when considering the highest values and normative standards of modern international, European, and national law. Raising awareness about gender equality issues means investing in the creation, interpretation, and implementation of legislation that is more fair, just, and equitable and will also contribute to a comprehensive understanding of social reality, as well as to gender-competent political, legal and economic decision-making and public policies.

The series accepts monographs focusing on a specific topic, as well as edited collections of articles covering a specific theme or collections of articles.

Ivana Krstić • Marco Evola • Maria Isabel Ribes Moreno
Editors

Legal Issues of International Law from a Gender Perspective

Co-funded by the Erasmus+ Programme of the European Union

LAWGEM
Master`s Study Program
Law and Gender

Springer

Editors
Ivana Krstić
University of Belgrade
Belgrade, Serbia

Marco Evola
Department of Law
LUMSA
Palermo, Italy

Maria Isabel Ribes Moreno
University of Cádiz
Cadiz, Spain

This project has been funded with support from the European Commission. This publication [communication] reflects the views only of the author, and the Commission cannot be held responsible for any use which may be made of the information contained therein.

ISSN 2731-8346 ISSN 2731-8354 (electronic)
Gender Perspectives in Law
ISBN 978-3-031-13458-6 ISBN 978-3-031-13459-3 (eBook)
https://doi.org/10.1007/978-3-031-13459-3

This Springer imprint is published by the registered company Springer Nature Switzerland AG
The registered company address is: Gewerbestrasse 11, 6330 Cham, Switzerland

Preface

The book series *Gender Perspectives in Law* is a systemic attempt to provide all-encompassing gender-competent legal knowledge. The term gender-competent legal knowledge is used to accentuate the reconsideration of different fields of legal knowledge from the point of gender equality approach and with offering relevant and convincing arguments in that regard. This term is sometimes replaced with the term "gender-sensitive", which also refers to awareness about the importance of gender equality approach and to its implementing in theoretical and scientific knowledge production. Having a gender-competent approach in legal education is required when considering the highest values and normative standards of modern international, European, and national law. Raising awareness about gender equality issues among researchers and academic scholars in the field of law and other multidisciplinary fields relevant for legal theory and practice, educating in a gender-sensitive manner law students (future lawyers, judges, prosecutors, public officials, members of parliament, and governmental bodies), as well as students of humanities-social sciences, means investing in the creation, interpretation, and implementation of legislation that is more fair, just, and equitable. Prosecutors and judges in particular, but also other legal professionals in all fields of legal practice, public administration, and policy decision-making need to be trained and sensitized in order to encourage a gender-sensitive approach. This will contribute to a more rich and comprehensive understanding of social reality, as well as to gender-competent political, legal, and economic decision-making and public policies. In other words, it means investing into the future based on more gender justice and more social justice and human rights protection in general. In the end, it will help fulfil the essence of contemporary law—equal respect and protection for all individuals, which leads to their equal opportunities and diminishes the possibility of gender discrimination.

This book series, *Gender Perspectives in Law*, attempts to cover all relevant subjects of legal knowledge from a gender equality perspective. The plural designation is entitled because there is a plurality of feminist understanding of gender equality issues generally speaking and insofar also within the law. The call for papers was open for professionals in legal, political, sociological, and historical fields of interest with an attempt to cover, as much as possible, specific relevant topics, in order to provide an overview of the gender competent deconstructing and reconsidering the way they are articulated in the dominant thought, i.e. the mainstream within the law. The authors in the series' volumes try to establish a gender equality approach to different fields of law while taking into consideration specific issues of their interest and attempting to consider chosen different aspects of legal knowledge and practice in a paradigmatic gender-competent manner. They attempt to critically reconsider the dominant moulds of legal knowledge and present innovative gender-sensitive and gender-competent insights relating to different issues within all fields of law, in order to introduce new research topics relevant for gender equality in law, as well as to stimulate the development of a legal and institutional framework for achieving gender equality in real life. The degree to which mainstream knowledge has been reconsidered from a gender equality perspective differs between contributors. Moreover, a variety of relevant legal subjects and other closely related subject matters are covered in varying degrees by the selected texts.

This book series *Gender Perspectives in Law* encouraged scholars and experts from different fields of law and humanities-social sciences to reconstruct their legal and multidisciplinary knowledge from the standpoint of gender equality. This book series should inspire further attempts of this kind, as a reconsideration of legal and multidisciplinary knowledge from a gender perspective has become an axiomatic task. If contemporary law is defined primarily from the human rights point of view, then it is necessary to take a gender equality perspective; the human rights foundation of law cannot be regarded as the civilizational standard without also incorporating women's rights and gender equality approach in general, articulating them in the mainstream legal and political thought, and eliminating gender-based biases and discrimination within the dominant legal systems.

This third book in the series *Gender Perspectives in Law*, which is titled *Legal Issues of International Law from a Gender Perspective,* offers a new perspective on international law, that was, for a long time, male-dominant and gender-neutral. However, this gender blindness led to many injustices, non-recognition of certain rights, and to impunity for serious crimes. The book covers the development of gender perspectives in different branches of international law. Thus, some universal standards are covered and explained. However, particular attention is reserved for the European human rights system. Therefore, the book provides an explanation of external policies of the EU in relation to sex, sexual orientation, and gender identity. Also, special focus is given to the relevant jurisprudence of the European Court of Human Rights in relation to gender and sexual orientation, female reproduction, and sexuality. The authors explain not only the importance of an adequate legal framework for combating gender inequality but also the detrimental effect of deeply rooted gender stereotypes and prejudices. Afterward, the development of particular branches is presented, such as a gender-sensitive approach to the prevention of war crimes, gender perspectives in refugee law, as well as the development of gender-sensitive environmental law. Additionally, the problematic situation of discrimination in the workplace is addressed from different approaches. Many discussions, especially among EU member states, are reserved for the issue of women's participation in the company boards, while another interesting topic is growing awareness of gender equality in an international trade agreement. Finally, the book also offers a historical perspective of the development of international law in the interwar period, with a particular focus on the situation in Yugoslavia. This book aims to critically reconsider the dominant moulds of legal knowledge and present innovative gender-sensitive and gender-competent insights relating to different issues within international law, in order to introduce new research topics relevant to gender equality, as well as to stimulate the development of an international legal and institutional framework for achieving greater gender equality in practice. The collection of essays offered in this book will be of interest to all those working in the field of international law, as well as to students and academics who can broaden and deepen their research on different legal issues of international law from gender perspectives.

This book includes papers written by Marco Evola, Ivana Jelić, Ludovica Poli, Berfu Yalçın and Alparslan Özaltuğ, Rigmor Argren, Ivana Krstić, Bojana Čučković, Linde Verhoeven and Alexandra Timmer, Mareike Froehlich, and Sanja Djajić.

Marco Evola deals with the scope and content of the EU external action. He evaluates how non-discrimination provisions based on sex, sexual orientation, and gender identity are framed within EU external relations and concludes that the approach is neither holistic, nor homogeneous. EU external action covers issues such as political participation, family law, marriage, birth registry, registration of same-sex partnerships, same-sex marriage, property rights, and inheritance. The author argues that gender equality is enshrined in all fields of its external relations, while non-discrimination on the ground of sexual orientation and gender identity is limited only to EU accession and the EU Neighbourhood Policy. Evola thus finds that non-discrimination on mentioned grounds is not important per se, but only in terms of its contribution to the EU's broader set of goals that it has set itself. The EU's external gender quality action is exposed to two different approaches: one based on economic reasons, which have been the driving force since the establishment of the organization, and the other based on human rights protection in the EU, which has just recently come into focus. It is crucial to strike the balance between these two approaches towards non-discrimination. The author argues that the EU institutions' practice shows that the economic approach has weakened the rationale of advancing human rights and combating prejudices and root causes of discrimination against women and LGBTIQ persons. Evola identifies several factors that decrease the capacity of the EU's external action to enhance human rights protection and concludes that these factors influence EU strategies and can seriously affect the attainment of the objective of promoting gender equality and the LGBTIQ community's rights.

Ivana Jelić evaluates the jurisprudence of the European Court of Human Rights (ECtHR) in relation to gender equality. The author's starting position is that gender equality is one of the main principles enshrined in the European Convention on Human Rights (ECHR), and its promotion demonstrates the evolving interpretation of the Convention as a living instrument. Non-discrimination in the Court's view was broadened by recognizing indirect discrimination and positive measures as a means of achieving substantial equality. According to the author, this is crucial as direct discrimination cases are rare and women are exposed to inequalities usually as a result of gender-neutral norms and practices. Jelić classifies jurisprudence of the ECtHR in relation to gender equality into three segments: (1) case-law in relation to Article 14 of the ECHR that covers direct gender discrimination; (2) domestic violence and trafficking that disproportionately affect women in practice and require their special protection; and (3) specific issues that affect women, such as violence against women and reproductive rights. An overview of the most relevant cases shows that, unlike gender religious identity cases, the Court provides extensive protection in cases that concern domestic violence, when the States' margin of appreciation is limited. Jelić also notes that the ECtHR very much relies on international jurisprudence on gender equality protection, and that cases of other international bodies influence gender sensitivity in the interpretation of norms by the Court itself. However, the author claims that feminist justice is still underdeveloped, when compared to what is needed to truly protect women, and argues that the Court avoids discovering the gendered aspects of violations, especially in cases of indirect discrimination against women. Nevertheless, the author concludes that the most recent gender-sensitive judgments are quite significant from the perspective of feminist justice and can help in the creation of a gender equality culture.

Ludovica Poli considers the impact of gender stereotypes on women's rights. Her starting point is that the female role in reproduction pushes and incites gender stereotypes about motherhood and sexuality. Childbearing and motherhood have a strong cultural dimension, given that in many societies, they represent a requirement and a clearly defined social function ascribed to women. She explores the jurisprudence of the European Court of Human Rights (ECtHR) and UN treaty bodies, which is divided into three segments: (1) reproductive capacity of girls and women; (2) access to reproductive health services; and (3) preconceptions about female sexuality. As for the last segment, the author devotes a section to the analysis of the Carvalho Pinto v. Portugal case, where the ECtHR recognized the violation of the ECHR, considering that the national court's decision to reduce the compensation amount was based on the applicant's age and sex, confirming prejudices held by the Portuguese judiciary with regard to the applicant's sexuality. Poli highlights the detrimental effect that gender stereotypes about female sexuality and reproduction have on women's fundamental rights, as they can lead to child marriage, female genital mutilations, ostracism, and other harmful practices. She believes that their growing recognition increases attention to obstetric violence, where she cites the CEDAW Committee's case S.F.M. v. Spain. She also refers to the CEDAW Committee's findings that denying access to contraception is considered to be gender discrimination. However, addressing the issue of abortion requires a deeper understanding of gender discrimination, as well as women's right to sex life separate from reproduction. Poli claims that violent acts in reproductive healthcare are persistent due to the lack of knowledge on the sexual and reproductive rights of women.

Berfu Yalçın and Alparslan Özaltuğ contributed to this volume with a paper dealing with discrimination in the workplace for LGBTQ persons. Yalcin and

Oyaltug claim that sexual orientation discrimination can occur in the workplace in many forms. The authors focus on European standards enshrined in the EU law and the relevant jurisprudence of the European Court of Human Rights (ECtHR). They contend that while the right to work is not guaranteed by the European Convention on Human Rights (ECHR), the ECtHR has assessed certain employment relationships within Article 8 (the privacy rights). On the other side, they present some of the most important provisions of the Employment Framework Directive (2000/78/EC), which provide protection from discrimination in the EU, and which is further supported by a broad interpretation of the Court of Justice of the EU (CJEU). Although the authors acknowledge the Directive's importance, they also highlight some challenges, such as discrimination during job interviews, discrimination in the workplace, whether sincere statements from the victim be sufficient for the prima facie case, the degree of victim status, and the degree of ratione personae. They argue that the victim status should be interpreted broadly in order to provide proper protection. Their position is also that both courts accept that the impartiality of the enterprise might be a justification for some rules that are discriminatory. The obligation to conform to heteronormative social rules, on the other hand, is not considered a legitimate cause. The same judgement holds true for an employer's homophobic speech, which directly hinders LGBTQ individuals' access to work and is not protected under Article 10 of the ECHR, which guarantees the freedom of expression. Moreover, it can bring about the positive obligation of States in order to protect the LGBTQ population. Finally, the authors devote a segment to the analyses of the Directive's exception for churches, which has been accepted by many European States and, they argue, allows the homophobic dynamics to survive. Their conclusion is that national courts, as well as influences and trends in human rights law, can minimize the effect of this exception.

Rigmor Argren offers a reconsideration of the Law on Armed Conflict (LOAC) from the feminist viewpoint. The analysis applies the feminist legal theory to the LOAC as a preventive legal regime. The author argues that a refined understanding of gender perspectives could contribute to enhancing resilience and strengthening the overall respect for the LOAC, thus increasing the protection of all persons in an armed conflict. The intention of this paper is to explore what insights a feminist reading of the obligation to prevent war crimes might bring to the table. The author seeks to address the gap in research by applying a gender lens to the (civil) legal obligation that States have to prevent war crimes in the first place. For that purpose, Argren considers critically the gendered nature of public international law. She assumes that from both a historical and contemporary perspective, the fundamental observation of international law as decidedly masculine still holds true, which can be evidenced in both organizational and normative terms. Public law has its roots in public/private dichotomy, insofar as the whole area of public international law has been described as gendered: the public being male, the private being female. It follows that the State has been seen as intrinsically male. She accentuates the social/political reality that war brings monumental suffering, directly and indirectly, which is not limited to civilian women only. But it is important to remember that when the veil of victimhood is lifted from women in armed conflict, wars can also serve as springboards, especially for women to gain access to the public domain, for example, as indispensable workers. However, as soon as the war is over, the need for women's return to the private realm of household duties resurfaces. The author also points to the differences in how males and females experience living through conflict. However, the differences in experiences of armed conflict do not stop at gender: its impact will also vary depending on race, class, socioeconomic circumstances, urban or rural location, family situation, age, employment, sexuality, and health. The author remarks that the LOAC should be applied without discrimination on any ground, as is customary in international and non-international armed conflicts.

Ivana Krstić focuses on the international refugee law and the recognition of women who need international protection. Although a large number of women have been forced into displacement and face many challenges, the international refugee law, which is based on the 1951 Convention on the Status of Refugees and its 1967 Protocol, has been gender-neutral for a long time. The five grounds explicitly recognized in the 1951 Convention as prosecution grounds do not include "sex/gender". However, the author argues that refugee women are protected by the 1951 Convention either as a "social group", or in a more individualized and at the same time more complex manner when gender-related claims intersect with other prohibited grounds, such as race, nationality, ethnicity, or religion. Krstić also claims that gender-based persecution has very specific forms, and it needs to be recognized in national legislation and understood by public authorities in order to provide adequate protection to women refugees. In addition, the author emphasizes that this protection cannot be granted without the introduction of a gender-sensitive procedure, development of gender-sensitive reception procedures and support services, and the issuing of gender guidelines. However, the author underlines that this does not mean that women are subjected to different asylum procedures than men, but that their specific position is recognized and that some phases in the procedure are designed to remove obstacles to their access to asylum and an efficient and just procedure. The author concludes that it is fair to say that despite its significant development, the refugee law is "not yet there" in terms of providing the full recognition and protection of women. Krstić points to the major challenges to the refugee regime for women, such as the existence of stereotypical views, lack of understanding of different forms of gender-based violence and their consequences to women, the need for a better assessment of asylum claims through the lenses of female refugees, and the acceptance that actors of persecution can also be private actors.

Bojana Čučković analyzes international law through gender lenses claiming first, that international regulations are gradually incorporating the gender equality perspective, and second, that international law has become gender-sensitive but not yet gender-responsive and gender responsible. The author also finds that the international environmental law (IEL) is more gender-sensitive than other branches of public international law. The initial silence on the matter has been steadily overcome with international instruments adopted from the 1990s onward. These instruments first acknowledged the influence that environmental degradation has had on women and the role they play in addressing it, and later included gender equality as an integral part of the treaty commitments. The author challenges the practical implications of gender-sensitive provisions contained in international environmental instruments and the potential for achieving concrete results from the point of "their capability to enhance the prospects of a more successful implementation of gender-responsive international environmental commitments". The author also remarks that many international environmental instruments have either acknowledged the vital role of women in environmental management or required States to consider gender-responsiveness of specific measures stipulated by international environmental treaties. The author highlights the shift from "man" to women, then from women to gender, as well as from gender-sensitive to gender-responsive approach in the IEL. She also mentions the shift from the dominant focus on a more gender-balanced participation in decision-making, to a focus on more essential issues of gender equality, as well as the shift from gender being considered an ad hoc issue to one that is permanently discussed. The background idea is that there is an internal link between gender (in)equality and the environmental issue. In addition, Čučković notes that environmental degradation impacts women in general, especially certain categories of women, in a much more detrimental way than men. At the same time, women in general had far less access and control over resources, and participated lesser in decision-making, than men had. The author concludes that gender issues need to be addressed by taking into account other relevant criteria for differentiation, as well as that it is necessary to shift from gender-sensitive towards a gender-responsive IEL.

Linde Verhoeven and Alexandra Timmer consider women's right to participate on company boards to be a human rights law issue. They present their approach as new, while offering a critical reflection on the question as to the extent in which international human rights law mandates the use of positive measures to improve the participation of women on company boards, as well as what obligations this entails on the state and on companies themselves. The authors argue that there is no human right as such to become a company board member, and that human rights bodies pay little attention to the subject of women's underrepresentation on company boards. They state that this issue is not taken seriously, unlike, for example, violence against women. This is due to women's underrepresentation in company boards not directly affecting a large group of women, and even more, the fact that women who gain directly from positive measures to improve gender balance on company boards are already privileged. Verhoeven and Timmer argue in favour of gender diversity in boardrooms due to financial benefits from diversity in decision-making, societal economic prosperity, and improvement of (sustainable) development outcomes. Additionally, inclusive and diverse leadership is needed to solve the complex challenges that decision-makers face today. Corporate social responsibility policy (CSR) and the policy on business and human rights (BHR) overlap to some extent as both strive towards socially beneficial action by businesses beyond profit maximization and increasing wealth. The authors highlight the CEDAW's focus on formal equality (equality of opportunity or close to it), substantive equality (equality of results or close to it), and transformative equality (questioning gendered power relations in practice), and state that these three obligations are intertwined and each is essential in itself to accomplish full gender equality in regard to equal participation in boards, enjoying the same income levels, equality in decision-making and political influence. Substantive equality includes a three-step gender framework—gender-responsive assessment, gender transformative measures, and gender transformative remedies. The authors point to the obligation of the States to explain to business enterprises what is expected from them in terms of human rights compliance by giving concrete and specific guidance, such as indicating expected outcomes and sharing best practices.

Mareike Fröhlich suggests that international trade agreements used to be gender-blind, but have lately started to include gender or gender-related provisions. This process has been sparked by the inclusion of the themes of sustainability and environmental protection, which require a multi-faceted approach. The author argues that trade facilitation has both a positive and a negative effect on women's economic activity and, therefore, on gender equality. Froehlich covers four distinct aspects: (1) types of agreements and main actors; (2) types of regulations; (3) enforcement of regulations; and (4) impact of gender provisions in trade agreements. The author explains that gender provisions are found in different parts of the agreements, in the preamble with the general references to gender equality, and as specific gender-related provisions in particular gender chapters. She also claims that it is imperative to take the gender perspective of trade liberalization into account, as different trade barriers can make a notable difference for gender equality and women's economic empowerment. The removal of these barriers, especially in female-dominated trade sectors, could lead to higher wages and better working conditions. Furthermore, improved access to education and finances leads to the better inclusion of women in male-dominated sectors and as entrepreneurs. The author notes that this will bring economic prosperity, as well as respect of gender equality. However, the author argues that this development requires a better understanding of the impact of trade barriers, which may be achieved by gender-related assessments, as the global standard in the ex-ante and ex-post evaluation of all trade negotiations. The author's primary focus is the 2021 gender-only Global Trade and Gender Arrangement between Canada, Chile, and New Zealand, but she says that there are various other agreements that include gender provisions or gender-related provisions. Therefore, she concludes that some major progress has been made, but that there are still many countries and regions that continue to completely ignore the gender perspective.

Sanja Djajić presents the personal history of Anka Godevac Subotić, the first and only female international lawyer of interwar Yugoslavia. She was not only an international lawyer and scholar but also an activist, feminist, journalist, and novelist, active both in Yugoslavia and abroad. Her inclusion in the book is warranted because of her pioneering work in combining feminism and international law in the Balkans, as well as because of the need for overcoming the invisibility of distinguished women in the history of legal theory and practice. The author first illustrates the position of women in Serbia and Yugoslavia through Anka Godevac Subotić's biography. Anka Godevac is the first woman to receive a doctoral degree at the Belgrade Faculty of Law in 1932, covering the field of international public law. This was the first doctorate in public international law ever awarded to a woman. Anka's passion and interest for women's rights and feminist movements are explained through the presentation of her academic work, but also through an explanation of that time period and the disadvantaged status of women in law in the interwar period. The second part of the paper is dedicated to gender exclusion and women's feminist solidarity in international law. Here, the author explains different feminist movements that gravitated towards international law and succeeded in making women's status an international concern. Their role in the League of Nations was highlighted in particular. In this part, the author explains women's movements in the Balkans through the activities of Anka Gođevac, including her engagement in international feminist movements. Academic, intellectual, and political interests of Anka Gođevac Subotić are presented, especially her interest in the issues of peaceful settlement of international disputes, the responsibility of states, nationality, and cooperation in the Balkans. She was the only female member of the Yugoslav Association of International Law during that time and the only woman who published texts on international law. Through this personal history, the contribution effectively illustrates the trajectory of Yugoslavia's history and the development of interwar international law.

The papers obviously deal with very different topics related to the field of international law. Interesting and indicative enough is also the fact that there are authors from many countries. The converging aim and axis is gender equality—its clarification, articulation, promotion within public law theory and practice. The global relevance of the gender equality perspective in legal education, legislation, and legal professions has been expressed and confirmed in the content and authorship of this book.

The editors of the book series *Gender Perspectives in Law* are grateful to the authors of this volume for offering relevant insights related to different fields of international law. They owe them appreciation for demonstrating a strong motivation and devotion to outlining, clarifying, and affirming the gender equality perspective in different fields of international law and through various issues of interest.

The series editors owe a great debt of gratitude and appreciation to the editors of this third volume *Gender Perspective in International Law*, for their enthusiasm and great contributions. They are also grateful to the publisher, who believed in and supported this pioneering attempt to collect gender-competent and gender-sensitive legal and multidisciplinary analyses. Finally, they believe that the synergy and successful cooperation between authors, reviewers, editors, and the publisher contributed to the quality of all papers in this book and the book series as a whole.

Belgrade, Serbia
June 2022

Dragica Vujadinović
Ivana Krstić

Contents

About the Editors

Ivana Krstić is a Full Professor of International Human Rights Law and International Public Law at the University of Belgrade, Faculty of Law. She is a Director of the Human Rights Centre and the Institute for Social and Legal Sciences at the University of Belgrade, Faculty of Law. She obtained her LLM (2003) at the School of Law, University of Pittsburgh (USA), along with an LLM (2004) and Ph.D. (2008) at the University of Belgrade, Faculty of Law. In the academic year 2006/2007, she was a Chevening Scholar working on her Ph.D. research at Exeter College, Oxford University. She teaches several courses, including the European Immigration Law and Policy, Non-Discrimination, Law, International Jurisprudence, International Humanitarian law, Gender Equality, and Minority Rights. She is also a member of several governmental bodies, including the Republic Commission for Transgender Persons. As a leading Serbian expert in human rights, she is engaged in many projects run by various international organizations and agencies, such as OHCHR, UNDP, UNICEF, UNWOMEN, and OSCE. She closely cooperates with Serbian Commissioner on Protection of Equality and with the Judicial Academy, coordinating and directing many trainings for judiciary, but also for other public officials. Since 2015, she is engaged as a Serbian expert for both non-discrimination and gender quality stream at the European Equality Law Network (EELN). She has published monographs and textbooks, around 20 handbooks, and more than 60 articles in international human rights law, international refugee law, and international public law.

Marco Evola is an Associate Professor of European Union Law at the LUMSA Department of Law Palermo. He obtained his Ph.D. (2008) at the University of Palermo. He was a post-doctoral researcher at the University of Palermo (2009–2013). He has been teaching European Union Law, European Union Private International Law, Human Rights, and European Migration Law. He was a member of different research groups within the framework of projects of research of national interest. He is a professor in Masters and post-lauream courses. He is a member of the Editorial Board of the review Diritti umani e diritto internazionale and a Member of the Scientific Committee of the review La Magistratura. He is a member of the College of Professors of the Ph.D course "Mediterranean Studies. History, Law and Economics". His scientific research focuses on human rights, migration, non-discrimination, accession to and withdrawal from the EU, Rule of Law. He has published a monograph on the legal status of third-country migrant workers in the EU legal system.

Maria Isabel Ribes Moreno is an Associated Professor of Labour Law and Social Security Law in the University of Cádiz. She holds a Bachelor's Degree on Law from the University of Sevilla, Master in Company's Legal Advice from I.E. (Madrid), and a Ph.D. in Law from the University of Sevilla (with honours). Her research activities have focused mainly on the analysis of Maritime Labour Law and all aspects of social and working conditions of seafarers, posted-workers, workers in port services, fishermen, and general workers, both in their labour and social security dimensions, and about European Labour Law and non-discrimination law regarding gender and disability. She is the author of a monograph and a co-author of many articles published by scientific reviews and chapters included in collective monographs dealing with these issues. Since 2000, she has been a researcher in various Research and Development Projects. She has carried out research stays at some of the most prestigious universities, such as the Institute of European and Comparative Law in the University of Oxford, Institute of Labour Law at KU Leuven, London School of Economics and Political Science, and University of Sheffield. She has experience of teaching in different areas of Labour, Employment, and Social Security Law, giving lectures for master, bachelor degrees and Jean Monnet Module (574698-EPP-1-2016-1-ES-EPPJMO-MODULE) in different degrees and Universities. She is a Mediator in the Extrajudicial Autonomous Service of Resolution of Labour Conflicts of Andalusia, a Member of the International Network Maritime Work Watch (MWW), the CIELO community, a member of the Spanish Association of Labour and Social Security Law and the INDESS (University Institute of Research for Social Sustainable Development) at the University of Cádiz.

The Fight Against Discrimination on the Grounds of Sex, Sexual Orientation and Gender Identity in the External Relations of the European Union

Marco Evola

Contents

Abstract The paper assesses how non-discrimination on the grounds of sex, sexual orientation and gender identity is conceived within European Union (EU) external relations and the legal issues it encompasses. An analysis of the multifarious instruments the EU avails itself in shaping its external action makes it clear that the EU approach towards equality is neither holistic nor homogeneous.

The EU promotes gender equality in all fields of its external relations, but action to outlaw discrimination on grounds of sexual orientation and gender identity is limited to accession to the EU and the European Neighbourhood Policy. EU external action to advance equality of women and LGBTIQ persons is suspended in a limbo between the protection of human rights and the economic rationale, which has rooted internal action in non-discrimination. The paper argues that the tension between the two approaches and the inconsistencies in promoting human rights in its external

M. Evola (✉)
Department of Law, LUMSA, Palermo, Italy
e-mail: m.evola@lumsa.it

I. Krstić et al. (eds.), *Legal Issues of International Law from a Gender Perspective*, Gender Perspectives in Law 3, https://doi.org/10.1007/978-3-031-13459-3_1

relations have prevented EU external action from eradicating the prejudices and stereotypes regarding discrimination on the grounds of sex, sexual orientation, and gender identity.

1 Introduction

EU engagement in the protection and promotion of the rights of women and lesbian, gay, bisexual, trans, non-binary, intersex and queer (hereinafter LGBTIQ) persons in its relationships with the outer world has been growing more and more over the last years. Notwithstanding this rising importance, scholars have not paid great attention to the activities the EU has been carrying out in this field.[1] The paper aims at contributing to filling up this lacuna in legal literature through an analysis of the scope and content of the EU external action.

Equality is one of the core values of the process of European integration. Pursuant to Article 2 TEU the Union is founded on a series of values, such as "respect for human dignity (. . .) equality (. . .) human rights" which are common "to the Member States in a society in which pluralism, non-discrimination, tolerance, justice, solidarity and equality between women and men prevail." Despite the express reference to the relationship between women and men, the value of equality is wider in scope so that it also encompasses the fight against discrimination on grounds of sexual orientation and gender identity. Both of the said outcomes flow from the many provisions of the founding Treaties committing the EU to outlawing and eradicating discrimination on grounds of sex and sexual orientation. The said understanding of the value of equality is also based on the Charter of Fundamental Rights, which prohibits any discrimination on grounds of sex and sexual orientation, highlighting that LGBTIQ persons' rights are to be protected.

Several rules of the Treaties feature the role of equality within the EU legal system. Article 8 TFEU refers the aim of eliminating inequalities to all activities of the Union. In the same vein, Article 10 TFEU establishes that in defining and implementing its policies and activities the Union shall aim to combat discrimination on a bundle of grounds including sex and sexual orientation. To counteract discrimination on the said grounds, Article 19, para. 1 TFEU confers upon the Union the competence to take appropriate action.

In regulating external action, Article 3, para. 5 TEU establishes that the Union shall uphold and promote its values, and contribute to protection of human rights in its relations with the wider world. The reference to the values of European integration and the guarantee of human rights has to be construed as a commitment to foster the rights of women and LGBTIQ people in external action.

The Lisbon Treaty introduced specific provisions on EU external relations, making equality their centre of gravity. Article 21, para. 1 TEU envisages that the

[1] Thies (2020), p. 431.

universality and indivisibility of human rights and the principle of equality are comprised within the guiding principles of EU external action, so that the Union is called on to advance them in third countries. Moreover, Article 21, para. 2 TEU implicitly bolsters the role of equality, setting it as one of the objectives of the EU's common policies and action, for it enlists the following aims: safeguarding the values of the Union, consolidating and supporting human rights, fostering sustainable economic, social and environmental development, and promoting good global governance. The system is complemented by the provision contained in the last paragraph of Article 21, establishing that respect for the principles and attainment of the objectives paragraphs 1 and 2 refer to also cover the external aspect of the internal policies of the Union.[2]

Furthermore, equality is part and parcel of the legal framework of different external polices of the EU. The rules on development cooperation[3] and humanitarian aid,[4] as well as the laws on the common commercial policy (hereinafter CCP)[5] implicitly commit the EU to its attainment by anchoring all of them to the principles and objectives of the EU.

A similar drafting marks Article 24, para. 2 TEU which provides that the Union shall conduct, define and implement a common foreign and security policy "within the framework of the principles and objectives" of the EU's external action. The rule clarifies that equality also underpins the Common Foreign and Security Policy (CFSP).

The reforms of the Lisbon Treaty spurred the EU institutions to pay greater and greater attention to discrimination on grounds of sex, gender identity and sexual orientation in the shaping of external relations.[6] In fact, non-discrimination became part of external action.[7] The Commission stressed that "the promotion of equality between women and men is a task for the Union, in all its activities" in the recent Strategy on equality 2020–2025.[8] The new impetus marking the Strategy lies behind the Agenda for gender equality and women's empowerment in the EU's external action (GAP III). In addition, the Commission elaborated the Agenda considering gender equality as a crucial objective of the Union's external relations, calling it "a core value of the EU and a universally recognised human right, as well as an imperative to well-being, economic growth, prosperity, good governance, peace and security."[9]

[2]Pech and Grogan (2020), p. 332; Thies (2020), p. 434; Cremona (2014), p. 17 *et seq.*; Cremona (2011), p. 280.

[3]Article 208 para. 1. subpara.1 TFEU.

[4]Article 214 para. 2 TFEU.

[5]Article 207 para. 1 TFEU.

[6]Council of the European Union (2008), Council of the European Union (2013) and European Commission and High Representative of the Union for Foreign Affairs and Security Policy (2015a).

[7]European Commission (2010), p. 27; European Commission (2015b), p. 17.

[8]European Commission (2020a), p. 1.

[9]European Commission (2020b), p. 1.

Furthermore, the LGBTIQ Equality Strategy 2020-2025, which is the first-ever strategy in this field of the EU's anti-discrimination policies, emphasiezed the need for moving towards "a Union of Equality.[10] The Strategy also impacts upon external action since it stressed the aim of making the EU lead the call for LGBTIQ equality around the world. In laying down this target, the Commission stressed that "LGBTIQ rights are human rights and LGBTIQ people should be able to fully enjoy their rights everywhere, at all times."[11]

The EU's external action covers a wide array of international relationships. Practice shows that the EU avails itself of several different instruments in discharging its commitment to gender equality, combining hard law with soft law.[12] Some of these instruments are bilateral or multilateral in nature, such as association agreements or trade agreements, while others are unilateral in nature, such as the General System of Preferences (GSP), financial assistance, and conditionality within the framework of admission to the EU or the European Neighbourhood Policy (ENP). Furthermore, the EU endorses many international treaties on human rights, such as the CEDAW and ILO Conventions, and cooperates with international organizations in outlawing discrimination on grounds of sex, sexual orientation and gender identity.

The intertwining of external relations with the commitment to eradicate discrimination against women and LGBTIQ persons and the practice which has been developed, pursuant to those provisions, raise interesting legal problems. The first of these legal issues refers to the scope of the EU's engagement in outlawing discrimination on grounds of sex, sexual orientation and gender identity within its external relations. The EU approach could be universal in nature or vary as a consequence of the features of each field of action within which the issue of non-discrimination arises. In this second scenario protection of the rights of women and LGBTIQ persons would not be promoted in all external relations. The second issue of interest is the definition of the content of non-discrimination on grounds of sex, sexual orientation and gender identity. In this perspective it is of utmost importance to identify the areas the EU's external action covers and the legal items the EU takes into consideration in setting up its external relations.

The third issue embraces the relationship between the advancement of gender equality and the LGBTIQ community's rights in the EU's external relations and the international system of protection of human rights.

The fourth item concerns the relationship between the concept of non-discrimination in the external relations of the EU and the concept of non-discrimination in its internal action.

All of the said matters will be examined in the following pages, but a preliminary step is the assessment of the legal framework featuring the EU's internal action in

---

[10] European Commission (2020k), p. 1.

[11] European Commission (2020k), p. 19.

[12] Pech and Grogan (2020), p. 343 *et seq;* Thies (2020), p. 439 *et seq.*

order to identify the legal items it encompasses and the rationale lying behing the rules that have been enacted.

2 Non-discrimination on Grounds of Sex in the EU's Internal Action

The Treaty founding the European Economic Community prohibited discrimination between female and male workers (Article 119 EEC) to prevent proper working of the internal market and fair competition from being affected by the pay gap.

The EU's policy on gender equality has evolved along two intertwined lines of development.

The first of these lines is to be found in the widening of the scope of the rules outlawing discrimination between women and men. The reforms of the Treaty provisions extended the prohibition of discrimination on the ground of sex beyond the original boundaries. As a consequence, the EU has enacted a comprehensive bundle of directives aiming at enhancing the legal status of female workers and promoting gender equality in areas other than employment and professional life. This set of secondary laws comprises the following issues: equal treatment of men and women in employment and occupation,[13] equal treatment of men and women in social security[14] and occupational social security schemes,[15] pregnant workers,[16] parental leave,[17] equal treatment between men and women in an activity in

[13]Directive 2006/54/EC of the European Parliament and the Council of 5 July 2006 *on the implementation of the principle of equal opportunities and equal treatment of men and women in matters of employment and occupation (recast)*, OJ L 204, (2006), 23–36.

[14]Council Directive 79/7/EEC of 19 December 1978 *on the progressive implementation of the principle of equal treatment for men and women in matters of social security*, OJ L 6, (1979), 24–25.

[15]Council Directive 86/378/EEC of 24 July 1986 *on the implementation of the principle of equal treatment for men and women in occupational social security schemes*, OJ L 225, (1986), 40–42.

[16]Council Directive 92/85/EEC of 19 October 1992 *on the introduction of measures to encourage improvements in the safety and health at work of pregnant workers and workers who have recently given birth or are breastfeeding (tenth individual Directive within the meaning of Article 16 (1) of Directive 89/391/EEC)*, OJ L 348, (1992), 1–7.

[17]Council Directive 2010/18/EU of 8 March 2010 *implementing the revised Framework Agreement on parental leave concluded by BUSINESSEUROPE, UEAPME, CEEP and ETUC and repealing Directive 96/34/EC (Text with EEA relevance)*, OJ L 68, (2010), 13–20; Directive (EU) 2019/1158 of the European Parliament and of the Council of 20 June 2019 *on work-life balance for parents and carers and repealing Council Directive 2010/18/EU*, OJ L188, (2019), 79–93.

self-employed capacity,[18] and equality between men and women in access to and supply of goods and services.[19]

The laws involved are grounded on the principle of non-discrimination and uphold attainment of the objective of promoting gender equality in the areas they regulate.

As has been rightly observed,[20] the connection the Directives establish between the rules they lay down and the principle of non-discrimination is of utmost importance from a legal point of view since the Court of justice has stated that the directives on non-discrimination are an expression of Article 21 of the Charter of Fundamental Rights[21] and a specific expression of the general principle of non-discrimination,[22] so that they have a direct effect on horizontal disputes.

The target of enhancing gender equality sheds light on the second line of development of EU law: securing women's fundamental right to equality. However, the shift from the original economic approach to the guaranteeing of human rights has been achieved just in part since EU rules fail to eradicate stereotypes and to reshape gendered roles in workplace, family and society. As a consequence the economic rationale still underpins the laws on equality between women and men.[23] A few examples will clarify this point.

Directive 79/7 on social security and Directive 86/378 on occupational social security schemes support the process of market integration because the social policy is subordinated to the economic policy and stresses the promotion of economic targets, mainly as regards the labour market.[24] EU law does not cover social assistance benefits so that there is no protection against the risk of poverty which affects women more than men.[25]

Directive 2004/113 aims to guarantee the principle of equal treatment of men and women in access to and supply of goods and services by providing a legal framework based on the prohibition of direct and indirect sex discrimination, harassment and sexual harassment and any instruction to discriminate. However, the Directive

---

[18] Directive 2010/41/EU of the European Parliament and the Council of 7 July 2010 *on the application of the principle of equal treatment between men and women engaged in an activity in a self-employed capacity and repealing Council Directive 86/613/EEC*, OJ L 180, (2010), 1–6.

[19] Council Directive 2004/113/EC of 13 December 2004 *implementing the principle of equal treatment between men and women in the access to and supply of goods and services*, OJ L 373 , (2004), 37–43.

[20] Bell and Waddington (2021), p. 1406.

[21] Case C-391/09, *Malgožata Runevič-Vardyn and Łukasz Paweł Wardyn v. Vilniaus miesto savivaldybės administracija and Others*, (ECJ 12 May 2011), para 43; Case C-414/16, *Vera Egenberger v Evangelisches Werk für Diakonie und Entwicklung eV* (ECJ 17 April 2018), para. 47.

[22] Case, C-507/18, *NH v Associazione Avvocatura per I diritti LGBTI – Rete Lenford*, (ECJ 23 April 2020) para. 38; Case C-555/07, *Seda Kücükdeveci v Swedex GmbH & Co. KG.*, (ECJ 19 Juanuary 2010), para. 21.

[23] Numhauser-Henning (2007), p. 147; Busby (2018), p. 120.

[24] Hodson and Maer (2001) and Carmel (2003).

[25] Hervey (2005), p. 310.

envisages a wide-ranging set of exceptions.[26] Unlike the other laws on discrimination, Directive 2004/113 has not a closed system of legitimate derogations to direct discrimination (Article 4, para. 5). Furthermore, the laws lay down specific provisions on actuarial factors in insurance contracts which legitimize different offers to men and women. This arrangement severely curtails the potential for reshaping private contractual relationships[27] since in the fields of goods and services, mainly insurance services, the treatment granted to women differs from the treatment men received.[28]

Lastly, the recently adopted Directive 2019/1158 on the work-life balance, notwithstanding the several provisions aiming at reshaping the traditional sharing of gender roles, leaves to Member States' discretion the enforcement of various key rules. As a consequence, it is doubtful that the Directive will determine "significant changes to the currently gendered reconciliation of work and family."[29]

The CJEU case law on the rules on gender equality has been swinging between the economic stance and the the human rights-based approach that are embedded in the laws on equality between women and men. As a consequence of this interpretative attitude "the Court has not taken opportunities to expand the equality agenda or to challenge stereotypes which define women's roles and perhaps form some of the strongest barriers to equality."[30]

3 Non-discrimination on the Grounds of Sexual Orientation and Gender Identity in the EU's Internal Action

Similarly to gender equality, protection against discrimination on grounds of sexual orientation and gender identity is based on rules which combine the proper working of the economy with promotion of equality as a human right. Moreover, the case law of the CJEU has neither strengthened the human rights dimension of rules prohibiting discrimination, nor contributed to eradicating stereotypes.

EU law on sexual orientation and gender identity discrimination is less comprehensive than the rules on sex discrimination. After the entry into force of the Amsterdam Treaty the EU adopted Directive 2000/78 which aims at putting into effect the principle of equal treatment by establishing a general framework for combating discrimination on, amomg other grounds, sexual orientation (Article

[26] Burri and Prechal (2008), p. 12.

[27] Schiek (2007), p. 434.

[28] Hervey (2005), p. 310.

[29] Weldon-Johns (2021), p. 316.

[30] Guth and Elfving (2019), p. 110.

1).[31] Furthermore, LGBTIQ persons are protected within the framework of Directive 2011/95 on international protection.[32]

Protection of people who have undergone gender reassignment is provided for by Directive 2006/54 (the so-called Recast Gender Directive) on equal opportunities and equal treatment of men and women in matters of employment and occupation.[33] Recital 3 of the Preamble makes it clear that the rules equate discrimination on the ground of gender identity with discrimination on grounds of sex.[34] This approach is consistent with the case law of the Court of justice which pointed out that gender reassignment discrimination is a form of sex discrimination.[35] The equation was first affirmed in *P. v S.* in which the Court found that the dismissal of an employee following her decision to undergo gender reassignment surgery was in breach of the Equal Treatment Directive.[36] The Court held that "discrimination arising, as in this case, from the gender reassignment of the person concerned (...) is based, essentially if not exclusively, on the sex of the person concerned. Where a person is dismissed on the ground that he or she intends to undergo, or has undergone, gender reassignment, he or she is treated unfavourably by comparison with persons of the sex to which he or she was deemed to belong before undergoing gender reassignment."[37] The Court relied on the same considerations in the following cases of *KB v NHS Trust Pensions Agency*[38] and *Richards.*[39]

A different reasoning marked the Court's case law on sexual orientation discrimination. In the cases of *Grant*[40] and *D and Sweden*[41] the Court did not grant same-sex

[31] Council Directive 2000/78/EC of 27 November 2000 *establishing a general framework for equal treatment in employment and occupation*, OJ L 303, (2000), 16–22.

[32] Directive 2011/95/EU of the European Parliament and of the Council of 13 December 2011 *on standards for the qualification of third-country nationals or stateless persons as beneficiaries of international protection, for a uniform status for refugees or for persons eligible for subsidiary protection, and for the content of the protection granted (recast)*, OJ L 337, (2011), 9–26.

[33] See footnote 13.

[34] The text of the Recital reads as follows: "The Court of Justice has held that the scope of the principle of equal treatment for men and women cannot be confined to the prohibition of discrimination based on the fact that a person is of one or other sex. In view of its purpose and the nature of the rights which it seeks to safeguard, it also applies to discrimination arising from the gender reassignment of a person."

[35] Bell (2012), p. 129 *et seq.*

[36] Council Directive 76/207/EEC of 9 February 1976 *on the implementation of the principle of equal treatment for men and women as regards access to employment, vocational training and promotion, and working conditions*, OJ L 39 (1976), 40–42.

[37] Case C-13/94, *P v S and Cornwall County Council*, (ECJ 30 April 1996), paras. 20–21.

[38] Case C-117/01, *K.B. v National Health Service Pensions Agency and Secretary of State for Health*, (ECJ 7 Juanuary 2004).

[39] Case C-423/04, *Sarah Margaret Richards v Secretary of State for Work and Pensions*, (ECJ 27 April 2006).

[40] Case C249/96, *Lisa Jacqueline Grant v South-West Trains Ltd*, (ECJ 17 February 1998).

[41] Joined Cases C-122/99 P and C-125/99 P, *D and Kingdom of Sweden v Council of the European Union*, (ECJ 31 May 2001).

couples the protection afforded for discrimination on the ground of sex. Following the legal recognition of same-sex partnerships in many Member States, the Court seemed apt to revise its stance. In the *Maruko*[42] and *Römer*[43] cases the Luxembourg Judge stated that if the surviving spouses and surviving life partners are in a comparable situation the refusal of a benefit would amount to an unlawful discrimination on the ground of sexual orientation. However, this progress towards the enhancement of LGBTIQ people's rights is limited since the Court's reasoning is based on the public/private dichotomy. As a consequence the conferral of rights to individuals does not entail any social recognition.[44] The difficulties in challenging stereotypes became evident in the *Léger* case[45] in which the Court ruled that the imposition on gay and bisexual men of a blanket ban on blood donations is lawful to the extent that there are no effective techniques for detecting infectious diseases that can be transmitted by blood. The reasoning is fraught with prejudices on the lifestyle of gay and bisexual men, which is considered to be at a high risk.[46]

However, the CJEU revived the human right dimension in the more recent *F* case referring to Principle 18 of the Yogyakarta Principles on the application of International Human Rights Law in relation to Sexual Orientation and Gender Identity in deciding on the lawfulness of the recourse to a psycologist's expert's report in the assessment of an application for asylum for fear of persecution on grounds of sexual orientation.[47]

To put it in a nutshell, the laws shaping EU internal action against discrimination on the grounds of sex, sexual orientation and gender identity as they are interpreted by the CJEU do not enshrine a fully-fledged human rights approach. EU internal action is based on a variable balance between the economic rationale and the most recent human rights-based stance.

The next sections will assess how these two approaches toward non-discrimination affect the external action of the Union.

---

[42] Case C-267/06, *Tadao Maruko v Versorgungsanstalt der deutschen Bühnen*, (ECJ 1 April 2008), para. 72.

[43] Case C- 147/08, *Jürgen Römer v Freie und Hansestadt Hamburg*, (ECJ 10 May 2011), paras. 42-51.

[44] Bell (2012), p. 140.

[45] Case C- 528/13, *Geoffrey Léger v Ministre des Affaires sociales, de la Santé et des Droits des femmes and Etablissement français du sang*, (ECJ 29 April 2015).

[46] Guth and Elfving (2019), p. 124.

[47] Case C-473/16, *F v Bevándorlási és Állampolgársági Hivatal*, (ECJ 25 Juanuary 2018), para. 62. The Yogyakarta principles were draft by the International Panel of Experts in International Human Rights Law and on Sexual Orientation and Gender Identity. They are available at yogyakartaprinciples.org.

4 The Scope of Protection and Promotion of the Rights of Women and LGBTIQ Persons in the EU's External Relations

The engagement of the EU in the protection and promotion of the rights of women and LGBTIQ persons is neither holistic nor homogeneous, for its scope varies in each of the fields of external action. Gender equality is embedded in the external action of the Union as a whole, but non-discrimination on the basis of sexual orientation and gender identity only covers admission to the EU and the ENP.

The guarantee of women's rights plays an important role in procedures of accession into the EU, as the recently-adopted Zagreb Declaration of 6 May 2020 clarified. The leaders of the EU and its Member States stated that "the EU welcomes the strong commitment by the Western Balkan partners to the primacy of democracy and the rule of law (. . .) as well as respect for human rights, gender equality (. . .)."[48]

The annual Reports on the progress of candidate countries and potential candidates take into consideration women's rights under the headings of the political criteria and the ability to assume the obligations of membership. The assessment is grounded on the internal action dual approach towards gender equality since women's rights are considered not only a matter of compliance with human rights standards of protection, but also as part of the duty to align the domestic legal systems with the Union *acquis*. In the section of the Reports dealing with human rights the EU evaluates the Gender Equality Strategies and Action Plans the candidate countries and potential candidates have adopted and implemented to secure protection and promotion of women's rights, making use of European and international standards as benchmarks.[49] In the latest Communication on EU enlargement policy the Commission observed that "the Western Balkan partners need to demonstrate that they are continuing efforts to promote and strengthen gender equality and to address gender-based violence."[50] In developing this general remark the Commission observed in the 2021 Montenegro Report that "the evaluation of the 2017-2031 action plan revealed shortcomings in the implementation, lack of awareness and commitment among institutions, poor gender mainstreaming, discrepancies in the application of the legal framework and weak coordination with other national strategies".[51]

As already highlighted, achievement of gender equality is equated with consistency of domestic laws with EU secondary laws on women's rights. The check is

[48]Zagreb Declaration, 6 May 2020, para. 7.

[49]See the latest Progress Reports European Commission (2021c), p. 32; European Commission (2021d), p. 30; European Commission (2021e), p. 34; European Commission (2021f), p. 37; European Commission (2021g), p. 37; European Commission (2021h), p. 33; European Commission (2021i), p. 32.

[50]European Commission (2021b), p. 8.

[51]European Commission (2021e), p. 34.

carried out within the framework of the ability to assume the obligations of membership and focuses on the reforms states aspiring to membership have enacted.[52]

The protection of LGBTIQ people's rights is part and parcel of the evaluation of candidate countries and potential candidates under the heading of human rights. The EU takes into consideration the legal arrangements that have been established and the strategies and action plans adopted to outlaw discrimination against LGBTIQ people. In the Albania Report 2021 the Commission pointed out that "(d)-iscrimination against lesbian, gay, bisexual, transgender, intersex and queer (LGBTIQ) persons remains pervasive and dominant in the Albanian society, especially regarding access to health care, education, justice, employment and housing. (...) Albania does not have legislation recognising civil cohabitation and same-sex marriage, which would require amendments to the family code. The national action plan for LGBTIQ persons, which came to end in 2020, did not produce visible results, due to the lack of financial resources and political will. However, the inter-ministerial team responsible for monitoring the action plan has not held any meeting since May 2019. Police officers, prosecutors and gender 'focal points' in line ministries continued receiving training on preventing discrimination on the basis of sexual orientation and gender identity. The shelter for LGBTIQ persons has continued to provide care, support and advocacy to homeless LGBTIQ individuals. The support from the state budget has increased, covering up to 40% of the core budget of the shelter, but continued dependence on donors creates uncertainty on the continuation of services."[53]

Gender equality and the LGBTIQ community's rights also mark the development of the ENP. The EU targets the objective of supporting the iniatives of its partners. In the 2020 Communication on Eastern Partnership Policy the Commission and the High Representative of the Union for Foreign Affairs and Security Policy (hereinafter High Representative) argued that "the EU will step up action to combat all forms of discrimination including on grounds of sex (...). The EU will also continue to support the partner countries in (...) promoting gender equality."[54] Moreover, strengthening of the rights of women and LGBTIQ persons is one of the benchmarks the EU avails itself of in evaluating compliance with human righs. In assessing Algeria's legal system the Commission and the High Representative argued that the constiituion of the State provides for gender equality, but notwithstanding such

[52] See the latest Progress Reports European Commission (2021c), p. 95; European Commission (2021d), p. 86; European Commission (2021e), p. 89; European Commission (2021f), p. 94; European Commission (2021g), p. 101; European Commission (2021h), p. 89; European Commission (2021i), p. 83.

[53] European Commission (2021c), p. 34. See also European Commission (2021d), p. 31; European Commission (2021e), p. 31; European Commission (2021f), p. 39; European Commission (2021g), p. 38; European Commission (2021h), p. 35; European Commission (2021i), p. 34; European Commission (2020c), p. 36; European Commission (2020d), p. 38; European Commission (2020e), p. 40.

[54] European Commission and High Representative of the Union for Foreign Affairs and Security Policy (2020a), p. 15.

provision, several reccomendations on discrimination on grounds of sex were addressed to Algeria during the 2017 Universal Periodic Review Process. Furthermore, the Report highlights that breaches of gender equality are still established by the family code in areas such as marriage, divorce, child custody and inheritance.[55] In the same vein the Report on Armenia pointed out that "on equal treatment and anti-discrimination, the new Constitution stipulates that discrimination on all grounds is prohibited. (. . .). A mechanism to protect lesbian, gay, bisexual, transgender and intersex (LGBTI) rights in Armenia is yet to be put in place. Discrimination against LGBTIQ persons remains an issue."[56] The Report on Tunisia shed light on the lack of a proper regulation addressing LGBTI people and the connected violation of their rights since they are not expressely laid down by the constitution. Furthermore, Tunisian law grant LGBTIQ persons no equality and arrest and anal tests are currently practised.[57]

The limited application of non-discrimination in the fields of trade and development cooperation is part and parcel of a broader practice of international commercial agreements which are embedded in an essentialist conception of equality that limits its achievement to guaranteeing women's equality.[58]

In the fields of common commercial policy (CCP) and development cooperation gender equality is channelled through a general reference to human rights as an essential element of the agreement the EU enters into with third countries or other international organizations,[59] but some agreements devote specific provisions to gender equality. Article 9, para. 2 of the Cotonou Agreement only refers to equality between women and men, without any consideration of LGBITQ persons' rights.[60] Moreover, some agreements promote gender equality through gender mainstreaming. This way of protecting women's rights marks the EU-Vietnam, agreement which regulates cooperation related to gender equality establishing that "(t)he Parties shall cooperate in strengthening gender related policies and programmes, as well as institutional and administrative capacity building and supporting the implementation of national strategies on gender equality including

[55]European Commission and High Representative of the Union for Foreign Affairs and Security Policy (2020b), p. 5; European Commission and High Representative of the European Union for Foreign Affairs and Security Policy (2019b), p. 8.

[56]European Commission and High representative of the Union for Foreign Affairs and Security Policy (2018a), pp. 4–5.

[57]European Commission and High representative of the Union for Foreign Affairs and Security Policy (2018b), p. 8; European Commission and High Representative of the Union for Foreign Affairs and Security Policy (2017a), p. 5.

[58]Fortas (2016), p. 361 *et seq.*

[59]Bartels (2005); Cremona (1996).

[60]Partnership Agreement between the members of the African, Caribbean and Pacific Group of States of the one part, and the European Community and its Member States, of the other part, signed in Cotonou on 23 June 2000 OJ L 317, 15.12.2000, p. 3-286. See also art. 8.10 para. 2 (d) of the Comprehensive Economic and Trade Agreement between Canada of the one part and the European Union and its Member States of the other part, OJ L 11,14.1.2017, 23-1079.

women's rights and empowerment, in order to ensure the equitable participation of men and women in all sectors of economic, cultural, political and social life."[61] The exclusive focus on gender equality marks the so called GSP+ scheme, which is based on the EU granting tariff preferences, provided under the special incentive arrangement for sustainable development and good governance, to those countries which have ratified 27 international conventions including CEDAW and ILO Convention no. 100 (1951) on equal remuneration of male and female workers for work of equal value and ILO Convention no. 111 (1958) on discrimination in respect of employment and occupation.[62]

This approach excluding LGBTIQ persons from the scope of the EU's external action in the CCC and development cooperation is the hallmark of the initiatives the EU adopted towards future agreements. In its position paper on the negotiations of the Association Agreement with MERCOSUR, the Commission focused on women and evaluated the impact on gender equality arguing that "women are expected to benefit from the AA".[63] Moving from this expectation the Commission outlined the future scenario in which the agreement is to produce its effects stating that "(h)-owever, as women are underrepresented in tradeable sectors, and increases in agricultural and industrial exports may result in technical upgrading, women are expected to benefit from employment and income gains less so than men."[64] Restricting equality to gender equality is also witnessed by the recently negotiated Partnership Agreement between the EU and the Members of the Organizations of ACP States. The text, which was initialed by the negotiators on 15 April 2021,[65] lays down an extensive regulation on gender equality,[66] obliging the Parties to pay special attention to it in promotion, protection and fulfilment of human rights

[61] Framework Agreement on Comprehensive Partnership and Cooperation between the European Union and its Member States of the one part and the Socialist Republic of Viet Nam of the other part, OJ L 329, 3.12.2016, 8-42. See also art 38 h) of the Interim Agreement Establishing a Framework for Economic Partnership between Eastern and Southern African States on one part and the European Community and its Member States on the other part, OJ L 111, 24.4.2012, 3-1172; art. 44 Political Dialogue and Cooperation Agreement between the European Community and its Member States on one side and the Andean Community and its Member Countries (Bolivia, Colombia, Ecuador, Perù and Venezuela) on the other (the agreement has not entered into force – see the Joint Proposal for a Council Decision on the conclusion of a Political Dialogue and Cooperation Agreement between the European Community and its Member States, of the one part, and the Andean Community and its Member Countries (Bolivia, Colombia, Ecuador, Peru and Venezuela), of the other part, JOIN (2016) 4 final, 2016/0025 (NLE).

[62] Regulation (EU) No 978/2012 of the European Parliament and of the Council of 25 October 2012 applying a scheme of generalised tariff preferences and repealing Council Regulation (EC) No 732/2008, OJ L 303, 31.10.2012, 1–82.

[63] i.e. Association Agreement.

[64] European Commission (2021a), p. 5.

[65] The text of the initialled agrement is available at: https://ec.europa.eu/international- partnerships/system/files/negotiated-agreement-text-initialled-by-eu-oacps-chief-negotiators-20210415_en.pdf.

[66] See Articles 1 (objectives), 2 (principles), 7 (cross-cutting themes), 10 (gender equality), 17 (conflicts and crises), 21 (education), 36 (gender equality and women's and girl's empowerment), 77 (global alliances and international cooperation), 80 (areas of international action).

(Article 1, para. 3 lett. a). In actual fact, all of the rules the negotiated text contains are conceived in order to counteract discrimination against women and girls. Article 36 is a litmus paper, for the provisions it lays down provide the duty to undertake reforms to give "women equal rights to economic and financial resources, as well as access to ownership of and control over land and natural resources, inheritance, and other forms of property." Furthermore, Article 36 aims at increasing women's full and effective participation in political life, equal access to employment and decent work conditions. The focus on women is also embedded in the obligation to promote the recognition of unpaid care work and the sharing of responsibilities within the household and the family at large.[67]

EU institutions' practice is grounded on the same rationale. In the Guidelines on Trade the Commission held that "pre-existing conditions of insecurity, stress or vulnerability, including of women or of particular groups (e.g. low-income, children, people with disabilities, ethnic minorities, indigenous peoples, those living in a particular territory) should be highlighted."[68]

Furthermore, women and girls are the main reference point of the CFSP strategy the EU has been framing. The Action Plan on Women, Peace and Security recognised that gender equality and women's empowerment are "a prerequisite for dealing with prevention, management and resolution of conflict" and identifies the key priorities areas of prevention, protection, relief and recovery, making exclusive reference to the problems women and girls face.[69]

The EU endorsed the United Nations Secutiry Council Resolution 1325 on Women, Peace and Security[70] calling on states to prevent infringements of women's rights, to support the participation of women in peace negotiatons/post-conflict, and to protect them from gender-based violence.[71] The objectives of the Resolution are part and parcel of the EU's external action.[72]

The EU also endorsed the Bejing Declaration, which requires states to act in order to empower women as a matter of social justice, development and peace.[73] The EU commitment to the 2030 Agenda for Sustainable Development of 2015[74] is entrenched in the promotion of women's rights because Goal 5 of the Agenda pursues the targets of achieving gender equality and empowering women and girls.[75]

---

[67] It has to be observed that women are the only individuals considered in the provision on education (Artcile 28), and universal access to sexual and reproductive health commodities (Article 29), and human and social development fields (Article 27), and inclusive and sustainable growth (Article 43), and entrepreneurship (Article 45), and trade and sustainable development (Article 49).

[68] European Commission (2015a), p. 9.

[69] Council of the European Union (2019).

[70] United Nations Security Council Resolution 1325 (2000).

[71] United Nations Security Council Resolution 1325 (2000).

[72] Council of the European Union (2018a); European Commission (2015a), para. 2.

[73] European Commission 2015a, para. 2.

[74] United Nations General Assembly Resolution (2015).

[75] United Nations General Assembly Resolution (2015), para. 3.

Furthermore, the EU has entered into strategic partnerships with other international organizations to advance women's rights (see *infra* Sect. 8).

Assessment of the practice clarifies that there is a perfect correspondence between the scope of the EU's internal policies and the scope of the enlargement process and the ENP. The reasons for the different moulding of the EU's external action to protect and promote the rights of women and LGBTIQ people are to be found in the specific features of each policy and the objectives the EU aims to attain in every field of action.

Only recently has the EU started cooperation with international organizations to protect LGBTIQ people's rights. In implementing the Guidelines the Council adopted in 2013,[76] the EU promoted political and human rights dialogues, enacted awareness-raising activities and granted financial assistance, all activities that achieved poor results in raising the standards of protection to be granted to the LGBTIQ community.[77]

5 Intersectionality As a Common Feature of the EU's External Action in the Fight Against Discrimination on the Basis of Sex, Sexual Orientation and Gender Equality

Intersectionality is the key approach toward the advancement of women's and LGBTIQ people's equality in all of the areas of external relations.

In the recent GAP III the Commission stressed that "women and girls with disabilities, of minority groups, migrant women and girls, LGBTIQ are among the groups particularly at risk,"[78] whereas "lack of access to schools further increases the gaps for girls with disabilities."[79] Furthermore, "women and girls with disabilities

[76] Council of the European Union (2013).

[77] European Commission (2020j), p. 14. A joint European Commission-World Bank roundtable was held on 23 September 2019 within the framework of admission. Furthermore, the EU provided support to the regional LGBTI Equal Rights Association for Western Balkans and Turkey (ERA) conference that took place on 7–9 November 2019 in Albania. Under the ENP meetings with civil society organizations were held at the EU headquartes to promote the rights of LGBTI people. The EU also funded a regional LGBTI conference on 27–29 September 2019 which gathered activists and civil society organisations from the Middle East and North Africa regions. As regards relations with third countries it is worth mentioning the side event to the Commission on the Status of Women (CSW) and the equality of transgender people that was organised in March 2019. The Commission also supported the ILGA Europe Annual LGBTI Conference, which took place in Prague in October 2019. The dialogue that was developed and the assistance to the working of LGBTIQ organisations contributed to the spread of awareness on the problems of the LGBTIQ community, but fighting stereotypes needs radical changes that cannot be brought about by the said initiatives.

[78] European Commission (2020b), p. 8.

[79] European Commission (2020b), p. 14.

are at heightened risk due to inaccessible information on prevention and assistance and acute barriers to accessing health or basic water, sanitation and hygiene services."[80] The LGBTIQ Strategy 2020-2025 refers to the particular attention the Commission is to devote to LGBTIQ people "experiencing intersectional discrimination" since "(t)hose who have disabilities, are elderly, migrants, or come from ethnic or religious minority background are particularly vulnerable to discrimination."[81]

Intersectionality is key in understanding assessment of candidate countries within the enlargement procedures. In the Serbia 2019 Report, the Commission observed that "older, rural and Roma women, as well as women with disabilities continued to be among the most discriminated against in society,"[82] and in dealing with education added that "the drop-out rate remains high, especially for Roma girls."[83] Similar considerations were expressed in the more recent Serbia 2021 Report. The Commission observed that "Roma women, older women, poor women, women with disabilities, refugee and internally displaced women, continue to experience intersecting forms of discrimination, which was further exacerbated by the COVID-19 crisis."[84] The Commission spurs candidate countries to consider non-discrimination in the light of intersectionality. A good example of this stance is to be found in the Turkey 2021 Report in which the Commission urged Turkey "to develop intersectoral campaigns on rights of Roma women, as a gender-sensitive approach is missing in the National Roma Strategy."[85]

The need for to pay attention to intersectionality also marks the EU approach towards trade. The Guidelines on Trade argue that "pre-existing conditions of insecurity, stress or vulnerability, including of women or of particular groups (e.g. low-income, children, people with disabilities, ethnic minorities, indigenous peoples, those living in a particular territory) should be highlighted."[86] This approach was retained during the negotiations with the ACP countries. The negotiated Partnership Agreement purports to commit the parties to put "special emphasis on women in vulnerable situations" (art. 10 para. 3).

The problems stemming from the challenges embedded in intersectionality were also explored in the field of the CFSP. The European Commission and the High Representative stressed that "the gender gap is even larger when gender inequality

---

[80]European Commission (2020b), p. 15. See also European Parliament (2021), para. 8.

[81]European Commission (2020k), p. 5–7 .

[82]European Commission (2019a), p. 27.

[83]European Commission (2019a), p. 29; European Commission (2020d), p. 37; European Commission (2020e), p. 40; European Commission (2020f), p. 32.

[84]European Commission (2021g), p. 38.

[85]European Commission (2021f), p. 41. See also European Commission (2021e), p. 35.

[86]European Commission (2015a), p. 9.

intersects with other forms of exclusion such as disability, age, caste, ethnicity, sexual orientation, geographical remoteness or religion."[87]

Making intersectionality the grounding factor of the EU external action is of the utmost importance in order to shape an effective strategy aiming at advancing women's and LGBTIQ people's equality. Discrimination is more and more the outcome of the breach of several prohibited criteria because of concurring phenomena, ranging from migration flows to rising poverty.[88]

It is worth pointing out that intersectionality is one of the features marking the approach towards gender equality and non-disrimination on the ground of sexual orientation or gender identity in the EU's internal action so that it embodies a commonality between the two actions. In the Gender Equality Strategy 2020-2025 the Commission connected intersectionality to gender-based violence, stating that "women who have a health problem or disability are more likely to experience various forms of violence."[89] Furthermore, the Commission held that "some women are structurally underrepresented in the labour market, often resulting from the intersection of gender with additional conditions of vulnerability or marginalisation such as belonging to an ethnic or religious minority or having a migrant background."[90] The LGBTIQ Strategy 2020–2025 points out that "(d)iscrimination is often multidimensional and only an intersectional approach can pave the way to sustainable and respectful changes in society."[91]

However, this common approach does not entail a perfect coincidence between the areas internal action and external action cover.

6 The Content of Gender Equality in External Relations of the European Union

EU practice has been establishing an extensive framework in which some areas are of the utmost importance. The first area is gender-based violence. The EU's engagement is grounded on the right to live a life free from all forms of violence. All of the external relations of the EU target the attainment of the said objective and counteract any form of gender-based violence, ranging from domestic violence to sexual harassment, to rape, to conflict-related violence to children, early and forced marriage (CEFM), female genital mutilation (FGM), forced abortion, forced sterilisation, and gender-biased selection (preferring sons at birth). Such an extensive stance was adopted in the Turkey 2020 Report in which the Commission dealt with

[87] European Commission and High Representative of the Union for Foreign Affairs and Security Policy (2015a), p. 3.

[88] Atrey (2019), p. 78 *et seq.*

[89] European Commission (2020a), p. 4.

[90] European Commission (2020a), p. 7.

[91] European Commission (2020k), p. 5.

domestic violence and observed also that “child, early and forced marriages remain a source of concern, as does discretionary mitigation in court cases of violence against women, possibly mirroring sexist prejudice and victim blaming. Incest is reported by civil society to be increasing but there is no policy action or acknowledgement of this by the authorities.”[92] The extensive coverage of gender-based violence is witnessed by the recent Bosnia and Herzegovina 2021 Report which pointed out that “Bosnia and Herzegovina needs to accelerate the prosecution of crimes of sexual violence, provide reparation to women victims of war crimes, and secure witness protection.”[93] In the aforementioned perspective, the Report on Lebanon, which was drafted within the ENP, argued that “the State Ministry for Women’s Affairs prepared a draft national strategy for women’s rights to be endorsed by the Council of Ministers. Article 522 of the Penal Code (exempting rapists from punishment if they marry their victims) was abolished in August 2017 and preparations are underway to amend the law regulating the minimum age for marriage and raise it to 18. Domestic violence remains under-reported.”[94]

Despite the attention that has been devoted to violence against women, the EU has fragmented gender-based violence in the different fields of its external engagement. As a consequence the unitary character of violence is missed. Gender-based violence constitutes the power of men over women and its exercise perpetuates male dominance.[95] Against this pattern of gender-based violence, the strategy of the Union fails to advance women’s equality because it has not been conceived to eradicate the stereotypes from which violence originates.

The said limit marks the way in which the EU operates in the second area gender equality covers: the promotion of sexual and reproductive health. The EU pursues the aim of ensuring women’s and girls’ right to self-determination, through elimination of practices such as FGM, which are an entrenched form of gender-based violence, and through access to sexual and reproductive health services and information. The connection between violence and sexual and reproductive health has been watered down in implementation of the external action because of the attention which is paid to access to services. Such an outcome is witnessed by the Serbia 2021 Report which detaches violence from health stating that “(a)n action plan on the national programme for safeguarding and improving sexual and reproductive health has yet to be adopted. Additional funding is needed to ensure it is implemented as regards improving access to quality services in this area.”[96] In the same perspective,

---

[92] European Commission (2020e), p. 39; European Commission (2020c), p. 34; European Commission (2020d), p. 37; European Commission (2020g), p. 34 *et seq.*; European Commission (2020b), p. 8 *et seq.*; European Commission (2019b), p. 5; Council of the European Union (2019), p. 10 *et seq.*

[93] European Commission (2021d), p. 30.

[94] European Commission and High Representative of the Union for Foreign Affairs and Security Policy (2018c), p. 5.

[95] On the relationship between sexuality, violence and male power over women see MacKinnon (1987), p. 32 et seq.

[96] European Commission (2021g), p. 38.

Article 41 of the Political Dialogue and Cooperation Agreement between the EU and the Andean Community provides that "partnerships with organised civil society, NGOs and the private sector are also needed to address sexual and reproductive health and rights in a gender-sensitive approach and to work with young people to prevent sexually transmitted diseases and unwanted pregnancies."[97]

Economic and social rights are the third area of action of the Union, which pursues the aim of strengthening women's rights and empowering them in the economic area. The recent GAP III sheds light on the rationale of the Union's stance, for the Commission stated that "women and men in all their diversity should have equal opportunities, equal access to employment, decent work, equal pay for equal work in order to be economically independent. Furthermore, women and men should equally share care responsibilities and have access to adequate social protection, public services, and financial and business opportunities."[98]

In order to attain the stated objectives, the EU aims at eliminating the gender pay gap, revising the allocation of roles within family through parental leave, fostering women's and girls' accession to employment and occupation, and prohibiting their discrimination as regards working conditions and social protection in all of the areas of the external relations.[99]

Furthermore, the EU champions empowerment of women in the field of entrepreneurship, which is based on setting up an environment sustaining women's economic activities and granting access to productive resources and finances.[100]

---

[97] See also the negotiated Partnership Agreement between the EU and members of the Organization of ACP countries establishing cooperation between the Parties with the aim of delivering universal access to sexual and reproductive health-care services within the context of gender equality and empowerment of girls and women (Article 48 para. 7; Article. 29 para. 5, Article 32 para. 2, Article 40 para 6).

[98] European Commission (2020b), p. 12.

[99] European Commission (2021b), p. 4; European Commission (2020c), p. 91 *et seq.*; European Commission (2020d), p. 96 *et seq.*; European Commission (2020f), p. 82 *et seq.*; European Commission and High Representative of the European Union for Foreign Affairs and Security Policy (2019a), p. 4 *et seq.*; European Commission and High Representative of the Union for Foreign Affairs and Security Policy (2018b), p. 6; Article 1 para.1 Draft provisions on Trade and Gender Equality in the context of the Modernisation of the EU-Chile Association Agreement; Council of the European Union, (2018a) para. 75; Article 33 of the negotiated Partnership Agreement between the EU and ACP.

[100] European Commission (2015a); Article 31 of the Cotonou Agreement; Articles 36 and 45 of the negotiated Partnership Agreement between the EU and ACP; Article 35 of the Interim Agreement between Eastern and Southern African States and the EC; Article 33 of the Agreement between the EU and Viet Nam; Articles 3 and 4 Draft provisions on Trade and Gender Equality in the context of the Modernisation of the EU-Chile Association Agreement; European Commission (2019b), p. 4; European Commission and High Representative of the Union for Foreign Affairs and Security Policy (2015b), p. 6.

In the same vein the EU has progressively extended the scope of its action in the related fields of education[101] and health.[102]

This field of action is characterized by tension between promoting equality as a fundamental right and removing discrimination because of its negative effect on the economy. In the enlargement procedure gender equality is also identified with alignment with the EU *acquis*,[103] thus reflecting the difficulties in setting aside the economic underpinning of internal action. Similarly, promoting women's empowerment in the fields of trade and development cooperation does not only purport advancing women's equality, but aims at dismantling. unfair competition, which stems also from the low standards of protection of women's rights.

Women's empowerment is not limited to economic activities, but encompasses the realm of the public sphere, which is the fourth area of the EU's engament in promoting gender equality in its external action. Underrepresentation is a point of departure of a series of activities the EU has been putting into place in order to increase the level of women's participation, representation and leadership in politics. Such a multifaceted engagement does not only pursue the target of promoting women's political rights, as it may appear at first sight, but is a contribution to a functioning economy. The Commission clarified the dual nature of the EU's action in the recent GAP III stating that "(w)omen and girls should participate equally in the public and private sphere, to achieve a functioning democracy and economy, and to fulfil human rights for all."[104] The participation of women in public life is a legal item common to all of the branches of external action. The Commission considers the role of women in politics and political parties in assessing candidate countries progress in establishing democratic institutions.[105] Furthermore, women's empowerment is taken into consideration in framing the ENP[106] and the CFSP.[107] In the end, as a consequence of the connection between improving women's participation in political life and the economy, women's empowerment also marks trade policy.

[101] Article 28 of the negotiated Partnership Agreement between the EU and ACP; Article 4 para 3 (V) Draft provisions on Trade and Gender Equality in the context of the Modernisation of the EU-Chile Association Agreement.

[102] European Commission and High Representative of the Union for Foreign Affairs and Security Policy (2021), p. 4; European Commission (2020c), p. 33; European Commission (2020d), p. 37; European Commission (2020f), p. 32.

[103] European Commission (2021g), p. 38.

[104] European Commission (2020b), p. 15.

[105] European Commission (2021c), p. 10; European Commission (2021d), p. 8; European Commission (2021e), p. 5; European Commission (2021f), p. 12; European Commission (2021g), p. 10; European Commission (2021h), p. 8; European Commission (2021i), p. 9; European Commission (2020e), p. 13 and 39; European Commission (2020h), p. 31-32 .

[106] European Commission and High Representative of the Union for Foreign Affairs and Security Policy (2021), p. 4; European Commission and High Representative of the Union for Foreign Affairs and Security Policy (2020b), p. 5; European Commission and High Representative of the Union for Foreign Affairs and Security Policy (2018a), p. 5; European Commission and High Representative of the Union for Foreign Affairs and Security Policy (2018b), p. 6.

[107] Council of the European Union (2019), p. 3 *et seq.*

Article 31 of the Cotonou Agreement, Article 33 of the EU-Viet Nam Agreement and Article 49 of the negotiated Partnership Agreement between EU and ACP countries make reference to ensuring, improving and expanding equal participation and opportunities for men and women in all spheres of political, economic, social and cultural life.

The relation between women, peace and security is the fifth area of the EU's external action in advancing gender equality. The focus on peace and security does not overshadow the intertwining between this item and those already examined. The Commission clearly stated that "conflict, crisis and fragility hamper progress towards sustainable peace and security and to achieving the SDGs. The WPS agenda focuses on the links between gender inequality and conflict, how they are mutually reinforcing, and emphasises the need to understand gender inequality as a root cause and driver of conflict and fragility. Inequalities coupled with exclusion of women from power, opportunities, services and security create a fertile ground for conflict and gender-based violence, especially when linked to weak state capacity or legitimacy."[108] As a consequence of this understanding, the issue at stake, though mainly covered by the CFSP,[109] is a matter of concern in the other fields of external relations.[110]

The Commission identified a sixth area of action in the advancement of women's rights in its external relations: environment and digital economy.

The connection between gender equality and these two fields was established taking into consideration the particular impact on women and girls of both of the said phenomena. The Commission observed that "(w)omen and girls in developing countries are particularly affected by the impact of climate change and environmental degradation," but are prevented "from participating equally in related governance processes for multiple reasons, including harmful gender norms, inadequate legal frameworks, low access to education and land ownership."[111] Furthermore, the digital divide could destroy the potential digital technologies offer to women's empowerment and gender equality, thus becoming a further reason for discrimination.[112]

In GAP III environment and digital economy are at the crossroads of the other areas of action because the involvement of women and girls in the green transition and the digital transformation entails political and economic empowerment, access to education, employment and entrepreneurship and the struggle against gender-based violence. The strategy of the Commission aims at improving practice.[113] Article 49 of the negotiated Partnership Agreement between the EU and ACP

[108] European Commission (2020b), p. 18.

[109] Council of the European Union (2019), p. 3 *et seq*; Council of the European Union (2018a), para. 1.

[110] Article 17 negotiated partnership Agreement between the EU and ACP.

[111] European Commission (2020b), pp. 18–19.

[112] European Commission (2020b), p. 19.

[113] European Commission (2020b), pp. 19–21.

provides that the Parties work towards "building women's resilience to climate change impacts" and envisages inclusive and sustainable economic growth and development. However, awareness of the way in which climate change impacts upon women has not given rise to the imposition of specific duties on the contracting parties that could enforce women's rights. Practice shows the difficulties the EU is facing in advancing a human right-based approach towards gender equality. Furthermore, it is quite surprising that the Commission took into no consideration the way in which the green transition and the digital transformation impact upon LGBTIQ persons.

7 The Content of Non-discrimination on Grounds of Sexual Orientation and Gender Identity in the EU External Action

The cautious approach of the EU's institutions in enacting laws protecting the rights of the LGBTIQ community and of the CJEU in application of the principle of non-discrimination on grounds of sexual orientation and gender identity has curtailed the external action of the EU in advancing the rights of LGBTIQ people so that few areas have been covered by the activity of the Union.

Great attention has been paid to the various forms of violence to which LGBTIQ persons are exposed. This legal item is common to the different areas of the EU's external action since it is considered the most important discrimination to which LGBTIQ persons are exposed. In the LGBTIQ Equality Strategy 2020-2025 the Commission stated that the EU makes "specific efforts to combat violence, hatred and discrimination and ensure that LGBTIQ rights are upheld in partner countries."[114]

In applying this approach the Commission considers whether or not candidate countries and potential candidates have laid down criminal laws to prosecute hate crimes, hate speech and violence against LGBTIQ persons.[115] In the same vein the EU focused on violence in UN fora.[116]

Furthermore, the EU's fight against discrimination has targeted the laws criminalizing same-gender relations and trans identities. The existence of criminal laws prohibiting homosexual relationships is one of the benchmarks the EU applies in the ENP. The Report on Tunisia referred to "(l)es condamnations d'homosexuels sur la

[114]European Commission (2020k), p. 20.

[115]See the latest Progress Reports European Commission (2021c), p. 34; European Commission (2021d), p. 31; European Commission (2021e), p. 36; European Commission (2021f), p. 39; European Commission (2021g), p. 39; European Commission (2021h), p. 35; European Commission (2021i), p. 34.

[116]European Commission (2019b), p. 14.

base du Code pénal (article 230) et la mise en œuvre des tests médicaux forcés, prévus dans le Code penal."[117]

The scrutiny of countries in the context of enlargement takes into consideration further issues relating to the legal status of LGBTIQ persons. The assessment moves from the alignment of internal law with the EU *acquis*, but it is not limited to the legal items EU law regulates. The Commission has taken into consideration the enactment and enforcement of laws on life partnerships of same-sex partners,[118] registration of same-sex partnerships, regulation of social and economic rights of same-sex couples, including family rights,[119] birth registry and gender recognition,[120] access to social services,[121] health care and housing.[122] The guarantee of the freedom of assembly and association and of freedom of expression is also a matter of concern.[123]

An overall assessment of practice and the perspectives which were outlined in the Strategy 2020–2025 clarified that the EU avails itself of vague criteria in evaluating the advancement of non-discrimination in third countries and takes into no consideration matters that are crucial in counteracting non-discrimination and eradicating stereotypes such as political representation, access to education, employment, entrepreneurship, social services, the protection of physical, mental and sexual health of LGBTIQ persons, and protection of the environment.

8 Protection of the Rights of Women and LGBTIQ Persons in the EU's External Action and the International Human Rights Protection System

International treaties protecting human rights and the practice of international human rights courts and treaty bodies play an important role in the promotion of gender equality and LGBTIQ persons' rights in EU external relations.[124] The Commission argued in GAP III that gender equality is "a universally recognised human right"[125] paving the way for making reference to international treaties in the improvement of external action. The Council stressed that the rights of LGBTI persons are "protected

[117] European Commission and High Representative of the Union for Foreign Affairs and Security Policy (2017b), p. 5.

[118] European Commission (2021e), p. 35.

[119] European Commission (2021d), p. 31.

[120] European Commission (2021g), p. 39.

[121] European Commission (2021e), p. 35.

[122] European Commission (2021c), p. 34.

[123] European Commission (2021f), p. 40.

[124] Thies (2020), p. 429.

[125] European Commission (2020b), p. 1.

under existing international human rights law" so that the action of the Union is built on these "international standards."[126]

In the admission procedure the EU assesses candidate countries' progress in the field of non-discrimination, making reference to compliance with the international instruments of protection of human rights and those referring to women and LGBTIQ persons such as the ECHR, the Istanbul Convention, the UN Security Council Resolution 1325 or the ILO Conventions on decent work and equality of women and men, the International Covenant on Civil and Political Rights, and the International Covenant on Economic, Social and Cultural Rights.[127] In the recent Turkey 2021 Report the Commission took into consideration the effects of the decision to withdraw from the Instanbul Convention pointing out that "(i)n the area of gender equality there was important backsliding on women's rights. Turkey's withdrawal from the Council of Europe Convention on preventing and combatting violence against women and domestic violence (the Istanbul Convention), followed by the adoption of a presidential decision in March 2021, represents a clear regression on the rights of women and girls. This decision compromises the women and girls' rights and combatting gender-based violence in Turkey, and sets a dangerous precedent. Following the withdrawal, hate speech increased in the media against women organisations."[128] The decision also affected the situation of the LGBTIQ community since "(h)ate speech and smear campaigns by government officials and media against the LGBTIQ community increased, notably following the withdrawal from the Istanbul Convention."[129]

The same international legal framework grants the EU several benchmarks within the ENP. In the Report on EU-Jordan relations the Commission and the High Representative pointed out that "(t)he country took legislative and executive steps to ensure more protection for individual rights in areas such as women's rights and women's empowerment. Jordan's progress on human rights was discussed at the Universal Periodic Review (UPR) in November 2018. The UPR encouraged Jordan to make further progress in areas such as gender-based violence and gender equality."[130]

In GAP III the Commission identified the objective of promoting "gender equality through trade policy, including through the EU's engagement in the World Trade Organisation and its work on Aid for Trade."[131] In the field involved the EU

[126] Council of the European Union (2013), paras. 1, 8.

[127] European Commission (2020d), p. 37; European Commission (2020e), p. 38; European Commission (2020f), p. 32; European Commission (2020i), p. 38 *et seq*; European Commission (2020k), p. 20; Council of the European Union (2013).

[128] European Commission (2021f), p. 38.

[129] European Commission (2021f), p. 40.

[130] European Commission and High Representative of the European Union for Foreign Affairs and Security Policy (2019b), p. 8; European Commission and High Representative of the Union for Foreign Affairs and Security Policy (2018a), pp. 4–5.

[131] European Commission (2020b), p. 14.

supports the 2030 Sustainable Development Goals (SDGs),[132] the ILO Conventions and the Decent Work Agenda,[133] the Beijing Declaration and Platform for Action,[134] the Helsinki Final Act and the Charter of Paris, and promotes the ratification of the United Nations Convention against Transnational Organized Crime and the Protocol to Prevent, Suppress and Punish Trafficking in Persons especially Women and Children,[135] and of CEDAW.[136]

The EU, UN and UN Women started the Spotligh Initiative in 2017,[137] aiming at attaining the objective of eliminating all forms of violence against women and girls. Moreover, the EU, UN Women and ILO launched the 3-year programme Promoting women's economic empowerment at work through responsible business in G7 countries,[138] which supports sustainable, inclusive and equitable economic growth. The cooperation with the UN is also witnessed by the UN-EU Strategic Partnership on Peace Operations and Crisis Management priorities (2019–2021).[139]

As already observed, multilateralism is also the guiding principle of the Union in advancing LGBTIQ equality. The EU supported the December 2008 United Nations General Assembly (UNGA) Statement on human rights, sexual orientation and gender identity, the 2006 joint statement at the Human Rights Council and the resolution on human rights, sexual orientation and gender identity the UN Human Rights Council adopted in 2011,[140] while the EU Member States unanimously supported a Recommendation of the Committee of Ministers of the Council of Europe on LGBTI rights.[141] Furthermore, the EU cooperates with several international organizations such as UN, Council of Europe and OSCE in the field of non-discrimination on the grounds of sexual orientation and gender identity.[142] This way of working is to be enhanced since the LGBTIQ Equality Strategy 2020-2025 stated that "(t)he EU will take action on LGBTIQ equality in international fora, build international partnerships based on the principles of equality and non-discrimination and engage regularly with partner countries in political and human rights dialogues in line with its guidelines to promote and protect LGBTI

---

[132] Article 1 of the negotiated Partnership Agreement between the EU and ACP.

[133] Article 33 of the negotiated Partnership Agreement between the EU and ACP.

[134] Article 36 of the negotiated Partnership Agreement between the EU and ACP.

[135] Article 72 of the negotiated Partnership Agreement between the EU and ACP.

[136] Article 66 of the negotiated Partnership Agreement between the EU and ACP.

[137] See www.spotlightinitiative.org.

[138] See https://www.empowerwomen.org/en/projects/we-empower-g7.

[139] Council of the European Union (2018b).

[140] Council of the European Union (2013), para. 10.

[141] Recommendation CM/Rec (2010)5 of the Committee of Ministers to member states on Measures to combat discrimination on grounds of sexual orientation or gender identity, adopted without a vote on 31 March 2010.

[142] Council of the European Union (2013).

people's human rights, in line with its human rights guidelines on non-discrimination in external action."[143]

It has to be added that the EU either avails itself of the opinions and recommendations delivered by the monitoring bodies international conventions on human rights set up, or requires third countries to report to these bodies with the aim of advancing gender equality and eradicating discrimination against LGBTIQ persons.[144]

Reference to the international system of protection of human rights and treaty bodies' practice contributes to attainment of the objectives the EU pursues in each field of its external relations. It also strengthens EU leverage in exporting its values and their connection to economic aims in admission to the Union and the ENP, whilst in the other fields of external action it supports achievement of the objectives the TEU lays down in Article 3, para 5 and Article 21, paras. 1 and 2: contributing to the development of international law, including respect for the principles of the UN Charter, promoting multilateral solutions to common problems, in particular in the framework of the United Nations, supporting democracy, the rule of law and the protection of human rights and preserving peace, prevent conflicts and strengthen international security within the international legal framework.

The EU's contribution to the spreading of international standards of protection of human rights has to be considered as a positive step in the strengthening of the system as a whole. However some doubts can be cast on the effectiveness of the action the EU has been putting into place relying on the practice of international organizations. Ratification of international treaties does not entail proper implementation of the rules or adoption of policies consistent with the laws flowing from those instruments. An assessment that does not take into consideration the concrete functioning of the domestic legal order could fail to attain the objective of advancing equality. Furthermore, the system of periodic reports that is adopted by treaties on human rights is not compelling, so that states are not bound by the findings of human rights treaty bodies. A similar approach characterises the quasi-judicial pattern of individuals' communications that has been set up within the framework of various treaties protecting human rights since the views of treaty bodies impose no obligations on States. As a consequence, recommendations and views finding breaches of human rights may not be followed by States' adoption of appropriate measures to comply with their human rights obligations.

Reliance on the findings of human rights treaty bodies could make the EU's action effective only if it availed itself of its leverage *vis-à-vis* third countries, subjecting financial assistance or conditionality policy to those findings.

---

[143] European Commission (2020k), p. 20.

[144] European Commission (2020d), p. 37; European Commission (2020e), p. 38; European Commission (2020f), p. 32; European Commission (2020i), p. 38 *et seq*; European Commission (2019b), p. 4; European Commission and High Representative of the Union for Foreign Affairs and Security Policy (2018a), p. 5. European Commission and High Representative of the Union for Foreign Affairs and Security Policy (2015b), p. 6. On the GSP+ see European Commission (2018), p. 92 *et seq*; Council of the European Union (2013), p. 21 *et seq*.

9 Final Remarks

The approach of the EU towards non-discrimination on the grounds of sex, sexual orientation and gender identity in its external action is neither holistic nor homogeneous.

Gender equality is promoted in all fields of external action, but protection of LGBTIQ rights is pursued in a few of them. The difference in the scope of the EU's external action on non-discrimination makes it clear that outlawing discrimination on the grounds of sex, sexual orientation and gender identity is important not *per se*, but because of its contribution to achievement of the wider set of aims the EU has targeted.

EU external action covers areas which are not covered by internal action since the former includes legal items such as political participation, family law, marriage, birth registry, the registration of same-sex partnerships, same-sex marriage, property rights, inheritance.

Notwithstanding the new impetus on equality which followed the entry into force of the Lisbon Treaty, the connection that has been established between attainment of the EU's objectives and external action on gender equality and LGBTIQ people's rights has left the latter in a limbo between two different approaches. The first is the economic rationale which was rooted in the original attitude towards advancing women's rights. The second of the said approaches is the protection of human rights the Union has been developing in the most recent years. To put it in a nutshell, the EU's external action on non-discrimination reproduces the same tension characterising its internal action.

As a consequence, practice has been vested with the task of striking the balance between the two approaches towards non-discrimination.

In the admission procedure, there are two crucial steps. The first is weighing of the promotion of the values of the Union against full implementation of the EU *acquis* in national law in assessment of applications for membership. The second step relates to the importance which is given to gender equality and LGBTIQ rights within the wider framework of candidate countries' compliance with human rights.

Similarly, in the context of the ENP, promotion of the "ring of friends" through the export of the EU's values coexists with the economic targets that are embedded in the relationships the Union established with the countries taking part in this policy to promote its economic model. Integrating political considerations into the economic rationale leaves a certain margin of discretion to EU institutions.

The EU's contribution to multilateralism has revived the policies in the fields of CFSP, trade and development cooperation, but the economic rationale is still at their basis.

The analysis of EU institutions' practice clarifies that the difficulties in setting aside the economic approach which is embedded in the exporting of the *acquis* of the Union and the focus on women as economic actors have weakened the rationale of advancing human rights and the contribution of the Union in eradicating the prejudices and the root causes for discrimination against women and LGBTIQ persons.[145]

Several factors decrease the capacity of the EU's external action to enhance protection of human rights. The first is the exclusion of non-discrimination against the LGBTIQ community from the scope of several fields of external action. Although the LGBTIQ Equality Strategy 2020-2025 emphasizes that LGBTIQ rights are human rights, there is no attempt to widen the scope of the external initiatives of the EU.

The conception of gender-based violence is the second factor. The Union highlights the impact of gender-based violence in the various fields of economic, political and social life, but does not consider this violence as the main instrument for distributing role in society and perpetuating stereotypess, a limit affecting the EU policy to dismantle the male-dominated system of relationships that violence has set up.

A third factor flows from the legal arrangements of trade agreements. Non-discrimination is regulated in the chapters dealing with labour and environmental rights, so that protection of human rights and outlawing of discrimination do not underlie the entire legal framework.[146]

The fourth factor relates to the way in which the international agreements the EU entered into promote gender equality. Most of the provisions establish principles of conduct or objectives from which no indivudals' entitlements derive.

The fifth factor is related to the justiciability of the provisions outlawing discrimination. Most of the treaty rules regulating non-discrimination do not fall within the scope of the laws establishing dispute settlement systems.[147]

The last factor is intrinsic to EU policy on human rights within the framework of trade relations. The assessment of practice clarifies that clauses advancing women's rights are contained in the agreements the EU concluded with no politically or economically powerful countries.[148] States playing a pivotal role in the economic sphere and the political arena refuse any external interference with the laws and practice on women equality and LGBTIQ rights and the EU's acceptance of this policy prevents its action from advancing equality. The EU adopts a careful stance towards human rights in negotiating with states such as China or India, a choice which casts doubts not only on the consistency, but also on the credibility of the EU as a global promoter of the rights of women and LGBTIQ persons.

All those factors have an impact on the strategies the EU has adopted to enhance its external action and could seriously affect attainment of the objective of promoting gender equality and LGBTIQ community's rights.

---

[145] Garcia (2021), p. 285.

[146] Thies (2020), p. 447; Kube (2019), p. 226. On the lack of consistency of the EU approach towards human rights see Velluti (2016), p. 41 *et seq.*

[147] Thies (2019), p. 81.

[148] Thies (2020), p. 448.

Finally, there is a more general question lying behind the legal issue this paper focuses on and involving the EU's role as a global promoter of human rights. The EU's ability to contribute to the strengthening of gender equality and LGBTIQ persons' rights in the international arena has to be evaluated against the legal framework the Treaties lay down. The reforms the Lisbon Treaty enacted conferred no new competences upon the Union in the field of human rights.[149] As a consequence it is doubtful that the competences the EU holds enable it to contribute to counteracting the root causes for discrimination against women and LGBTIQ persons.[150]

References

Atrey S (2019) Intersectional discrimination. Oxford University Press, Oxford

Bartels L (2005) Human Rights conditionality in the EU's International Agreements. Oxford University Press, Oxford

Bell M (2012) Gender identity and sexual orientation: alternative pathways in EU equality law. Am J Comp Law 60:127–146

Bell M, Waddington L (2021) Similar, Yet Different: the Work-life Balance Directive and the Expanding Frontiers of EU Non-discrimination Law. Common Market Law Rev 58:1401–1432

Burri S, Prechal S (2008) EU gender equality law. Report of the European Commission. Office for Official Publications of the European Union, Luxembourg, pp 3–22

Busby N (2018) The evolution of gender equality and related employment policies: the case of work–family reconciliation. Int J Discrimination Law 8(2–3):104–123

Cannizzaro E (2014) The EU's Human Rights Obligations in Relation to Policies with Extraterritorial Effects: a Reply to Lorand Bartels. Eur J Int Law 25:1093–1099

Carmel E (2003) What is European and Social about European Social Policy? Some remarks on the open of co-ordination. Paper for ESP Anet Conference Copenhagen 14–17 November

Council of the European Union (2008) EU guidelines on violence against women and girls and combating all forms of discrimination against them

Council of the European Union (2013) Guidelines to promote and protect the enjoyment of all human rights by the lesbian, gay, bisexual, transgender and intersex (LGBTI) persons

Council of the European Union (2018a) Council conclusions on women, peace and security

Council of the European Union (2018b) Council conclusions reinforcing the UN-EU strategic partnership on peace operations and crisis management: priorities 2019–2021

Council of the European Union (2019) EU Action Plan on Women, Peace and Security (WPS) 2019-2024

Cremona M (1996) Human Rights Clauses in the EC's trade agreements. In: O'Keeffe D, Emiliou N (eds) The European Union and World Trade Law: after the GATT Uruguay Round. Wiley, Chichester, pp 62–77

Cremona M (2011) Values in EU Foreign Policy. In: Evans M, Koutrakos P (eds) Beyond the Established Orders: policy Interconnections between the EU and the Rest of the World. Hart Publishing, Oxford, pp 275–315

[149] Pech and Joelle (2020), p. 334; Velluti (2016), p. 46.

[150] Velluti (2016), p. 46; Cannizzaro (2014), p. 1098.

Cremona M (2014) A reticent court?: policy objectives and the Court of Justice. In: Cremona M, Thies A (eds) The European Court of Justice and external relations law: constitutional challenges. Hart Publishing, Oxford, pp 15–32
European Commission (2010) Strategy for equality between women and men 2010-2015
European Commission (2015a) Guidelines on the analysis of human rights impacts in impact assessments for trade-related policy initiatives
European Commission (2015b) List of actions by the Commission to advance LGBTI equality
European Commission (2018) Mid-Term Evaluation of the EU's Generalised Scheme of Preferences (GSP)
European Commission (2019a) Serbia 2019 Report Accompanying the document Communication from the Commission to the European Parliament, the Council, the European Economic and Social Committee and the Committee of the Regions 2019 Communication on EU Enlargement Policy
European Commission (2019b) Final Report 2015–2019 on the List of Actions to advance LGBTI equality
European Commission (2020a) Communication from the Commission to the European Parliament, the Council, the European Economic and Social Committee and the Committee of the Regions. A Union of Equality: Gender Equality Strategy 2020–2025
European Commission (2020b) Joint Communication to the European Council and the Parliament. EU Gender Action Plan (GAP) III – An Ambitious Agenda for Gender Equality and Women's Empowerment in EU External Action
European Commission (2020c) Albania 2020 Report Accompanying the Communication from the Commission to the European Parliament, the Council, the European Economic and Social Committee and the Committee of the Regions 2020 Communication on EU Enlargement Policy
European Commission (2020d) Serbia 2020 Report Accompanying the Communication from the Commission to the European Parliament, the Council, the European Economic and Social Committee and the Committee of the Regions 2020 Communication on EU Enlargement Policy
European Commission (2020e) Turkey 2020 Report Accompanying the Communication from the Commission to the European Parliament, the Council, the European Economic and Social Committee and the Committee of the Regions 2020 Communication on EU Enlargement Policy
European Commission (2020f) North Macedonia 2020 Report Accompanying the Communication from the Commission to the European Parliament, the Council, the European Economic and Social Committee and the Committee of the Regions 2020 Communication on EU Enlargement Policy
European Commission (2020g) Kosovo* 2020 Report Accompanying the Communication from the Commission to the European Parliament, the Council, the European Economic and Social Committee and the Committee of the Regions 2020 Communication on EU Enlargement Policy
European Commission (2020h) Bosnia and Herzegovina 2020 Report Accompanying the Communication from the Commission to the European Parliament, the Council, the European Economic and Social Committee and the Committee of the Regions 2020 Communication on EU Enlargement Policy
European Commission (2020i) Montenegro 2020 Report Accompanying the Communication from the Commission to the European Parliament, the Council, the European Economic and Social Committee and the Committee of the Regions 2020 Communication on EU Enlargement Policy
European Commission (2020j) Final Report 2015–2019 on the List of actions to advance LGBTI equality
European Commission (2020k) Communication from the Commission to the European Parliament, the Council, the European Economic and Social Committee and the Committee of the Regions. Union of Equality: LGBTIQ Equality Strategy 2020–2025
European Commission (2021a) European Commission services' position paper on the sustainability impact assessment in support of negotiations for the trade part of the European Union-Mercosur Association Agreement

European Commission (2021b) Communication from the Commission to the European Parliament, the Council, the European Economic and Social Committee and the Committee of the Regions. 2021 Communication on EU Enlargement Policy
European Commission (2021c) Commission Staff Working Document. Albania 2021 Report Accompanying the document Communication from the Commission to the European Parliament, the Council, the European Economic and Social Committee and the Committee of the Regions 2021 Communication on EU Enlargement Policy
European Commission (2021d) Commission Staff Working Document. Bosnia and Herzegovina 2021 Report Accompanying the document Communication from the Commission to the European Parliament, the Council, the European Economic and Social Committee and the Committee of the Regions 2021 Communication on EU Enlargement Policy
European Commission (2021e) Commission Staff Working Document. Montenegro 2021 Report Accompanying the document Communication from the Commission to the European Parliament, the Council, the European Economic and Social Committee and the Committee of the Regions 2021 Communication on EU Enlargement Policy
European Commission (2021f) Commission Staff Working Document. Turkey 2021 Report Accompanying the document Communication from the Commission to the European Parliament, the Council, the European Economic and Social Committee and the Committee of the Regions 2021 Communication on EU Enlargement Policy
European Commission (2021g) Commission Staff Working Document. Serbia 2021 Report Accompanying the document Communication from the Commission to the European Parliament, the Council, the European Economic and Social Committee and the Committee of the Regions 2021 Communication on EU Enlargement Policy
European Commission (2021h) Commission Staff Working Document. Kosovo 2021 Report Accompanying the document Communication from the Commission to the European Parliament, the Council, the European Economic and Social Committee and the Committee of the Regions 2021 Communication on EU Enlargement Policy
European Commission (2021i) Commission Staff Working Document. North Macedonia 2021 Report Accompanying the document Communication from the Commission to the European Parliament, the Council, the European Economic and Social Committee and the Committee of the Regions 2021 Communication on EU Enlargement Policy
European Commission and High Representative of the Union for Foreign Affairs and Security Policy (2015a) Gender Equality and Women's empowerment: Transforming the Lives of Girls and Women through EU External Relations 2016-2020
European Commission and High Representative of the Union for Foreign Affairs and Security Policy (2015b) Implementation of the European Neighbourhood Policy in Palestine Progress in 2014 and recommendations for actions Accompanying the document Joint Communication to the European Parliament, the Council, the European Economic and Social Committe and the Committee of the Regions. Implementation of the European Neighbourhood Policy in 2014
European Commission and High Representative of the Union for Foreign Affairs and Security Policy (2017a) Association Implementation Report on the Republic of Moldova
European Commission and High Representative of the Union for Foreign Affairs and Security Policy (2017b) Rapport sur l'état des relations UE-Tunisie dans le cadre de la Politique européenne de voisinage révisée Avril 2017
European Commission and High Representative of the Union for Foreign Affairs and Security Policy (2018a) Report on EU-Armenia relations in the framework of the revised ENP
European Commission and High Representative of the Union for Foreign Affairs and Security Policy (2018b) Rapport sur l'état des relations UE-Tunisie dans le cadre de la Politique européenne de voisinage révisée
European Commission and High Representative of the Union for Foreign Affairs and Security Policy (2018c) Report on EU-Lebanon relations in the framework of the revised ENP (2017-2018)

European Commission and High Representative of the European Union for Foreign Affairs and Security Policy (2019a) Report on EU - Azerbaijan relations in the framework of the revised European Neighbourhood Policy

European Commission and High Representative of the European Union for Foreign Affairs and Security Policy (2019b) Report on EU - Jordan relations in the framework of the revised European Neighbourhood Policy (2018-2019)

European Commission and High Representative of the Union for Foreign Affairs and Security Policy (2020a) Joint Communication to the European Parliament, the European Council, the Council, the European Economic and Social Committee and the Committee of the Regions. Eastern Partnership Policy beyond 2020

European Commission and High Representative of the Union for Foreign Affairs and Security Policy (2020b) Rapport sur l'état des relations UE-Algérie dans le cadre de la PEV renouvelée Avril 2018 – Août 2020

European Commission and High Representative of the Union for Foreign Affairs and Security Policy (2021) Association Implementation Report on Georgia

European Parliament (2021) The EU Strategy for Gender Equality. European Parliament resolution of 21 January 2021 on the EU Strategy for Gender Equality

Fortas A-C (2016) Droits international économique et genre. In: Jänterä-Jareborg M, Tigroudja H (eds) Women's Human Rights and the Elimination of Discrimination. The Hague Academy of International Law, The Hague, pp 354–389

Garcia M (2021) Trade Policy. In: Abels G, Krizsán A, MacRae H, van der Vleuten A (eds) The Routledge Handbook of Gender and EU Politics. Routledge, London, pp 278–289

Guth J, Elfving S (2019) Gender and the Court of Justice of the European Union. Routledge, London

Hervey TK (2005) Thirty Years of EU Sex Equality Law: Looking Backwards, Looking Forwards. Maastricht J Eur Comp Law 12:307–325

Hodson D, Maer I (2001) The Open Method as a New Mode of Governance: the Case of Soft Economic Policy Co-ordination. J Common Mark Stud 39:719–746

Kube V (2019) EU Human Rights, International Investment Law and Participation. Operationalising the EU Foreign Policy Objective to Global Human Rights Protection. Springer, Heidelberg

MacKinnon C (1987) Feminims Unmodified. Discourses on Life and Law. Harvard University Press, Cambridge

Numhauser-Henning A (2007) EU Sex Equality Law Post-Amsterdam. In: Meenan H (ed) Equality in an Enlarged European Union. Understanding the Article 3 Directives. Cambridge University Press, Cambridge, pp 145–177

Pech L, Grogan J (2020) EU External Human Rights. In: Wessel RA, Larik J (eds) EU External Relations Law. Hart Publishing, Oxford, pp 327–364

Schiek D (2007) Broadening the Scope and the Norms of EU Gender Equality Law: towards a Multidimensional Conceptions of Equality Law. Maastricht J Eur Comp Law 14:427–466

Thies A (2019) The Lisbon Treaty and EU External Relations Law. Accommodating Stakeholders Values, Principles and Objectives. In: Söderstein A (ed) The Lisbon Treaty 10 Years on: Success or Failure? Swedish Institute for European Policy Studies, Stockolm, pp 63–89. www.sieps.se/en

Thies A (2020) The EU's Law and Policy Framework for the Promotion of Gender Equality in the World. In: Griegerich T (ed) The European Union as Protector and Promoter of Equality. Springer, Heidelberg, pp 429–454

United Nations General Assembly Resolution (2015) A/RES/70/1, 29 September 2015

United Nations Security Council Resolution 1325 (2000) S/RES/1325, 31 October 2000

Velluti S (2016) The Promotion and Integration of Human Rights in EU External Trade Relations. Utrecht J Int Eur Law 32:41–68

Weldon-Johns M (2021) EU work-family policies revisited: Finally challenging caring roles? Eur Labour Law J 12(3):301–321

Marco Evola is an Associate Professor of European Union Law LUMSA Department of Law Palermo. He obtained his Ph. D (2008) at the University of Palermo. He was post-doctoral researcher at the University of Palermo (2009–2013). He has been teaching European Union Law, European Union Private International Law, Human Rights, European Migration Law. He was a member of different research groups within the framework of projects of research of national interest. He is professor in Masters and post-lauream courses. He is a member of the Editorial Board of the review Diritti umani e diritto internazionale and Member of the Scientific Committee of the review La Magistratura. He is a member of the college of professors of the Ph.D course "Mediterranean Studies. History, Law and Economics". His scientific research focuses on human rights, migration, non-discrimination, accession to and withdrawal from the EU, Rule of Law. He has published a monograph on the legal status of third-country migrant workers in the EU legal system.

Feminist Justice and the European Court of Human Rights

Ivana Jelić

Contents

Abstract Gender equality is clearly one of the pillar principles of the European Convention on Human Rights. Protection of women's rights can be treated through an individual right, dealing with its substantial and procedural limb (ex. sex discrimination cases), or as an (aggravated) aspect or an attribute of a violation of a right enshrined by the Convention (ex. gender equality in connection with rights to freedom of expression or religion). Despite its principled position and having in mind the present state of jurisprudence of the Strasbourg Court (ECtHR), it could be concluded that feminist justice is still underdeveloped in comparison with the growing need for the protection of women's rights, insisting on personal integrity.

Observing from a broader perspective, the ECtHR's case law regarding feminist justice can be categorized into three clusters: (1) cases relating to achieving formal equality between men and women and prohibiting direct gender discrimination, focusing on the idea of achieving "sameness with men" (jurisprudence under Article 14); (2) cases relating to issues that may, in theory, affect both men and women, but in reality, disproportionately affect women and require special (additional) protection, such as domestic violence and trafficking; and (3) cases relating to issues that

---

I. Jelić (✉)
European Court of Human Rights, Council of Europe, Strasbourg, France
e-mail: ivana.jelic@echr.coe.int

I. Krstić et al. (eds.), *Legal Issues of International Law from a Gender Perspective*, Gender Perspectives in Law 3, https://doi.org/10.1007/978-3-031-13459-3_2

are specific to women's rights, such as violence against women and reproductive rights.

The Court has gradually widened its approach concerning the protection of women's rights, giving rise to a 'living instrument doctrine' by interpreting the Convention "in the light of present-day conditions". This approach of evaluative interpretation of the Convention is necessary in order to address actual challenges of violation of human rights of women and girls, which were not envisaged in the text of the Convention 70 years ago.

The author tends to make an analysis on how contemporary international law deals with feminist justice, with a special emphasis on the most important ECtHR cases. The contribution should give an analytical overview through the prism of direct and indirect gender discrimination, having in mind the mentioned three clusters, with an emphasis on the recent case-law.

1 Introduction: Importance of Gender Sensitive Judgments

Gender-sensitive judgments of international courts, such as the European Court of Human Rights (ECtHR), certainly must contribute to more complete protection of women's rights, effective gender equality, breaking down prejudices and barriers stemming from the mentality of historically patriarchal societies. And, most of all, those judgments bridge the victims with justice where national judiciary failed to protect their rights and, thus, contributed to their violations.

The role of international human rights courts, albeit regional, and UN human rights treaty bodies is to correct mistakes done by national judiciaries in application of legal principles, and to point out shortcomings vis-à-vis national procedures and legislative frameworks harming the protection of human rights. The ECtHR as a European corrective judicial mechanism, but also the most developed regional human rights court, has achieved to provide for better protection of women's rights and gender equality, by virtue of interpretation of the European Convention on Human Rights (ECHR, Convention) as a living instrument, so the interpretation is realized 'in the light of present-day conditions',[1] which is the approach applicable to the ECHR as a whole

The Court's determination to interpret the Convention according to its intention i.e. teleological approach in legal interpretation, is pertinent in particular for those rights that were not explicitly codified when the Convention was born over seventy years ago. As the Court stated 'The Convention is intended to guarantee not rights that are theoretical or illusory but rights that are practical and effective',[2] which is one of the main signposts on the way to justice. Indeed, complex issue of gender equality protection requires interpretation of concrete, practical and effective rights.

[1] Tyrer v. The United Kingdom, para. 31.

[2] *Airey v. Ireland*, para. 24.

2 How Much Has the ECtHR's Jurisprudence Achieved?

Although the Convention neither contains provisions on protection of women's rights nor codifies explicitly the principle of gender equality, it is evident from the case-law of the Strasbourg Court, which actually makes the Convention alive or interpreted as a living instrument that is adjustable to the present-day conditions, that one of major goals in the member states of the Council of Europe is the advancement of gender equality.[3] The Court is not at all blind for the cases of violation of certain gender sensitive rights or ill-treatment mainly affecting women and girls. Considering the 'living instrument' doctrine the Court has adopted an evolutive interpretation method of the Convention and the Protocols thereto, by integrating different aspects of women's rights into the protection already provided for the existing rights in the Convention. In more and more gender sensitive judgments, "the Convention's special features as a human rights treaty and the fact that it is a living instrument which should be interpreted in the light of present-day conditions" has been emphasized. [4] Having in mind this approach, gender equality has become one of the pillar principles of the Convention system.

However, the issue at stake is how much has actually changed, since the time of justified criticism that "the Court's jurisprudence has been largely impotent in challenging gender discrimination and achieving gender equality",[5] and how the ECtHR follows the development trend of gender protection. The recent practice of the Court speaks in favor of the fact that topics of feminist justice are becoming more and more present, because women are becoming more self-aware and assertive.

Unlike the ECHR, women's rights are specifically codified in a number of international human rights instruments that require High Contracting Parties (HCPs) to take necessary steps to ensure that women's human rights are protected by law and that discrimination on the basis of gender is prohibited. Those instruments also provide legal framework for combating gender inequalities and practices that negatively affect women's and girls' rights.

It is topical to emphasize that universal human rights legal framework in respect of women's rights is more developed that the European.[6] However, in respect to the

[3] *Konstantin Markin v. Russia* (GC), para. 12; *Jurčić v. Croatia*, para. 65.

[4] *S.M. v. Croatia* [GC], para. 292. See also: *Khamtokhu and Aksenchik v. Russia* [GC], para. 73.

[5] Radacic (2008), p. 842.

[6] The most comprehensive treaty on the rights of women, the United Nations Convention on the Elimination of Discrimination against Women (CEDAW) condemns any form of discrimination against women and reaffirms the importance of guaranteeing equal political, economic, social, cultural and civil rights to women and men. Equality is guaranteed to woman regardless of their marital status also by requiring the HCPs to enact national legislation banning discrimination (Articles 1, 2, and 3). By allowing the HCPs to take temporary special measures to accelerate the achievement of equality in practice between men and women (Article 4), and to take actions to modify social and cultural patterns that perpetuate discrimination (Article 5), the CEDAW gives adequate general framework for the protection of women's rights, while permitting the states to determine and design concrete steps, actions and measures in order to implement the principles

regional instruments on woman's rights protection, there are significant developments.[7]

Regional courts on human rights, the Court of Justice of the EU, as well as the UN human rights treaty bodies, have developed useful jurisprudence, which the ECtHR refers to in its judgments in respect of the gender sensitive issues.[8]

Despite the fact that the Strasbourg Court's case-law left great space to margin of appreciation to the states, in particular is the issues regarding religious gender sensitive rights,[9] it has recently shown more sensitivity in protecting gender oriented rights, where domestic courts had stayed tacit. Actually, the Court has considered the protection of women's rights beyond pure gender equality concept and placed them on the level of deserved gender sensitive protection. For example, the recent

---

there set forth. An emphasis on need for equal access to education has its provision (Article 10), which is crucially important for woman's independence and emancipation. The need for childcare facilities and other social services to help women fulfil family obligations along with work responsibilities and participation in public life (Article 11) and non-discriminatory health services for women, including family planning services (Article 12) are emphasized. In addition, by accepting binding effect of the CEDAW, the HCPs obliged themselves that contracts and other private instruments that restrict the legal capacity of women "shall be deemed null and void" (Article 15), and that appropriate measures to eliminate discrimination in matters relating to marriage and family shall be undertaken, stressing the equal responsibilities of men and women in family life (Article 16).

[7]The following three are notable. First, The Inter-American Convention on the Prevention, Punishment and Eradication of Violence Against Women (the *Convention of Belém do Pará*) recognizes the rights of women to be free from violence in both public and private. The right of all women to enjoy and exercise the rights protected by other regional and international human rights instruments is specifically codified (Article 4). The Convention introduces the HCPs' obligation to undertake affirmative steps to prevent, punish and eradicate violence against women and to progressively undertake measures to address the social and cultural factors contributing to violence or discrimination against women (Article 7). Second, the Protocol to the African Charter on the Rights of Women in Africa (the *Maputo Protocol*) puts an emphasis on the particularly important issues for Africa, such as genital mutilation. There women's dignity is elevated to the level of a particular right (Article 3), which is in harmony with general standing that human dignity is a material or substantive source of all human rights. Having in mind that the feminist justice should reflect gender equality, woman's integrity and independence, it is topical to underline two specific rights that the Protocol codifies: right to equality in marriage (Article 6) and the right to decide whether to have children (Article 14). Finally, The Council of Europe Convention on Preventing and Combating Violence against Women and Domestic Violence (the *Istanbul Convention*) is a further step towards protection of woman's rights, stipulating that sexual harassment, rape, forced marriage, honor crimes, genital mutilation and other forms of violence constitute serious human rights violations. The issue of implementation of these provisions is a theme *per se*, with lots of challenges, such as the attitude of some HCPs towards their obligations deriving from these treaties.

[8]Exempli causa: *Molla Sali v. Greece* (GC, judgment in merits), paras. 70-72 (reference to Concluding observations CEDAW and the UN Human Rights Committee), *Dubská and Krejzová v. The Czech Republic* (GC) paras. 65-66. (referring to concluding observations of CEDAW), *S.M. v Croatia*, para. 191 (Case law of the Inter-American Court), *Christine Goodwin v. UK*, Application no. 28957/95, para. 43 (reference to the ECJ), *Konstantin Markin v. Russia*, Application no. 30078/06, paras. 65-68. (reference to ECJ).

[9]Exempli causa: Leyla Şahin v. Turkey, *S.A.S. v. France*.

case-law highlights the first verdicts on internal prostitution,[10] where an ineffective investigation in the context of rights protected by Article 4 was found, and the first verdict on bullying in the workplace,[11] with a strong aspect of gender endangerment.

Still, there is much room for development of the case law on gender-sensitive judgments. Considering the feminist justice's state under international human rights law, as well as a comparison with the case-law of the Luxembourg Court, it could be concluded that the ECtHR's case-law concerning gender equality is still to be developed. It suffers from certain shortcomings, whether the gender sensitive issue is treated in the context of an individual human woman's right or as an aspect or an attribute of a violation of a right which was already codified in the Convention law. Having in mind growing need for the protection of ample variety of women's rights insisting on personal integrity, dignity, participatory rights and effective equality in almost all spheres of social and family life, as well as in the working environment, the previous statement could be a signal for more efforts to be dedicated to this issue. In addition, the ECtHR should make more use of the jurisprudence of the international judicial and quasyjudicial bodies to go beyond the structural limits of the Convention and the Protocols thereto, in dealing with the above mentioned issues. That would certainly make contribution to establishing more comprehensive gender sensitive approach. The ECtHR's case-law relevant to feminist justice encompasses limited number of direct discrimination cases and much more cases regarding specific types of indirect discrimination, such as domestic violence, sex trafficking, sexual violence, wearing of religious symbols like burka, work related rights and reproductive rights. These are gender-based harms that have been raised before the Court, in which the Court has historically been unwilling to examine in conjunction with Article 14, as they do not fall under the traditional view of what constitutes gender discrimination. However, in recent years the Court has begun to examine these issues in conjunction with Article 14 to a limited extent.

For the purpose of the paper, the Court's jurisprudence relevant to feminist justice will be analyzed in respect of two categories: (1) direct gender discrimination and gender equality, and (2) specific types of indirect discrimination against woman.

3 Direct Gender Discrimination and Gender Equality in Jurisprudence of the ECtHR: Protection Under Article 14 and Protocol 12

Analyzing the jurisprudence, which is relevant to feminist justice, it is obvious that the Court rarely deals with direct forms of discrimination against women under the umbrella of Article 14 of the Convention or Protocol 12 thereto. On the other side, the Court has, in recent years, progressively examined and recognized indirect forms

[10] *S.M. v. Croatia [GC].*

[11] *Špadijer v. Montenegro.*

of discrimination against women under other rights enshrined in the Convention, such as in *Jurčić. v. Croatia.*

While the language used by domestic laws and judgments in direct discrimination cases is openly gender discriminatory against women, treating overtly the two genders differently, in the cases of indirect discrimination the language of the domestic laws and judgments could be considered as gender neutral, but actually it disproportionately disadvantages women, often reinforcing traditional female stereotypes. For example, an indirect discrimination can be found in law that grants certain benefits only to full-time employees, but not to part-time employees, and the latter are predominantly women, as in the case *Isabel Elbal Moreno v. Instituto Nacional de la Seguridad Social (INSS) and Tesorería General de la Seguridad Social (TGSS).*[12]

Direct discrimination ECtHR's case-law relevant to feminist justice in its major part concerned domestic laws and practices regarding legally based inequalities, such as the inability of women to choose a surname as a married woman and distinctions in immigration rules.[13] Recent case-law has also given examples of difference in treatment on ground of pregnancy, which—if not justified—falls under characterization of direct discrimination on a ground of sex.[14]

Out of three conditions for discrimination, two are mandatory to exist: difference in treatment and ground of discrimination. Existence of a comparator, as the third condition, is an optional one. If the comparator is inadequate, that could cause more problems than inexistence of one.[15]

In order to examine cases of direct discrimination, the Court adopted a formal equality approach, which focuses on achieving equal access and opportunity for both genders. In the first case on gender discrimination before the Court, *Abdulaziz, Cabales and Balkandi v. the United Kingdom,* a gender distinction in immigration rules aiming to protect the labor market was considered to be factually valid but not legitimate.[16]

The Court has also examined what constitutes "legitimate aim" of rules that directly discriminate against women. Whereas the ECtHRthus quite broadly accepts an aim as legitimate, it examines more thoroughly whether that aim is actually reached in the concrete case as can be seen in *Abdulaziz, Cabales and Balkandi v. the United Kingdom.* The Court there considered two aims as legitimate: the protection of the labour market[17] and the aim of advancing public tranquillity.[18]

[12]CJEU, C-385/11, *Isabel Elbal Moreno v. Instituto Nacional de la Seguridad Social (INSS) and Tesorería General de la Seguridad Social (TGSS)*, 22 November 2012.

[13]*Ünal Tekeli v. Turkey.*

[14]*Jurčić v. Croatia*, para. 69.

[15]Recent case of *Napotnik v. Romania* has provoked, rightly, a lot of academic controversial discussions in this regard.

[16]*Abdulaziz, Cabales and Balkandi v. the United Kingdom,* para 78.

[17]*Abdulaziz, Cabales and Balkandi v. the United Kingdom,* para. 78.

[18]*Abdulaziz, Cabales and Balkandi v. the United Kingdom,* para. 82.

However, "the advancement of the equality of the sexes is today a major goal in the member States of the Council of Europe. This means that very weighty reasons would have to be advanced before a difference of treatment on the ground of sex could be regarded as compatible with the Convention"[19] and concerning the first aim the Court was not convinced that "[. . .] the difference that may nevertheless exist between the respective impact of men and of women on the domestic labour market is sufficiently important to justify the difference of treatment, [. . .]".[20] Concerning the second aim, the Court was "not persuaded that this aim was served by the distinction drawn in those rules between husbands and wives."[21]

In another gender discrimination case, *Ünal Tekeli v. Turkey,* Turkish women's inability to choose their surname, as married women, due to difference in treatment on grounds of sex established by national law, was treated as violation of the Convention, as such difference in treatment could not be justified.

When the Court, during its earlier period, dealt with national legislation recognizing the legal relationship between a child and its unmarried mother by procedures which were not applied to children born of married mothers,[22] it found that the difference in treatment regarding the private and family life of the applicant unmarried mother compared to married mothers was not justified by the assumption that some unmarried mothers do not wish to care for their children, and the desire to preserve traditional families. While the Court recognizes that each State is afforded a margin of appreciation in the implementation of its social policy, this margin is narrowed where it is based on reasons that are not relevant or sufficient to justify differential treatment. Traditionalism and assumptions on unmarried mothers' wish to be parent cannot justify such treatment, and the Court is clear that such explanations have no place in a Convention system designed to secure rights to all.

The Court has proven in many cases[23] that particular traditions, general assumptions, prevailing social attitudes, mentality or financial interests in a state could not be used to justify the difference in treatment on ground of sex. Also, there is no space for religion, tradition or other identity connected issues to be used as grounds for justification of discrimination. This is obvious in *Molla Sali v. Greece*, where the Court found violations of Article 14 and Article 1 of Protocol 1 regarding inheritance right of a Muslim widowed woman, who was discriminated against by a legally based priority to application of sharia, as dominant law in family matters in her religious community, which was against civil law giving legal priority to her late husband's will, that was in her favor.[24] This approach confirms universality of

[19] *Abdulaziz, Cabales and Balkandi v. the United Kingdom,* para. 78.

[20] *Abdulaziz, Cabales and Balkandi v. the United Kingdom,* para. 79.

[21] *Abdulaziz, Cabales and Balkandi v. the United Kingdom,* para. 81.

[22] *Marckx v. Belgium.*

[23] *Exempli causa*: *Ünal Tekeli v. Turkey,* para. *63, Jurčić v. Croatia,* paras. *73 and 84, Konstantin Markin v. Russia (GC),* para. *127.*

[24] *Molla Sali v. Greece* (GC, Judgment in Merits), paras. 158, 161.

human rights and values that are common to all, regardless of one's belongings and affiliations, or society's determinations such as tradition or religion.

In the cases regarding Article 14 in conjunction with Article 1 of Protocol 1, the Court established the test of "manifestly without reasonable foundation"[25] in situations where certain measures aiming to correct a historical inequality caused allegedly a difference in treatment, like in the case of *Stec and Others v. UK* regarding the entitlement to social security benefits in UK.[26] The Court grants in these cases a wide margin of appreciation and deems the national authorities as better suited to examine and determine the case. Therefore, it restricts its control on the question whether the national authorities had acted "manifestly without reasonable foundation".[27] The Court thereby accepts "reasonably and objectively grounds"[28] for a justification, and for example this can be the aim to correct historical inequalities or the aim to compensate for reduced earning capacity during a person's working life.

Direct discrimination cases before the ECtHR, obviously, were those in which a different treatment, based on a discriminatory ground on gender, had derived from national laws with discriminatory provisions.

The limited representation of cases regarding the non-discrimination principle under Article 14 relevant to feminist justice in the ECtHR's jurisprudence could be explained in two ways. Firstly, such instances have become less and less common in Europe, notably due to (in some states, amended) national legislative and institutional frameworks that secured prohibition of gender discrimination in the member states of the Council of Europe. Secondly, due to the structure of the Convention, namely due to the character of Article 14 which is "subsidiary in nature and requires that the facts of the case broadly relate to issues protected under a right found in the Convention."[29]

Although the application of Article 14, which has its ancillary status to other substantive provision of the Convention and the Protocols thereto, "does not necessarily presuppose the violation of one of the substantive rights protected by the Convention",[30] the Court often practices refraining from examining issues under Article 14 if it has found a violation of other articles. The usual formulation that "there is no need to give a separate ruling on the remaining complaints",[31] known as Câmpeanu formula, is not as adequate as frequently used, which is visible also in separate opinions of the ECtHR judges.[32] However, if the concerned case contains a

[25] *Stec and Others v. UK,* para. 52.

[26] *Stec and Others v. UK,* paras. 61-66.

[27] *Stec and Others v. UK,* para. 52.

[28] *Stec and Others v. UK,* para. 59.

[29] Sjöholm (2017), p. 195.

[30] *E.B. v. France* [GC], para. 47.

[31] *Centre for legal resources on behalf of Valentin Câmpeanu v. Romania*, para. 156.

[32] Joint Partly Dissenting Opinion of Judges Ziemele and Bianku to the *Câmpeanu case*, para. 1.

"clear inequality of treatment",[33] the approach of the Court is different and it considers the merits regarding the claims under Article 14, as well.

On the other side, the introduction of Protocol 12 to the ECHR has limited effect so far, as the Court has not practiced invoking Protocol 12 in cases regarding Article 14.

Finally, in gender sensitive cases where the applicants did not invoke one of the above provisions, the Court should use its power of being the master of characterization so to apply the virtue of the *jura novit curia* principle in respect of introducing those provisions. The principle implies that "the Court is not bound by the legal grounds adduced by the applicant under the Convention and the Protocols thereto and has the power to decide on the characterization to be given in law to the facts of a complaint by examining it under Articles or provisions of the Convention that are different from those relied upon by the applicant".[34]

4 Indirect Gender Discrimination and Gender Equality in Jurisprudence of the ECtHR

The Court has been increasingly confronted with cases of indirect forms of discrimination, in particular those treatments that disproportionately affect women, such as issues of gender based domestic violence, sex trafficking, work related rights in connection to pregnancy and bullying at workplace. In the cases concerning the exploitation of women as domestic servants without payment (and sometimes without their passports that were taken away), even though the Court emphasized the positive obligations of the state in this context, notably effective investigations and criminalisation of the aforementioned behaviour,[35] no mention is made to the gender dimension which would be pertinent. Even though the Court is aware of the gender dimension of the respective case,[36] it is evident that an emphasis on gender based discrimination is needed.The cases from this context share the fact that the victims in them were migrant girls/women but no mention is made to Art. 14 ECHR, even though the lack of legislation or effective investigations in these cases clearly could arise to intersectional discrimination as mostly migrant women are the victims.

Indirect discrimination against women has been examined primarily under existing rights, notably Articles 2, 3, 4, 8 and 9 of the Convention. In recent years, those articles have been examined also in conjunction with the principle of non-discrimination under Article 14, which is positive step towards comprehensive protection of gender equality and gender justice.

[33] *Airey v. Ireland* (1979), para. 30.

[34] *Radomilja and Others v. Croatia* [GC].

[35] For example, see *Siliadin v France*, paras. 89, 112.

[36] See *J. and others v Austria*, para. 33.

As Radačić noticed, although the Court's standing that indirect discrimination is covered by Article 14, firstly expressed in *Belgian Linguistic case*, years have passed before the Court started to apply the test concerned in *D.H. v. Czech Republic*.[37] This passage of almost four decades was a period where a living instrument doctrine was not frequently applied. As of 2007, the concept of indirect discrimination was more and more present in the Strasbourg court case-law. Moreover, as Etinski noticed, the concept became widespread through national legal systems of majority of the HCPs to the Convention, which development the EU contributed to.[38]

The Court's acknowledgement of the applicability of Article 14 in cases of indirect discrimination is important from a perspective of feminist justice. Namely, using that method the Court takes a more gender-sensitive approach to adjudication and recognizes systemic discriminatory effect on women even when the law seems as gender neutral, rather than to only acknowledge that a particular female applicant had suffered a violation of a substantive article.

However, the cases regarding sex trafficking and exploitation of women for the purpose of prostitution are regarded not in conjunction with Article 14, but exclusively under Article 4. Despite the fact that in *S.M. v. Croatia* the applicant did not allege violations in respect of discrimination, there was a space for considering an aspect of violence motivated by discrimination under Article 14,[39] as judge Turković wrote in her concurring opinion.[40]

Regarding reproductive rights, it is clear that the Court significantly lacks gender-sensitivity, having in mind that it did not once discuss the issue of gender discrimination in abortion cases, although this was raised in a number of the complaints. In *A, B, C. v. Ireland*, for example, even though the applicants did point on Art. 14 ECHR in their complaints, the Court did not examine the case under Art. 14 ECHR and justified this with a reference to its examination under Art. 8.[41]

In order to introduce comprehensive protection against discrimination, in more recent years, the ECtHR has also interpreted the scope of non-discrimination to include indirect discrimination and substantive equality. The substantive equality approach focuses on achieving burden-sharing in work and family life. In these cases, whether a violation exists depends on whether the law "aims to encourage gender equality or is perceived to disadvantage women."[42] Thus, the key is the Court's understanding of "equality" and "disadvantage". Sjöholm argues that the Court understands "equality" as "women and men following similar life-courses and balancing between work and family-life",[43] while "disadvantage" is seen as

[37] Radačić (2008), p. 843.

[38] Etinksi (2015), pp. 41–45.

[39] *Nachova and Others v Bulgaria* [GC], para. 161.

[40] Concurring Opinion of Judge Turković in *S.M. v. Croatia*.

[41] *Nachova and Others v Bulgaria* [GC], 270.

[42] Sjöholm (2017), p. 212.

[43] Sjöholm (2017), p. 212.

"maintenance of traditional gender roles."[44] As such, women and men are "seen as analogous in character, which requires the eradication of social and economic differences, mainly stemming from historical factors."[45]

Without tending to cover all the aspects and issues *vis- à -vis* indirect discrimination, this part will tackle the case-law in a brief analysis of the ECtHR feminist justice's regarding the issues that are specific to women's rights, with an emphasis on the most important or more recent cases.

4.1 Some Aspects of Articles 2 and 8 in the Context of Indirect Discrimination

Violence against women and girls is one of the most essential and challenging issues of gender equality. It shows all the weaknesses of humankind, such as dependence on mentality barriers, prejudices, insufficient national legislative and institutional framework, the unwillingness of the judiciary to apply international standards, giving priority to domestic particular law.

While there is no explicit prohibition of domestic violence under the Convention, the Court has integrated such prohibition into other rights in the Convention and examined the issue from the standpoint of the right to life, right to privacy and prohibition on inhuman or degrading treatment and, to a limited extent, non-discrimination in cases of systematic negligence by the state. The Court has not ruled that domestic violence constitutes a *per se* violation of the Convention but has taken a rather expansive view of what constitutes domestic violence, including physical, psychological and economic abuse. The Court reaffirmed in *Valiulienė v. Lithuania* that substantial emotional trauma is inherent in domestic violence and must not be discounted. In *Hajduova v. Slovakia,* the Court held that threats of violence *per se* were considered to constitute a violation of Article 8, as previous abuse had engendered a well-founded fear that the threats would be realized. The Court dealt with repeated acts of online violence in *Volodina v. Russia* (no. 2) in context of article 8, where special diligence in conducting proceedings in domestic violence cases, including cyberviolence, was emphasized.[46]

The Court examined the principle of non-discrimination under Article 14 in the landmark domestic violence case *Opuz v. Turkey,* which is often mentioned as the most gender-conscious case of the Strasbourg Court. The violation of Articles 2 and 3, as well as Article 14 read in conjunction to two mentioned substantive articles was found due to: fatal injuries sustained by applicant's mother in domestic violence case, in which the risk was foreseeable as the authorities had been aware of the perpetrator's history of violence, failure of authorities to take appropriate measures

---

[44] Sjöholm (2017), p. 212.

[45] Sjöholm (2017), p. 212.

[46] *Volodina v. Russia* (no. 2), paras. 62–67.

to protect the applicant and her family from domestic violence, and failure of judicial system to provide adequate response to serious domestic violence. Positive obligation of the authorities was emphasized regarding the protection of right to life in the context of their duty to prevent and suppress offences against the person.[47] With respect to evidence demonstrating indirect discrimination against women, the Court was receptive to the assessment by reputable organizations such as Amnesty International as well as UN CEDAW that indicated a disproportionate victimhood of women in a particular region of Turkey, as well as negligence on the part of the authorities in the same area. This practice is welcomed from a feminist justice perspective as the acceptance of cases of indirect discrimination proven on the basis of statistics and/or information from domestic or international organizations greatly increases the possibility of adjudicating gender-based harms.

The Court has examined domestic violence cases under Article 2 largely. It focuses on states' positive obligations towards preventing domestic violence, such as putting in place effective criminal law provisions to deter the commission of offences and effective law enforcement. The general principles applicable under Article 14 in conjunction with Article 2 in those cases where a gender-based violence ended in death of a victim, as emphasized in *Nachova and Others v. Bulgaria*,[48] have been applied in later case-law.

In more recent case *Tkheladze v. Georgia*, the Court reiterated the principle that "whenever there are any doubts about the occurrence of domestic violence or violence against women, an immediate response and further special diligence is required of the authorities to deal with the specific nature of the violence in the course of the domestic proceedings" as established in previous similar cases.[49],[50] The Court relied on the principles developed in *Opuz case* and emphasized that relevant consideration has to be given to "the need to ensure that the police exercise their powers to control and prevent crime in a manner which fully respects the due process and other guarantees which legitimately place restraints on the scope of their action to investigate crime and bring offenders to justice".[51]

In the most recent case of domestic violence *A and B. v. Georgia*, where a victim was murdered by her partner who was a police officer at the time and used that power to harm her, the Court found a violation of Article 2 in both substantive and procedural limb, as well as Article 14, due to the failure of the HCP to prevent gender-based violence by a police officer and to investigate the law-enforcement authorities' passive response. The Court concluded that "the present case can be seen as yet another vivid example of how general and discriminatory passivity of the law-enforcement authorities in the face of allegations of domestic violence can

[47] *Opuz v. Turkey*, para. 130.

[48] paras. 157–161.

[49] *Kurt v. Austria* [GC], § 165-66, and *Volodina v. Russia*, para. 92.

[50] *Tkheladze v. Georgia,* para. 48.

[51] *Opuz v. Turkey,* paras. 129–130, *Tkheladze v. Georgia* para. 49.

create a climate conducive to a further proliferation of violence committed against victims merely because they are women."[52]

4.2 Some Aspects of Articles 3 and 8 in the Context of Indirect Discrimination

The Court has also dealt with domestic violence issues under Article 3 and Article 8, where it examined the severity of the facts on a case-by-case basis, rather than to rule that domestic violence is a *per se* violation of the Convention. Judge Pinto de Albuquerque in *Valiulienė v. Lithuania* wrote a particularly insightful concurring opinion that argued for a more gender-sensitive approach to domestic violence. He argued that a gender-sensitive approach would not necessarily patronize women but would serve the important function of countering real factual inequalities. He believed that, as domestic violence disproportionately affects women, the "full useful effect of the Convention can only be achieved with a gendered interpretation and application, taking into consideration the factual inequalities between men and women and the way in which they affect the lives of women."[53] He believed that the inherent level of humiliation and psychological trauma associated with domestic violence automatically reaches the level of severity under Article 3, and that establishing solely a violation of Article 8 would "fall short of the real and full meaning of violence in the domestic context, and would thus fail to qualify as a 'gendered understanding of violence'".[54] He was critical of the majority's contextual approach that focuses on assessment of the level of severity based on the particular circumstances of the case, as it would create incoherent case law on finding violations of Articles 3 and 8 respectively.

The Court has found violations of Article 14 in conjunction with Article 3 regarding Russia's continued failure to adopt legislation to combat domestic violence against women or implement protection measures in *Volodina v. Russia* case. The Court found that the assumptions and flaws inherent in the legal framework surrounding the punishment of perpetrators of domestic violence to be based in discrimination based on sex. Particularly striking was the Russian authorities' decision to decriminalize battery which had led to a sharp drop in reports of domestic violence, in a context where women are overrepresented as victims in cases involving violence in the home. The Court's approach therefore took account of the dire situation of protection of women against gendered violence in Russia to find a violation.

The Court has integrated a prohibition on sexual violence within the scope of Article 3 and Article 8, a great number of cases being about rape and sexual abuse.

[52] *A and B. v. Georgia,* para. 49.

[53] Concurring opinion of Judge Pinto de Albuquerque, in *Valiuliene v. Lithuania*, paras. 28–29.

[54] Concurring opinion of Judge Pinto de Albuquerque, in *Valiuliene v. Lithuania*, paras. 28–29.

Generally, the Court has distinguished between physical acts of sexual violence, which normally falls under Article 3 (see *Y. v. Slovenia)*, and non-physical acts that fall within the scope of Article 8 (*Söderman v. Sweden*). The Court has also increasingly recognized harms of sexual violence as violations of Article 3 in recent years, regardless of the identity of the perpetrator. *X and Y v. the Netherlands* is one of the earliest cases where the Court developed positive obligations for states with regard to sexual violence. However, the Court's jurisprudence on this topic remains decidedly gender-neutral, mainly focusing on examining the procedural aspects of other rights, with little recognition of the indirectly discriminatory aspects of sexual violence under Article 14.

The general principle applicable under Article 14 in conjunction with Article 3, as summarized in *Sabalić v. Croatia,*[55] has particular significance regarding the HCPs' procedural obligations regarding effective investigation.

In cases where the applicant complained under, inter alia, Article 3, but the Court assessed that the case primarily the complaint under Article 8, the principle of *jura novit curia* was applied.[56] The most recent example is the case of bullying at work, which harmed the applicant's psychological integrity, violating her dignity, honour and reputation and personal and professional integrity, and the failure of the relevant domestic bodies to protect her.[57] As the Court concluded "by virtue of the *jura novit curia* principle the Court is not bound by the legal grounds adduced by the applicant under the Convention and the Protocols thereto and has the power to decide on the characterization to be given in law to the facts of a complaint by examining it under Articles or provisions of the Convention that are different from those relied upon by the applicant".[58]

5 Positive Measures

The Court accepts specific measures which involve difference in treatment between men and women that are justified by their correcting effect regarding factual and historical inequalities and injustice between the two sexes. Under the condition of being objectively and reasonably justified, those special or positive measures are treated as affirmative action for promotion of effective gender equality.

Having in mind the Court's case-law, difference in treatment concerns specific aspects of gender related features where only a woman could have certain role, such as pregnancy and motherhood, or where a woman could be additionally targeted and victimized, such as immigration rules, pension, social security and taxation schemes,

[55] *Sabalić v. Croatia,* para. 93–98.

[56] *Špadijer v. Montenegro*, paras. 1, 66 and 69, *Sandra Janković v. Croatia*, para. 27, and *Dolopoulos v. Greece*, paras. 35–37.

[57] *Špadijer v. Montenegro*, paras. 1, 66, 34 and 69.

[58] *Špadijer v. Montenegro,* para. *68, Radomilja and Others v. Croatia*, para. 126.

imprisonment, disability, medical error, belonging to national, cultural or ethnic minority, or employment.

Neither Article 14 nor Protocol No. 12[59] contain prohibition of different treatment of groups if they were established in order to correct "factual inequalities" between the groups.[60] However, it appears that the Court has been more ready to accept historical social differences rather than biological differences between the two genders. The Court accepted affirmative action in *Stec v. the United Kingdom,* which concerned special measures directed to different retirement ages for men and women, which were introduced in order to ease financial difficulties that women might suffer due to their traditional role in the family and often monetary dependence. Similarly, in *Pearson v. the United Kingdom,* the Court found no violation of the right concerned, because the difference in pension age between men and women stipulated in law aimed to mitigate financial inequality arising from a woman's traditionally unpaid role in a family rather than earning money in the workplace. In these types of cases, the Court's jurisprudence plays a corrective role *vis-à-vis* factual inequalities and historical social differences.

The Court acknowledged in many cases that only women could be treated differently on grounds of pregnancy and that the states have to provide for the principle of effective equality bearing in mind that fact.

Regarding difference in treatment because of pregnancy, there is obvious need in some countries for introduction of special positive measures for protection of equality during pregnancy and maternity. In *Jurčic v. Croatia*, where the applicant's employment-related benefits were rejected and her employment declared fictitious, because she got pregnant with help of *in vitro* fertilization before her employment started, the Court found a violation of Article 14 in conjunction with Article 1 of Protocol No. 1. Temporary negative effect on the employer cannot be sufficient justification for different treatment on the grounds of pregnancy. In that spirit the Court concluded "that, as a matter of principle, even where the availability of an employee is a precondition for the proper performance of an employment contract, the protection afforded to a woman during pregnancy cannot be dependent on whether her presence at work during maternity is essential for the proper functioning of her employer or by the fact that she is temporarily prevented from performing the work for which she has been hired" and that "introducing maternity protection measures is essential in order to uphold the principle of equal treatment of men and women in employment".[61]

However, the concept of positive measures does not work in every gender sensitive case. The Court did not conclude in favor of discrimination in those situations in which the difference in treatment could be objectively and reasonably justified. In that regard, the termination of a diplomatic employment of a pregnant

[59] See the Preamble of Protocol No. 12.

[60] *Belgian Linguistic case* (No. 2); *Stec and Others v. The United Kingdom.*

[61] *Jurčic v. Croatia,* para. 76.

diplomat was justified as necessary for protection of the functioning capacity of the employer.[62]

Considering the potentials for further developments, Etinski concluded that the ECtHR had underscored the importance of the obligations of HCPs to take positive measures against *de facto* indirect discrimination.[63]

Positive measures need to be introduced in many states, as they are indispensable means to effect full equality. Failure to recognize them in national legislation and practices could lead to violation of women's rights.

6 Conclusion

The European Court of Human Rights has come a long way in introducing an evolutive interpretation of the Convention in gender sensitive cases. The Convention has its real meaning only "in the light of present day conditions" and feminist justice is one of the burning topics of nowadays.

By expanding of the Court's understanding of non-discrimination, while including indirect discrimination and positive measures *vis-à-vis* achieving substantive equality, it has been shown that the meaning of law has priority over pure normative interpretation. This is in line with the Court's evolutive treaty interpretation of the Convention as a living instrument. That way the protection of women has been increased beyond the issues that were explicitly stipulated in the Convention.

The Court's case-law illustrates increased protection of women, in particular concerning domestic violence and the HCPs' positive obligations concerned, where there is no room for taking into consideration broad notion of margin of appreciation, like in the cases regarding gender religious identity.

One of the key achievements of the Court has been in gradually recognizing indirect forms of gender-based violations that women usually experience and integrating these issues into existing rights in the ECHR. The Court accepted both a formal and substantive approach to equality and direct and indirect discrimination. This is crucial because cases of direct discrimination are becoming rarer and women continue to experience factual inequalities based on facially gender-neutral domestic laws.

In addition, the Court has increasingly referred to international jurisprudence in respect to gender equality protection, notably international treaties and practice of UN Treaty Bodies. That has greatly enhanced gender-sensitivity in norm interpretation by the Court.

Although the Court has been successful in integrating issues of feminist justice into existing rights in the Convention, there is room for improvement of women's rights protection. So far, the Court has mostly avoided acknowledging gendered

[62] *Napotnik V. Romania*, para. 77.

[63] Etinski (2015), p. 56.

aspects of the violations it has found and has consistently refrained from adopting a more gendered approach to relevant issues. The relatively limited use of Article 14 across various types of harms, as discussed above, is demonstrative of the Court's tendency to avoid explicitly ruling where there has been a violation of the principle of non-discrimination, especially in cases of indirect discrimination against women. The Court's assessment of states' obligations is also gender-neutral and similar regardless of the offence.

Nevertheless, there are more achievements to be commended than flaws to be corrected. That could be stated in particular having in mind the most recent gender sensitive judgment, that accommodated issues such as protection from gender-based bullying and harassment at work because of the applicant's "whistle-blowing" activities,[64] as well as working relating rights and social benefits concerned in the case of pregnancy that was caused by in vitro fertilization shortly before the applicant started to work.[65]

To conclude, the Court's readiness to apply a living instrument doctrine in addressing gender sensitive cases resulted in more gender sensitive rulings. It expanded its legal correcting role in the areas which were traditionally viewed as a matter of domestic laws and typically did not rise to the level of international human rights law, such as domestic violence. This is exactly essential contribution to the feminist justice where special role belongs to international human rights courts. By bringing justice to victims of human rights violations, the courts contribute also to broader aim—development of human rights culture. In the context of feminist justice, this means the culture of gender equality where effective equality and acceptance of positive measures for women are part of the rule of law, civic standard and average citizen's state of mind. That also means full realization of "the constitutional principle of the equal citizenship stature of men and women", as famous Ruth Bader Ginsberg defined women's rights.

References

Etinski R (2015) Concept of indirect discrimination under Article 14 of the European Convention on Human Rights. Zbornik radova Pravnog fakulteta u Nišu 70:41–58

Radačić I (2008) Critical review of jurisprudence: an occasional series, gender equality jurisprudence of the European Court of Human Rights. Eur J Int Law 19(4):841–857

Sjöholm M (2017) Gender-sensitive norm interpretation by regional Human Rights Law Systems. Brill Nijhoff, Leiden

[64] *Špadijer v. Montenegro.*

[65] *Jurčic v. Croatia.*

Online Database

The HUDOC database of the European Court of Human Rights case-law, https://hudoc.echr.coe.int

de Albuquerque Paulo P (2013) Concurring opinion of Judge Pinto de Albuquerque, in the case of *Valiuliene v. Lithuania*. https://hudoc.echr.coe.int/fre?i=001-117636

Turković K (2020) Concurring Opinion of Judge Turković in the case of *S.M. v. Croatia.* https://hudoc.echr.coe.int/fre?i=001-203503

Ziemele I, Bianku L (2014) Joint Partly Dissening Opinion of Judges Ziemele and Bianku in the case of *Câmpeanu v. Bulgaria*. https://hudoc.echr.coe.int/fre?i=001-145577

Cases

A and B v. Georgia - 73975/16, Judgment 10 February 2022

Abdulaziz, Cabales and Balkandali v. The United Kingdom, Nos. 9214/80, 9473/81, 9474/81, Judgment 28 May 1985

Airey v. Ireland, No. 6289/73, Judgment 9 October 1979

Belgian Linguistic case (No. 2). No. 2126/64, Judgment 23 July 1968

Centre for legal resources on behalf of Valentin Câmpeanu v. Romania, No. 47848/08, Judgment 17 July 2014

D.H. and others v. The Czech Republic [GC], No. 57325/00 Judgment 13 November 2007

Dolopoulos v. Greece (dec.), No. 36656/14, Decision 17 November 2015

E.B. v. France [GC], No. 43546/02, Judgment 22 January 2008

Hajduova v. Slovakia, No. 2660/03, Judgment 30 November 2010

Jurčić v. Croatia, 2021, 54711/15, Judgment 4 February 2021

Khamtokhu and Aksenchik v. Russia [GC], Nos. 60367/08 and 961/11, Judgment 24 January 2017

Konstantin Markin v. Russia (GC), No. 30078/06, Judgment 22 March 2012

Kurt v. Austria [GC], no. 62903/15, Judgment 15 June 2021

Leyla Şahin v. Turkey, No. 44774/98, Judgment 10 November 2005

Marckx v. Belgium, No. 6833/74, Judgment 13 June 1979

Molla Sali v. Greece [GC], No. 20452/14, Judgment 18 June 2020

Nachova and Others v Bulgaria [GC], Nos. 43577/98 and 43579/98, Judgment 06 July 2005

Napotnik v. Romania 33139/13, Judgment 20 October 2020

Opuz v. Turkey, No. 33401/02, Judgment 09 June 2009

Pearson v. the United Kingdom, No. 8374/03, Judgment 22 August 2006

Radomilja and Others v. Croatia [GC], Nos. 37685/10 and 22768/12, Judgment 20 March 2018

Sabalić v. Croatia, No. 50231/13, Judgment 14 January 2021

Sandra Janković v. Croatia, No. 38478/05, Judgment 5 March 2009

S.A.S. v. FRANCE, No. 43835/11, Judgment 1 July 2014

S.M. v. Croatia [GC], No. 60561/14, Judgment 25 June 2020

Söderman v. Sweden [GC], No. 5786/08, Judgment 12 November 2013

Stec and Others v. The United Kingdom [GC], No. 65731/01, Judgment 12 April 2006

Špadijer v. Montenegro, No. 31549/18, Judgment 9 November 2021

Tkhelidze v. Georgia, No. 33056/17, Judgment 08 July 2021

Tyrer v. The United Kingdom, No. 5856/72, Judgment 25 April 1978

Valiuliene v. Lithuania, No 33234/07, Judgment 6 March 2013

Volodina v. Russia, No. 41261/17, Judgment 9 July 2019

Volodina v. Russia (No. 2), No. 40419/19, Judgment 14 September 2021

Ünal Tekeli v. Turkey, No. 29865/96, Judgment 16.11.2004

X and Y v. the Netherlands, No. 8978/80, Judgment 26 March 1985

Y. v. Slovenia, No. 41107/10, Judgment 28 May 2015

Ivana Jelić is a judge of the European Court of Human Rights. She studied law at University of Montenegro, University of Belgrade and University of California in Berkeley. She holds LL.M (2004) and PhD (2007) in public international law from Belgrade Law School, University of Belgrade. Before joining the Court, she was teaching international law and human rights at the Faculty of Law, University of Montenegro. She was a member (2015–2018) and Vice President (2017–2018) of the UN Human Rights Committee. She publishes extensively on the European and international protection of human rights, the rule of law, gender equality.

Female Reproduction and Sexuality: The Impact of Gender Stereotypes on Women's Rights in International Jurisprudence

Ludovica Poli

Contents

Abstract The female role in reproduction generates and fuels stereotypes on women's position as mothers, on their resulting situation in society and on their sexuality. The paper aims to consider how the European Court of Human Rights and UN human rights bodies have screened the impact of gender stereotypes on women's fundamental rights, dealing with three main profiles. First, it focuses on fertility as a 'qualitative standard' and on the specific violations to which girls and women are subjected, due to their reproductive capacity. Second, it considers stereotypes affecting women when accessing reproductive health services. Third, it deals with preconceptions about female sexuality, which—along with other biases—constitute a serious obstacle to the recognition of equality between the sexes. In conclusion, it argues that the capacity to give birth explains the centrality of reproductive rights for women. While these rights belong to all couples and individuals, they have the greatest meaning and impact on women: only by being able to take free, informed and responsible choices about sexuality and reproduction, women can fully exercise their rights to life, health, education and be free from torture and other forms of ill-treatment.

L. Poli (✉)
University of Turin, Department of Law, Turin, Italy
e-mail: ludovica.poli@unito.it

I. Krstić et al. (eds.), *Legal Issues of International Law from a Gender Perspective*, Gender Perspectives in Law 3, https://doi.org/10.1007/978-3-031-13459-3_3

1 Introduction: Reproduction, Motherhood and Stereotypes

As long as it is based on a free and independent decision, pregnancy can be a unique and precious event in life: while not all women have the desire to give birth to another human being, men are *de facto* precluded from gestation as a human relation experience. However, far from being a merely personal and intimate experience, childbearing and motherhood also have a strong cultural dimension: in many societies, they represent a qualifying condition and a clearly identified social function which is attributed to women. Motherhood combines women's 'reproductive capacity' and their 'reproductive function', entangling the biological dimension of gestation and social/cultural expectations with respect to the continuation of the species. In fact, women's role in reproduction generates and fuels stereotypes in the form of preconceptions and assumptions about the role of women as mothers and their resulting position in society, as well as on the definition of their sexuality.[1] Indeed, it is easy to see why reproduction has been at the core of the feminist discourse on women's rights, and why motherhood has been qualified as "one of the anchor points for denying women rights and equality and for discriminating against them".[2]

This analysis aims to assess how the European Court of Human Rights (ECtHR) and UN human rights bodies have screened the impact of gender stereotypes related to female reproduction on fundamental human rights. In particular, the focus will be placed on three main aspects. First, the paper will consider the identification of fertility as a 'qualitative standard' applied to women and the specific violations to which girls and women are subjected because of their reproductive capacity. Second, stereotypes affecting women when accessing reproductive health services will be considered. Finally, reference will be made to preconceptions about female sexuality, which, along with other gender biases, represent a serious obstacle to the recognition of equality between men and women.

2 Fertility As a 'Qualitative Standard' and Women's Human Rights Violations

The UN High Commissioner for Human Rights stressed that "patriarchal concepts of women within the family mean that women are often valued based on their ability to reproduce".[3] Kept away from productive activities and deemed unsuitable for work

[1]Cook et al. (2010), pp. 255–258; Marván et al. (2008), pp. 673–687; Chrisler et al. (2014), pp. 634–657.

[2]Neyer and Bernardi (2011), p. 164.

[3]Office of the Hight Commissioner for Human Rights, Sexual and reproductive health and rights, https://www.ohchr.org/en/node/3447/sexual-and-reproductive-health-and-rights.

and education, women are expected to contribute to community life by way of motherhood. Indeed, the capacity to procreate is seen as a 'qualitative standard' for women and infertility might easily be at the root of fundamental human rights violations. According to the World Health Organization (WHO), infertility affects up to 15% of reproductive-aged couples worldwide. Although male infertility is the cause of conception problems in about 50% of the cases, the social burden falls disproportionately on women.[4] In many cultures, where having children is a social obligation, childless women suffer discrimination, stigma and ostracism and are considered a socioeconomic burden for the entire community. Childless women are frequently excluded from decision-making within the family;[5] sometimes they are considered to be outcasts and treated accordingly.[6] They may be expelled from their husbands' house (with or without formal divorce),[7] lose the chance to have access to land[8] (and/or to financial or social security),[9] and be deprived of the ability to inherit their spouses' property.[10] In some cases, this dishonour extends to their wider family due to the loss of progeny. [11]

The representation of women as mothers and the identification of their role within family and society explain, at least in part, some of the human rights violations suffered by girls and women, such as child marriage and female genital mutilations/ cuttings.

As noted by the United Nations Office of the High Commissioner for Human Rights, child marriage is a form of forced marriage, given that one or both parties, being minors, are not in a condition to express full, free, and informed consent. [12] While, in many countries, this phenomenon also affects boys and is generally driven by many different factors (including poverty, the need to reinforce social ties, and the belief that marriage offers protection), it disproportionally affects girls worldwide [13] and is primarily due to "deep-rooted and intersecting gender inequalities, patriarchal

[4]World Health Organization, Addressing subfertility/infertility in developing countries, https://www.who.int/news-room/fact-sheets/detail/infertility.

[5]Okonofua et al. (1997), p. 216.

[6]Ademóla (1982), p. 16.

[7]Okonofua et al. (1997), p. 215.

[8]Feldman-Savelsberg (1994), pp. 463–474.

[9]Okonofua et al. (1997), p. 215.

[10]Okonofua et al. (1997), p. 216.

[11]On this topic see also Fledderjohann (2012), pp. 1383–1390; Marida and Larsen (2008), pp. 159–173.

[12]UN Office of the Hight Commissioner for Human Rights, Child and forced marriage, including in humanitarian settings, https://www.ohchr.org/EN/Issues/Women/WRGS/Pages/ChildMarriage.aspx.

[13]More than 650 million women alive today were married before reaching age 18: UNICEF. 2020. Four areas of influence driving child marriage. What the data tells us and how it can inform programming https://www.unicef.org/documents/four-areas-influence-driving-child-marriage.

values, discriminatory gender norms, stereotypes, perceptions and customs".[14] As explained very clearly by Rebecca Cook, "laws that prescribe younger ages for women to marry than for men maintain the stereotype of women as restricted to childbearing and service roles, while denying them the years of education, preparation, and experience made available to men".[15] Child marriage represents a violation of human rights, seriously threatening the future of girls and women; it deprives them of the ability to make decisions, it represents the main obstacle to their education and it makes them more vulnerable to violence, discrimination and abuse.[16] Moreover, child marriage is often accompanied by early and frequent pregnancy and childbirth, resulting in higher-than-average maternal morbidity and mortality rates.[17]

Female genital mutilations/cuttings (FGM/C) represent another clear example of human rights violations deriving from gender stereotypes on female sexuality and reproduction. According to the World Health Organisation, FGM/C include "all procedures that involve the partial or total removal of external genitalia or other injury to the female genital organs (. . .) for non-medical reasons".[18] The practice of FGM/C is driven by several socio-cultural reasons, which vary from one community to another. The reasons cited by authors as cultural motivation for this practice[19] include the need to prevent female promiscuity. In particular, the removal of sensitive tissues from genitals (the clitoris) is considered to attenuate sexual desire in girls, thereby promoting virginity before marriage and reducing the chances of sex outside of it.[20] Therefore, even more than for child marriages, in the case of FGM/C, cultural labels on the role of women in reproduction are closely linked with stereotypes of female sexuality, according to which women are "the principal guardians of

[14]Human Rights Council, Resolution on Consequences of child, early and forced marriage UN Doc. A/HRC/RES/41/8 19 July 2019.

[15]Cook (1993), pp. 73–86 at 74.

[16]Nour (2009), pp. 51–56; Raj (2010), pp, 931–935; Raj et al. (2018), pp. 3–19.

[17]Yaya et al. (2019); Nasrullah et al. (2014), pp. 534–543; Santhya (2011), pp. 334–339.

[18]World Health Organization (2018), p. 15. WHO classifies FGM/C into four main typologies: (1) partial or total removal of the clitoris (clitoridectomy) and/or the prepuce; (2) partial or total removal of the clitoris and the labia minora, with or without excision of the labia majora; (3) Narrowing of the vaginal orifice with the creation of a covering seal by cutting and positioning the labia minora and/or the labia majora, with or without excision of the clitoris (infibulation); this type includes the so-called re-infibulation, that is the procedure to narrow the vaginal opening in a woman after she has been deinfibulated (for example after childbirth); (4) All other harmful procedures to the female genitalia for non-medical purposes, for example: pricking, pulling, piercing, incising, scraping and cauterization. World Health Organization (2018), pp. 1–4.

[19]Maintenance of cleanliness, pursuance of aesthetic appeal, prevention of stillbirths in primigravidae and enhancement of fertility, promotion of social and political cohesion and increase in matrimonial opportunities, improvement of male sexual performance and pleasure: Green (2005), pp. 153–187, 155–158.

[20]El-Shawarby and Rymer (2008), pp. 253–255.

sexual morality, but with uncontrolled sexual urges".[21] FGM/C can have serious complications, leading to permanent physical and psychological health problems, including irreparable damage to the reproductive organs resulting in infertility and in sexual disfunction.[22] As such, this practice violates many fundamental rights of girls and women (including the right to health, right to equality and non-discrimination as well as the freedom from torture and other ill-treatment). It has, accordingly, been defined in human rights instruments and by human rights bodies as a form of gender-based violence, i.e. a form of violence motivated by the role culturally attributed to women.[23]

The cultural dimension of the above mentioned violations and the compelling social conventions that require them make it extremely difficult to design and implement preventive strategies.[24] In particular, it is clear that domestic legislation criminalizing phenomena such as FGM/C and child marriages is not sufficient to address such practices. As demonstrated by UN specialized agencies and programmes, a comprehensive approach promoting gender equality and children's rights,[25] which includes community-based interventions (like community dialogues with family members and religious leaders),[26] are more suitable strategies to address the root causes of such violations.

3 Gender Stereotypes and Reproductive Health Care: Contraception, Abortion and Obstetric Violence

Gender stereotypes affect, condition and limit how reproductive health services are offered to women and implemented for their benefit. As stressed by Rebecca Cook, traditional constructs according to which "if women could enjoy sexual relations while preventing pregnancy and avoiding sexually transmitted diseases, then (...) sexual morality and family security would be in jeopardy"[27] are often translated into

[21] Special Rapporteur on violence against women, its causes and consequences, Ms. Radhika Coomaraswamy, Report on Cultural practices in the family that are violent towards women UN Doc. E/CN.4/2002/83 31 January 2002, para. 14.

[22] Biglu et al. (2016), pp. 3–8; Raina et al. (2007), pp. 1273–1284.

[23] See, in particular, Article 2 of the Declaration on the Elimination of Violence against Women (General Assembly resolution 48/104), explicitly defining female genital mutilation as a form of violence against women and calling upon States to protect women against any form of violence that occurs within the family household or in other environments, and the Report of the Special Rapporteur on violence against women cit. [note 21], paras. 12–20.

[24] Preston (2013), pp. 585–607; Bunting (2005), pp. 17–38.

[25] UNFPA and UNICEF (2020).

[26] Matanda et al. (2021).

[27] Cook (1993), p. 73.

normative provisions aimed at controlling "women's behaviour by limiting or denying women's access to reproductive health services",[28] including abortion.

Denying access to contraception, for example, was considered a discrimination against women and a violation of their rights. In its Summary of the inquiry concerning the Philippines, the Committee on the Elimination of Discrimination against Women (CEDAW Committee) found that the implementation of two executive orders relating to reproductive health services in Manila were in violation of the Convention. The Executive Order No. 003 recalled the sanctity of life and the protection of the life of the mother and the unborn, as enshrined in the Philippine Constitution, and declared that the City of Manila would "promote responsible parenthood and uphold natural family planning not just as a method but as a way of self-awareness in promoting the culture of life while discouraging the use of artificial methods of contraception like condoms, pills, intrauterine devices, surgical sterilization, and other". [29] With the subsequent Executive Order No. 030, a funding ban was imposed on modern contraception. [30] The Committee concluded that the Philippines had violated their obligations under CEDAW Article 12 (which sets a prohibition to discrimination in access to health services, including those relating to family planning) and Article 5 (which requires States to promote the elimination of prejudices and stereotypes on the role of women). Indeed, the two executive orders reinforced gender biases prejudicial to women "given that they incorporated and conveyed stereotyped images of women's primary role as child bearers and child rearers". [31]

In addition, stereotypes regarding female reproduction often reinforce pro-life positions, militating against abortion and threatening the full recognition of women's right to self-determination. The views adopted by the CEDAW Committee in *L. C. v. Peru*[32] are remarkable not only because they stress the importance of guaranteeing access to lawful abortion services,[33] but also because they considered that the refusal to perform a therapeutic abortion was driven by stereotypes relating to reproduction and, thus, discriminatory. [34] The case concerned a thirteen-year-old girl, who became pregnant due to repeated sexual abuses by an adult man. As a result, L.C. fell into a state of depression and attempted to commit suicide by jumping from a building. The damage to her spinal column caused paraplegia of the lower and upper limbs requiring emergency surgery. However, the surgery was

[28] Cook (1993), p. 73.

[29] Committee on the Elimination of Discrimination against Women, Summary of the inquiry concerning the Philippines under Article 8 of the Optional Protocol to the Convention on the Elimination of All Forms of Discrimination against Women, 22 April 2015,, para 2.

[30] CEDAW, Summary, para 3.

[31] CEDAW, Summary, para 43.

[32] Committee on the Elimination of Discrimination against Women, *L.C. v. Peru*, Communication No. 22/2009, 4 November 2011.

[33] Ngwena (2013), pp. 310–324.

[34] Cusack and Pusey (2013), pp. 54–92 at 70; see also Bates (2013), pp. 640–656.

postponed due to the fear that the treatment could harm the foetus. The legal termination of the pregnancy, requested by the girl in accordance with domestic law, was rejected. It was only after she spontaneously miscarried that she underwent surgery for her spinal injuries, almost three and half months after it had initially been decided that the surgery was necessary, when much of the damage had already become irreparable.[35] The girl's mother, author of the communication, argued that the refusal to perform a therapeutic abortion on L.C. and the delayed scheduling of the surgery gave rise to a violation of Article 12 and Article 5 of the CEDAW. In particular, she claimed that "timely access to necessary medical treatment was made conditional on carrying to term an unwanted pregnancy, which fulfils the stereotype of placing L.C.'s reproductive function above her right to health, life and a life of dignity".[36] The conclusions reached by the Committee were in line with these arguments: recognizing the violation of Articles 12 and 5 of the CEDAW, it stressed that "owing to her condition as a pregnant woman, L.C. did not have access to an effective and accessible procedure allowing her to establish her entitlement to the medical services that her physical and mental condition required".[37] The Committee thus clarified that the decision to postpone urgent surgery due to the pregnancy was determined by the stereotype that the protection of the foetus should prevail over the health of the mother.[38]

Two other cases decided by the UN Human Rights Committee (HRC) deal with the impact of stereotypes concerning reproduction on the level of discrimination suffered by women. In *Mellet v. Ireland*[39] and *Whelan v. Ireland*[40] the authors of the communications, who had received diagnoses of fatal foetal impairments, could not legally terminate the pregnancies because, under Irish law in force at that time, abortion was only permitted when there was a real and substantial risk to the life, and not just to the health, of the pregnant woman. Therefore, to undergo the procedure, they had to travel (at their own expenses) to the United Kingdom. In its decisions, the HRC recognized the psychological, physical, and financial damage caused by Ireland's abortion laws and found that Ireland had violated Articles 7, 17 and 26 of the International Covenant on Civil and Political Rights (ICCPR).[41] According to the authors of the communications the criminalization of abortion in Ireland is based on a "gender-based stereotype that women should continue their pregnancies regardless of the circumstances, their needs and wishes, because their primary role is to be mothers and caregivers".[42] Indeed, this typecasting represents clear

[35]Committee on the Elimination of Discrimination against Women, *L.C. v. Peru* cit. [note 32], paras. 2.1-2.11.

[36]CEDAW, *L.C. v. Peru* cit. [note 32], para. 8.10.

[37]CEDAW, *L.C. v. Peru* cit. [note 32], para. 8.15.

[38]CEDAW, *L.C. v. Peru* cit. [note 32], para. 8.15.

[39]Human Rights Committee, *Mellet v. Ireland*, Communication No. 2324/2013, 17 November 2016.

[40]Human Rights Committee, *Whelan v. Ireland*, Communication No. 2425/2014, 12 June 2017.

[41]Sękowska-Kozłowska (2018), pp. 25–31.

[42]Human Rights Committee, *Mellet v. Ireland* cit. [note 39], para. 3.19.

discrimination given that "male patients and patients in other situations in Ireland are not expected to disregard their health needs and travel abroad in relation to their reproductive functions".[43] Significantly, individual members of the Commitee have upheld the applicants' position in their concurring opinions. In *Mellet,* Sarah Cleveland stated that "[r]equiring (. . .) to carry a fatally impaired pregnancy to term (. . .) underscores the extent to which the State party has prioritized (whether intentionally or unintentionally) the reproductive role of women as mothers".[44] Similarly, in *Whelan,* Yadh Ben Achour underlined that "[t]he act of reducing the author to an instrument of procreation constitutes discrimination and infringes at once her freedom of self-determination and her right to gender equality and personal autonomy".[45] Unfortunately, the Committee does not appear to be ready to embrace this approach. In fact, the majority of its members opted - in both cases - to consider that the treatment to which the authors were subjected created a discriminatory legal distinction between them and those women who carry to term unviable pregnancies, failing to adequately take into account Ms. Mellet and Whelan's medical needs as well as their socioeconomic conditions.[46]

Along with abortion and contraception, stereotypes affect other aspects of women's right to reproductive health. The concept of 'obstetric violence' has recently gained recognition, thanks to Latin American childbirth activism. In 2007, this form of violence against women was codified for the first time in a domestic legal instrument in the Venezuelan Organic Law on the Right of Women to a Life Free of Violence, which describes obstetric violence as "the appropriation of women's body and reproductive processes by health personnel (. . .) resulting in a loss of autonomy and ability to decide freely about their bodies and sexuality, negatively impacting their quality of life".[47] According to the WHO, many women experience abusive treatments during pregnancy and childbirth, including physical and verbal abuse, medical procedures (including sterilization) without consent or with consent obtained coercively, refusal to give pain medication, gross violations of privacy, denial of admission to health facilities, avoidable complications, and even detention in facilities after childbirth due to an inability to pay.[48] The Special Rapporteur on violence against women underlined that mistreatment in reproductive health services and during childbirth affects women all around the world and across

[43] Human Rights Committee, *Whelan v. Ireland* cit. [note 40], para. 7.12.

[44] Human Rights Committee, *Mellet v. Ireland* cit. [note 39], Individual opinion of Committee member Sarah Cleveland (concurring) para. 14.

[45] Human Rights Committee, *Whelan v. Ireland* cit. [note 40], Individual opinion of Committee member Yadh Ben Achour (concurring) para. 6.

[46] Human Rights Committee, *Mellet v. Ireland* cit. [note 39], para. 7.11; *Whelan v. Ireland* cit. [note 40], para. 7.12.

[47] Sadler et al. (2016), pp. 47–55, at 50.

[48] World Health Organization Statement (2015). The prevention and elimination of disrespect and abuse during facility-based childbirth, UN Doc. WHO/RHR/14.23.

all socioeconomic levels.[49] According to the Special Rapporteur's Report of 2019, mistreatments and violence during childbirth are part of the continuum of violations that are experienced by women and girls when they seek forms of sexual and reproductive healthcare (including abortion, fertility treatments and contraception), in a wider context of structural inequality, discrimination, and patriarchy.[50] In fact, "[h]armful gender stereotypes in reproductive health context on women's decision-making competence, women's natural role in society and motherhood limit women's autonomy and agency".[51] As explained by some authors, there is a profound relationship between gender stereotypes and the occurrence of obstetric violence: the idea of women as subdued individuals, physically and emotionally fragile, easily allows control and even abuses of their bodies, their sexuality and reproductive function.[52] In line with this cultural approach, childbirth is often perceived as an event requiring suffering: women are expected to be happy to give birth to a healthy baby, while their own physical and emotional well-being is ignored.[53]

In *S.F.M. v. Spain* the author of the communication maintained that she suffered obstetric violence due to the pathologizing of her labour and the consequent abuse of medication and medical interventionism (including many unnecessary vaginal examinations, administration of oxytocin, as well as the performance of episiotomy without information or consent).[54] In assessing a violation of Articles 2 (b), (c), (d) and (f), 3, 5 and 12 of the CEDAW, the Committee stressed that stereotyping seriously affects the right of women to be free from gender-based violence, including obstetric violence, and that the authorities called to assess responsibility for such acts should exercise particular caution in avoiding the repetition of stereotypes.[55]

Even if the international jurisprudence has produced important achievements in assessing the adequacy of reproductive health services, a number of factors make the violation of women's reproductive human rights difficult to detect. Indeed, in this field, gender biases intersect with other labels and typecasts, including unequal power relationships between health professionals and female users. As a matter of fact, "[the] health provider has the power of authoritative medical knowledge and the social privilege of medical authority, while the woman is largely dependent on the

[49] Special Rapporteur on violence against women, its causes and consequences, Ms. Dubravka Šimonović, Report on a human rights-based approach to mistreatment and violence against women in reproductive health services with a focus on childbirth and obstetric violence, UN Doc. A/74/137, 11 July 2019, para. 16; see also Council of Europe Parliamentary Assembly, Resolution 2306 (2019) Obstetrical and gynecological violence, 3 October 2019.

[50] Report of the Special Rapporteur on violence against women (2019), para. 9.

[51] Report of the Special Rapporteur on violence against women (2019), para. 46.

[52] Jardim and Modena (2018), p. 8.

[53] Report of the Special Rapporteur on violence against women (2019), para. 46.

[54] Committee on the Elimination of Discrimination against Women, *S.F.M. v. Spain*, Communication No. 138/2018, 28 February 2020, para 3.1.

[55] CEDAW, *S.F.M. v. Spain*, para 7.5.

provider for information and care"[56] and these power dynamics inevitably affects women's perception of their own rights and freedoms.

4 Not Only Reproduction: Female Sexuality

Women's contribution to reproduction strongly influences cultural views on sex and traditional morality, fuelling laws and practices aimed at controlling female sexuality or subjecting it to the needs and desires of their male partner. The so-called 'husband stitch' is a good example in this regard: it consists of adding an unnecessary extra stitch when repairing a vaginal tear after delivery, without first obtaining informed consent from the woman and with the aim of tightening the vagina and guaranteeing more sexual pleasure for the male partner.[57] Despite its glossy name, it is clearly—in essence—a form of female genital mutilation. The influence of gender stereotypes on sexual life and their impact on women's rights is clear even outside cases of violence or other forms of intervention without consent on a woman's body.

The judgement of the European Court of human rights in the case *Carvalho Pinto v. Portugal* provides an interesting reading on the relationship between female sexuality and reproduction as grounds for judicial stereotyping and discrimination. The applicant suffered from a gynaecological condition for which she had to undergo surgery. The operation failed and she began to experience severe pain and incontinence losing the ability to have sexual relations. Having brought legal action against the hospital, she obtained compensation for non-pecuniary damage. This compensation, however, was later reduced by the Supreme Administrative Court as the applicant already had two children and was 50 years old, an age—according to the domestic judges—when sex is not as important as in the younger years.[58] The applicant complained before the European Court that the Portuguese Supreme Administrative Court's judgment had discriminated against her on the grounds of her sex and age, relying on Articles 8 and 14 of the European Convention on Human Rights (ECHR).

The European Court recognized the violation considering that the decision of the Supreme Administrative Court to reduce the compensation amount was based on the applicant's age and sex and confirmed the prejudices prevailing amongst the judiciary in Portugal, already identified by other monitoring bodies.[59] The Court also noted that previous allegations of medical malpractice suffered by two male patients over 50 years of age had been approached very differently by another Portuguese judicial authority. In fact, in those cases, the Supreme Court of Justice had

[56] Report of the Special Rapporteur on violence against women (2019), para. 49.

[57] Kukura (2018), pp. 721–802, at 736; see also Ray (2021).

[58] *Carvalho Pinto de Sousa Morais v. Portugal*, ECtHR, App. No. 17484/15, Judgement 25 July 2017, para. 49.

[59] *Carvalho Pinto de Sousa Morais v. Portugal*, paras. 53–54.

considered that the resulting impossibility to have normal sexual relations affected the applicants' self-confidence and caused severe mental trauma, without considering whether or not they already had children or any other elements.[60] According to the ECtHR, therefore, while domestic courts may consider the age of applicants in deciding claims related to non-pecuniary damage in liability proceedings, the case in question was based on the assumption that sexuality was not important for a 50-year old woman and mother of two children, reflecting "a traditional idea of female sexuality as being essentially linked to child-bearing purposes and [ignoring] its physical and psychological relevance for the self-fulfilment of women as people".[61]

Judges Ravarani and Bosnjak argued, in their dissenting opinion, that the ECtHR should have considered a much larger number of judgments delivered by the Portuguese Court to determine if there was a pattern of discrimination in its decision-making.[62] However, as judge Yudviska highlighted, the language of the judgment was "discriminatory in and of itself. It [did] not refer to any differential physical needs of men and women, but to the persistent perception that the primary focus of a woman's sexual life is the reproductive function".[63]

This case helps us to identify two key aspects of gender stereotyping that affects women's fundamental rights. First, it explains that a comparator is not necessary to reveal discriminatory treatment when it is based on a stereotype.[64] In fact, as stressed by Alexandra Timmer, stereotypes do not derive from a comparison with other groups that are treated better, but they are fundamentally based on cultural pre-conceptions.[65] Second, the case clarifies that gender stereotypes on female sexuality and reproduction necessarily produce intersectional discrimination, whereby the various personal grounds determining a difference in treatment (in this case, sex and age) combine and generate a separate and peculiar form of discrimination. The Supreme Court's reasoning, declaring that the importance of sex had diminished in the applicant's life as she was 50 years old, was not only based on the stereotype that elder people have no interest in (or capacity for) sexual activity, or on the idea that sex for women is just instrumental to reproduction, but also on a misconception of female sexuality, which was—at the same time—both ageist and sexist.

[60] *Carvalho Pinto de Sousa Morais v. Portugal*, para. 55.

[61] *Carvalho Pinto de Sousa Morais v. Portugal*, para. 52.

[62] *Carvalho Pinto de Sousa Morais v. Portugal*, Joint dissenting opinion of Judges Ravarani and Bosnjak, para 18.

[63] *Carvalho Pinto de Sousa Morais v. Portugal*, Concurring opinion of Judge Yudviska.

[64] *Carvalho Pinto de Sousa Morais v. Portugal*, Concurring opinion of Judge Motoc, para. 18.

[65] Timmer (2015), pp. 239–284, at 252.

5 Concluding Remarks: The Meaning of Reproductive Rights for Women

The European Court of Human Rights and UN human rights bodies have already explored, at least in part, the scope of gender stereotypes and their detrimental effect on women's fundamental rights. Many important achievements in understanding human rights violations as an expression of gender stereotypes on female sexuality and reproduction have been reached. In particular, it is clear that the representation of women as mothers fuels human rights violations such as child marriage and female genital mutilations/cuttings. Reproductive stereotypes also attribute the 'blame' to women for couples' infertility, resulting in ostracism and other harmful consequences.

The recognition of the detrimental effect of gender stereotypes on sexual and reproductive health rights is also growing, with increasing attention devoted to obstetric violence and denied access to contraception. As far as abortion is concerned, a deeper understanding of discrimination—based on the reproductive role attributed to women—is desirable, as this form of inequality is not always clearly identified by human rights bodies. Furthermore, additional jurisprudence on women's right to a sex life, independent from reproduction, would contribute to close the current loopholes in the protection of women's fundamental rights.

A major reason for the persistence of violent acts in reproductive health-care is women's lack of knowledge of their sexual and reproductive rights.[66] Indeed, the capacity to give birth and its social/cultural meaning explain the centrality of reproductive rights for women.[67] While reproductive rights belong to all couples and individuals,[68] their protection for women has a different and stronger meaning, as it is functional to the promotion of other rights. Only by being able to take free, informed and responsible choices about sexuality and reproduction, women can fully exercise their rights to life, health, private life, education and freedom from torture and other ill-treatments. For women, much more than for men, reproductive rights are closely linked to the full enjoyment of other fundamental human rights.

---

[66] Jardim and Modena (2018), p. 9.

[67] On reproductive rights and their impact on women: Cook (1993); Temmerman et al. (2014), pp. e30–e31; Gebhard and Mora (2013), paras. 2–5. These rights basically rest upon the recognition of reproductive choice as codified under Article 16 (1) (e) of the CEDAW, which safeguards "the basic right of all couples and individuals to decide freely and responsibly the number, spacing and timing of their children and to have the information and means to do so, as well as to attain the highest standard of sexual and reproductive health".

[68] International Conference on Population and Development. 1994. Program of Action, UN Doc. A/CONF.171/13, par. 7.3.

References

Ademóla A (1982) Changes in the patterns of marriage and divorce in a Yoruba town. Rural Africana 14:1–24

Bates C (2013) Abortion and a Right to Health in International Law: L.C. v Peru. Camb J Int Comp Law 3(2):640–656

Biglu M-H, Farnam A, Abotalebi P, Biglu S, Ghavami M (2016) Effect of female genital mutilation/cutting on sexual functions. Sex Reproductive Healthcare 10:3–8

Bunting A (2005) Stages of development: marriage of girls and teens as an International Human Rights Issue. Soc Legal Stud 14(1):17–38

Chrisler JC, Gorman JA, Marván ML, Johnston-Robledo I (2014) Ambivalent sexism and attitudes toward women in different stages of reproductive life: a semantic, cross-cultural approach. Health Care Women Int 35(6):634–657

Cook RJ (1993) International Human Rights and Women's Reproductive Health. Stud Family Plan 24(2):73–86

Cook RJ, Cusack S, Dickens B (2010) Unethical female stereotyping in reproductive health. Int J Gynecol Obstetrics 109(3):255–258

Cusack S, Pusey L (2013) CEDAW and the rights to non-discrimination and equality. Melb J Int Law 14(1):54–92

El-Shawarby SA, Rymer J (2008) Female genital cutting. Obstet Gynaecol Reproductive Med 18(9):253–255

Feldman-Savelsberg P (1994) Plundered kitchens and empty wombs: fear of infertility in the Cameroonian grassfields. Soc Sci Med 39(4):463–474

Fledderjohann JJ (2012) 'Zero is not good for me': implications of infertility in Ghana. Human Reproduction 27(5):1383–1390

Gebhard J, Mora DT (2013) Reproductive rights, international regulation. Max Planck Encyclopedia of Public International Law

Green F (2005) From clitoridectomies to 'designer vaginas': The medical construction of heteronormative female bodies and sexuality through female genital cutting. Sex Evolution Gender 7(2):153–187

Jardim DMB, Modena CM (2018) Obstetric violence in the daily routine of care and its characteristics. Revista latino-americana de enfermagem 26:e3069

Kukura E (2018) Obstetric violence. Georgetown Law J 106(3):721–802

Marida H, Larsen U (2008) Motherhood in sub-Saharan Africa: the social consequences of infertility in an urban population in northern Tanzania. Culture Health Sexuality 10(2):159–173

Marván ML, Islas M, Vela L, Chrisler JC, Warren EA (2008) Stereotypes of women in different stages of their reproductive life: data from Mexico and the United States. Health Care Women Int 29(7):673–687

Matanda D, Groce-Galis M, Gay J, Hardee K (2021) Effectiveness of interventions designed to prevent or respond to female genital mutilation: a review of evidence. UNFPA, UNICEF, WHO and Population Council, Kenya

Nasrullah M, Muazzam S, Bhutta ZA et al (2014) Girl child marriage and its effect on fertility in Pakistan: findings from Pakistan demographic and health survey, 2006–2007. Matern Child Health J 18:534–543

Neyer G, Bernardi L (2011) Feminist perspectives on motherhood and reproduction. Historical Soc Res 36(2):162–176

Ngwena CG (2013) A commentary on LC v Peru: the CEDAW Committee's first decision on abortion. J Afr Law 57(2):310–324

Nour NM (2009) Child marriage: a silent health and human rights issue. Rev Obstet Gynecol 2:51–56

Okonofua FE, Harris D, Odebiyi A, Kane T, Snow RC (1997) The social meaning of infertility in Southwest Nigeria. Health Transition Rev 7(2):205–220

Preston DM (2013) Slapping the hand of cultural relativism: female genital mutilation, male dominance, and health as a Human Rights framework. William Mary J Women Law 19:585–607

Raina R, Pahlajani G, Khan S, Gupta S, Agarwal ACD, Zippe. (2007) Female sexual dysfunction: classification, pathophysiology, and management. Fertil Steril 88(5):1273–1284

Raj A (2010) When the mother is a child: the impact of child marriage on the health and human rights of girls. Archiv Dis Childhood 95:931–935

Raj A, Jackson E, Dunham S (2018) Girl child marriage: a persistent global women's health and Human Rights Violation. In: Choudhury S, Erausquin JT, Withers M (eds) Global perspectives on women's sexual and reproductive health across the lifecourse. Springer, Cham, pp 3–19

Ray S (2021) The Husband-Stitch: Could it be Female Genital Mutilation? https://www.durham.ac.uk/research/institutes-and-centres/ethics-law-life-sciences/about-us/news/obstetric-violence-blog/the-husband-stitch/

Sadler M, Santos MJDS, Ruiz-Berdún D, Leiva RG, Skoko E, Gillen P, Clausen JA (2016) Moving beyond disrespect and abuse: addressing the structural dimensions of obstetric violence. Reproductive Health Matters 24(47):47–55

Santhya KG (2011) Early marriage and sexual and reproductive health vulnerabilities of young women: a synthesis of recent evidence from developing countries. Curr Opin Obstet Gynecol 23:334–339

Sękowska-Kozłowska K (2018) A tough job: recognizing access to abortion as a matter of equality. A commentary on the views of the UN Human Rights Committee in the cases of Mellet v. Ireland and Whelan v. Ireland. Reproductive Health Matters 26(54):25–31

Special Rapporteur on violence against women, its causes and consequences, Ms. Dubravka Šimonović (2019) Report on a human rights-based approach to mistreatment and violence against women in reproductive health services with a focus on childbirth and obstetric violence. UN Doc. A/74/137

Temmerman M, Khosla R, Say L (2014) Sexual and reproductive health and rights: a global development, health, and human rights priority. Lancet 384(9941):e30–e31

Timmer A (2015) Judging stereotypes: what the European Court of Human Rights can borrow from American and Canadian equal protection law. Am J Comp Law 63:239–284

UNFPA and UNICEF (2020) Child marriage and the law: technical note for the global programme to end child marriage

World Health Organization Statement (2015) The prevention and elimination of disrespect and abuse during facility-based childbirth. UN Doc. WHO/RHR/14.23

World Health Organization (2018) Care of girls & women living with female genital mutilation. A clinical handbook

Yaya S, Odusina EK, Bishwajit G (2019) Prevalence of child marriage and its impact on fertility outcomes in 34 sub-Saharan African countries. BMC Int Health Hum Rights 19(1):33

Ludovica Poli is Associate Professor of International Law at the University of Turin, Department of Law, where she teaches Public International Law and International Human Rights Law. She holds a Ph.D. in Public International Law (2008), a Master's degree in Peacekeeping Management (2004), and a Master's degree in Bioethics and Clinical Ethics (2016). Her main field of research is human rights law, although she has also explored other international law domains, including humanitarian law, international criminal law, and the law of international organizations.

Workplace Discrimination Towards LGBTQ Employees and Employee Candidates in the Job Market: A European Approach to the Workplace Discrimination Towards LGBTQ

Alparslan Özaltuğ and Berfu Yalçın

Contents

Abstract The visibility and awareness of LGBTQ people in society as well as in the workplace increase steadily. While LGBTQ equality covers a wide range of issues, this paper will focus on workplace discrimination, such as homophobic speech at the workplace, the hindrance to access to work, LGBTQ worker's rights at the workplace in Europe. In this scope, EU law and the European Convention on Human Rights (ECHR) provide two important sources of protection from discrimination on the grounds of sexual orientation and gender identity. Under the ECHR, the right to work is not protected by the Convention; however, the European Court of Human Rights (ECtHR) had already accepted that in some situations, issues arising from employment relations might fall under the scope of Article 8 of the Convention. Furthermore, the ECtHR was confronted with the question of discrimination against LGBTQ individuals in the workplace. As for the EU Law, most notably, tackling sexual orientation-based discrimination at the workplace has been a duty of EU

A. Özaltuğ (✉)
Galatasaray University, Istanbul, Turkey
e-mail: alparslan.ozaltug@ogr.gsu.edu.tr

B. Yalçın
Europa-Institut, Saarbrucken, Germany

I. Krstić et al. (eds.), *Legal Issues of International Law from a Gender Perspective*, Gender Perspectives in Law 3, https://doi.org/10.1007/978-3-031-13459-3_4

Member States by the adoption of the Employment Framework Directive (2000/78/EC). In this direction, the Court of Justice of the European Union (CJEU) was already asked to interpret the Directive regarding homophobic speech in two recent cases.

1 Introduction

Access to the labor market is one of the utmost hardships faced by LGBTQ individuals. Indeed, evidence-based studies show that openly LGB applicants are 1.5 times less likely to be invited to a job interview. Furthermore, the call-back rate for a job offer of an applicant who is a cisgender woman is 50% higher than a trans woman.[1] In this context, direct insults, threats, harassment, dismissal, or wage inequality can be evaluated as some of the challenges faced by LQBTQ persons in the workplace.[2] While in recent years, populist anti-gay opinions are on the rise in some parts of Europe, the European Court of Human Rights (ECtHR) has taken a strong stance against discrimination of LGBTQ persons, especially in the context of homophobic hate speech. However, the protection of LGBTQ individuals in the workplace can be more of a challenge for the ECtHR. Although Article 14 of the European Convention on Human Rights (ECHR) provides a right to be free from discrimination, this is not a stand-alone right and should be only taken into consideration with a substantial right as protected under the ECHR. In this context, the right to work is not protected under the Convention *per se*. Nonetheless, the ECtHR had already evaluated the right to work under the scope of the right to private and family life (Article 8 of the Convention). Within this scope, we will analyze the Court's case-law on workplace discrimination in certain aspects. Subsequently, we will evaluate homophobic hate speech of the employer and set up criteria for the obvious conflict between the right to freedom of expression of the employer and the right to be free from hate speech based on sexual orientation in the labor context.

From the European Union's (EU) perspective, the right to equal treatment and the right to be free from discrimination at the workplace have been strengthened by utilizing EU Directives. Most notably 2000/78 EC Directive[3] establishes the fundamental rules pertaining to anti-discrimination schemes for LGBTQ workers. Since this Directive came into force relatively recently, the cases dealt with by the court are limited but also noteworthy. Therefore, there are still some grey zones that are

[1] CoE (2021a, b), p. 19; "25% of LGBTI persons have been the victim of at least one attack in the workplace due to their sexual orientation, gender identity or sex characteristics. Seventy-seven percent of LGBTI persons living with a partner acknowledge that they have voluntarily avoided revealing their sexual orientation, gender identity or sex characteristics in various work situations. Thirty five percent state that they are unhappy about not being visible."

[2] CoE (2021a, b), p. 18.

[3] Council Directive 2000/78/EC of 27 November 2000 establishes a general framework for equal treatment in employment and occupation. Official Journal L 303, 02/12/2000 P. 0016 – 0022.

awaited to be answered by the CJEU in the future, and some considerable questions concerning the attitude of the Court towards balancing freedom of expression and hate speech. The stance of the CJEU is way far from what it used to be when the Court has ruled on *Grant* and *D & Sweden* cases.[4] Although the reluctance of the CJEU to adopt progressive approaches to equality was evident in the former cases,[5] it can be said that the CJEU takes a more progressive and inclusive interpretation in favor of LGBTQ people and social realities in recent cases.[6] Thanks to the increasing visibility of LGBTQ people, compared to the past few decades, LGBTQ employees are now afforded more rights and more legal protection against homophobia and discrimination at the workplace on EU soil.[7] On the other hand, the surveys still show that LGBTQ individuals are less likely to be recruited compared to heterosexual individuals. In this direction, the Equal Treatment Directive mainly prohibits any discriminatory treatment against people on the grounds of religion or belief, disability, age, or sexual orientation throughout the recruitment process, during the recruitment and post-employment era.[8] In this scope, any sort of discrimination, either direct or indirect, shall be prohibited by the Member States, unless there are justification grounds provided by the Directive.[9] The scope of this Directive targets the unequal and/or discriminative treatments of any candidates, employees, or retired persons regarding occupational matters both in the public and private sector.

Subsequently, we will analyze the proof of discrimination, especially the establishment of a *prima facie* case and the victim status. Lastly, the exceptions afforded to the churches should be evaluated since LGBTQ people, especially the priests working in the churches, in some cases may be subject to discrimination at churches

[4]Mulder (2017), pp. 51–52. At the time when the Court ruled on these cases, the interpretation and references made by the Court were based on the 2000/43/EC Directive. The Court, therefore, has assessed the discrimination of LGBTQ employees' cases based sex rather than sexual orientation. When the court did so, it has concluded that different treatment between the unmarried lesbian employee in a partnership and unmarried heterosexual employee in a partnership would not constitute sex-based discrimination, since the former should be compared with a gay employee in a partnership in a similar situation. Consequently, neither a gay employee in a partnership nor a lesbian employee in a partnership would be entitled to the travel allowance granted by the company, the Court concluded that there was no discrimination of the comparable groups based on sex. See Case C-249/96, Grant v. South-West Trains Ltd., para. 36. However, it is also worth noting that the Court has further noted that same-sex relationships are not viewed, at that time, as equivalent to the marriages or relationships of people of the opposite sex. See the Equal Misery Argument adopted by the CJEU and its critics. Tryfonidou (2018), p. 232. The author argues that instead of comparing the concerned employee with a fictional gay colleague in a partnership, it would have been appropriate to use a male colleague with a female partner as a comparator. Otherwise, the sex of the claimant as well as the sex of the partner is changed.

[5]Mulder (2017), p. 52.

[6]In a similar vein see Tryfonidou (2018), p. 238. By these recent judgments, *N.H.* and *Asociația Accept,* the Court has also acknowledged and achieved substantive equality in sexual orientation-related matters.

[7]*NH v Associazione Avvocatura per i diritti LGBTI - Rete Lenford* and *Asociația Accept.*

[8]Recital para.33 and art.2/2 of the Directive.

[9]Muir and Waddington (2018), p. 27.

that are their workplace. Indeed, there are some exceptions afforded to the churches by some states that exclude the churches from the anti-discrimination rules, such as the recital of 2000/78/ EC Article 24 as well as Article 4(2).

2 Discrimination in the Workplace on the Basis of Sexual Orientation

Discriminative behaviors towards LGBTQ employees shall be avoided from the beginning of the recruitment process until the dismissal of the LGBTQ employee from the post. While discrimination towards LGBTQ individuals in the workplace is a fact of business life,[10] the fear of facing discrimination through the employment processes also has negative implications on LGBTQ individuals. Indeed, non-surprisingly, studies show the fear of discrimination affects the productivity of the employee in a negative manner.[11] With this awareness, many countries have enacted legislation prohibiting and punishing discriminative behaviors of employers at the workplace from the beginning of the recruitment process throughout the occupation. In this context, directives of the EU regulate and set the minimum standard of protection for LGBTQ employees EU-wide. Despite this fact, rather a recent survey conducted both in EU countries as well as Serbia and the North Macedonia suggests that 21% of LGBTQ individuals have felt discriminated against at work while 26% of them are not out of the closet at work.[12]

While anti-discrimination regulations are a step forward, the mere existence of legislation is not enough for the protection of LGBTQ employees. It is, therefore, necessary to provide the victim access to justice against the discriminative behavior as well as procedural guarantees such as securing the confidentiality of the procedure and guaranteeing access to the pieces of evidence required for the procedure.[13] Indeed, the employees are still expected to satisfy the needs of heteronormativity at the workplace.[14] Therefore, not complying with the rules conforming to the gender roles assigned by the heteronormativity could hinder the employee candidates' to access the labor market. Can an employee dress up the way he considers appropriate while it conflicts with sex roles? Is there a place for male employees with skirt suits, high-heels, and make-up in the workplace? May the employer intervene with the dress code merely based on sex? In such circumstances, what are the limits of intervention concerning a dress code? Or is it possible for an employer to claim a legitimate interest in the dress code of employees based on the expectations of stakeholders or customers? The answers to all of these questions are closely related

[10] ILO (May, 2015), p. 1.

[11] ILO (May, 2015), p. 1.

[12] European Union Agency for Fundamental Rights (2020), p. 31.

[13] European Union Agency for Fundamental Rights (2020), p. 35.

[14] European Union Agency for Fundamental Rights (2020), p. 31.

to combatting gender stereotypes that are enshrined both in legislation, gender stereotypes, and people's gender role perceptions. In line with the movement of combatting gender stereotypes and their repercussions on national and international instruments, some answers can be also drawn from legal practice.

From the ECtHR's perspective, while there is no explicit normative clause concerning the right to work in the ECHR, the Court interprets the scope of Article 8 as ample as to cover professional and business activities. Indeed, Article 8 covers the right to develop relationships with others and this includes relationships within the workplace.[15] In this direction, the ECtHR does not interpret the scope of the article as narrow as only covering the right to seek employment or unfair dismissal. On the contrary, the ECtHR provides a much wider scope and accepts different aspects of employment under Article 8. According to the Court, access to work, retirement pensions, work-related benefits, reduction in remuneration, dismissals, parental leave may benefit from the protection by the Convention.[16]

Accordingly, workplace discrimination based on LGBTQ identity can be evaluated under the right to respect for private life in conjunction with Article 14. Indeed, the Court had already decided on four cases[17] regarding the dismissal of civil servants based on their sexual orientation. These cases concerned dismissal from the United Kingdom Armed Forces merely based on the applicants' sexual orientation. According to the ECtHR, the sole reason for the applicants' dismissal and investigations conducted was the applicants' sexual orientation. As a consequence, not only the dismissal of the applicants was not in line with the Convention but also the investigation process regarding their sexual orientation was "exceptionally intrusive". In this scope, there is no doubt that one's sexual orientation constitutes one of the most intimate aspects of an individual's private life.[18] However, the United Kingdom offered neither specifically convincing nor weighty reasons for the investigation of applicants' dismissal or investigation of their homosexuality.[19] Consequently, the Court found that both the investigations on the applicants' sexual orientation and their discharge based on their homosexuality in accordance with the Ministry of Defence's policy were not in line with Article 8 of the ECHR.[20] Considering the outcome of these applications, it is clear that civil servants' dismissal based on their sexual orientation is not compatible with the Convention. Nevertheless, considering private sector employees' rights, the application of the Convention and the extent of it might be debated since employers would also benefit

---

[15] O'Connell (2012), p. 180.

[16] See the summary of the case-law on employment rights; CoE (2021a, b), pp. 1–5, 10, 17–20.

[17] *Perkins and R. v. the United Kingdom*, App. Nos. 43208/98, 44875/98, Judgment of 22 October 2002; *Beck, Copp and Bazeley v. the United Kingdom*, App. Nos. 48535/99, 48536/99, 48537/99, Judgment of 22 October 2002; *Lustig-Prean and Beckett v. the United Kingdom*, App. Nos. App. nos. 31417/96, 32377/96, Judgment of 27 September 1999; *Smith and Grady v. the United Kingdom*, App. Nos. 33985/96, 33986/96, Judgment of 27 September 1999.

[18] *Lustig-Prean and Beckett v. the United Kingdom*, para. 83.

[19] Para.98; *Smith and Grady v. the United Kingdom*, para. 110.

[20] *Smith and Grady v. the United Kingdom*, para. 111.

from the Conventional rights opposed to State actors. In this scope, the positive obligation of States to effectively protect rights enshrined in the ECHR should be taken into consideration.

3 Hate Speech of Employers: A Form of Workplace Discrimination Towards LGBTQ Individuals

When homophobic hate speech takes place at the workplace, LGBTQ employees might avoid disclosing their sexual orientation or gender identity. In this context, fear of discrimination and harassment can cause considerable anxiety and inevitably loss of production of the affected employee.[21] Undoubtedly, this reasonable fear created by inequitable homophobic behaviors conducted by the employer or even colleagues might affect LGBTQ employees' careers irrevocably.

Under the ECtHR's jurisprudence, the right to freedom of expression has been accepted as one of the essential foundations of a democratic society. In one of the first cases concerning freedom of expression, namely *Handyside* judgment,[22] the Court set the principles regarding the importance of freedom of expression in democracies.[23] One of the most important outcomes of the judgment is that not only favorably received, inoffensive expressions were under the protection of the right to freedom of expression but also offending, shocking, disturbing expressions deserve the protection of Article 10 of the Convention.[24] The importance of freedom of expression in a well-functioning democratic society has been repeated by the Court many times to this date.[25] However, freedom of expression is not an absolute right, and it is subject to limitations and hate speech constitutes one of the most important exceptions to the protection of freedom of expression. On the one hand, as it was stated in *Handyside* judgment, democracy relies on pluralism, tolerance, and broadmindedness, and on the other hand, hate speech itself goes against the values protected by democracy.[26] Even though hate speech is an important exception, the

---

[21] ILO (2015), p. 1.

[22] *Handyside v. The United Kingdom, Application No. 5493/72,* Judgment of 07 December 1976.

[23] Harris et al. (2014), p. 614.

[24] *Handyside v. The United Kingdom*, Application No. 5493/72, Judgment of 07 December1976, para.49.

[25] *Handyside v. The United Kingdom,* Application No. 5493/72, Judgment of 07 December 1976, para.49..; *Observer and Guardian v. The United Kingdom,* Application No. 13585/88, Judgment of 26 November 1991, para.59; *Ligens v. Austria*, Application No. 9815/82, Judgment of 08 July 1986, paras.41-42; *VgT Verein Gegen Tierfabriken v. Switzerland*, Application No.24699/94, Judgment of 28 June 2001, para.73.

[26] *Garaudy v. France*, Application No.65831/01, decision on admissibility, 24 June 2003; *Schimanek v. Austria,* Application No. 32307/96, decision on admissibility 01 February2000; *M'Bala M'Bala* v. France, Application No. 25239/13, decision on admissibility 20 October 2015; *Norwood v. The United Kingdom,* Application No. 23131/03, decision on admissibility 16 November 2004; *Pavel Ivanov v. Russia,* Application No. 35222/04, decision on admissibility 20 February 2007; *Belkacem v. Belgium,* Application No. 34367/14, decision on admissibility 20 July 2017.

ECtHR hasn't made a precise definition of it,[27] instead, the Court applies a case-by-case approach.

In the ECtHR's judgments, hate speech towards various minorities has been widely discussed. Although not in the labor context, homophobic hate speech, in general, has been subjected to the Court's jurisprudence to this date.[28] In the case of *Carl Johann Lilliendahl v. Iceland,*[29] the Court evaluated that speech that does not necessarily call for violence or other criminal acts but insulting, ridiculing, slandering specific groups of the population can still permit authorities to restrict freedom of expression.[30] And in the application of *Beizaras and Levickas v. Lithuania,*[31] concerning the positive obligation of the States, the ECtHR found that the sexual orientation of the applicants had played a role in the way they were treated by the domestic authorities, considering that Lithuanian authorities had referred the applicants' sexual orientation in their decisions.[32] These judgments suggest a cumulatively rigorous approach of the Court on homophobic hate speech issues. Indeed, while the Court was reluctant to determine the existence of hate speech in *Vejdeland and others*, in Lilliendahl's application, the ECtHR did not step back from identifying homophobic hate speech. And with the *Beizaras and Levickas* judgment, the Court emphasized the States' positive obligation to protect from such speech. Considering the Court's little tolerance against homophobic hate speech, one can make inferences on the Court's possible approach to anti-gay hate speech and discrimination based on LGBTQ in employment-relationship.

As for the CJEU, the Court has already concluded in two cases that hate speech that target LGBTQ people shall elevate to the violation of the Equal Treatment Directive in the given context. On its first judgment concerning hate speech against LGBTQ people, *Asociația Accept v Consiliul Național pentru Combaterea Discriminării,*[33] the CJEU confirmed that the speech of Gigi Becali, who is the director of a Romanian football club, has amounted to hate speech. The speech mainly targeted gay football players, how they shall find no place in the team since they are homosexuals. Subsequently, Becali has commented on a Bulgarian football player who is rumored to be gay and a possible transfer from a Bulgarian football club to the Romanian football club. He noted that even if he were not gay, there have been rumors circulating about his sexual orientation, and thus, he will never employ

---

[27] In some judgments, the ECtHR gives an indefinite definition of hate speech as "all forms of expression which spread, incite, promote or justify hatred based on intolerance". Tulkens (2015), p. 2, *Gunduz v. Turkey,* Application No. 35071/97, Judgment of 04 December 2003, para.40; Weber (2019), p. 3.

[28] *Vejdeland and others v. Sweden*, Application no. 1813/07, Judgment of 09 February 2012, *Lilliendahl v. Iceland,* Application No. 29297/18, Judgment of 12 May 2020, *Beizaras and Levickas v. Lithuania*, App. No. 41288/15, Judgment of 14 January 2020.

[29] *Lilliendahl v. Iceland,* Application No. 29297/18, Judgment of 12.05.2020.

[30] *Lilliendahl v. Iceland* , para. 36.

[31] *Beizaras and Levickas v. Lithuania,* App. No. 41288/15, Judgment of 14 January 2020.

[32] *Beizaras and Levickas v. Lithuania*, paras. 120–124.

[33] Case C-81/12, Judgment of the Court (Third Chamber), 25 April 2013.

him at the football club.[34] The CJEU has confirmed the conclusion of harassment of the national equality administration concerning the violation of equal treatment on employment.[35] Additionally, the Court most particularly noted that when it comes to the sanction, which needs to be effective, proportionate, and dissuasive in the meaning of Article 17 of the Directive,[36] the allegations of the plaintiff association concerning the warning measure imposed by the National Council for Combatting Discrimination (CNCD) were valid.[37] Given the impact and seriousness of the present case, the warning measure issued by CNCD did not satisfy the effectiveness and dissuasiveness criteria in terms of the Equal Treatment Directive.[38] In this direction, an important conclusion of the CJEU concerning hate speech at the workplace is that when the discrimination is established by the complainant, it is the burden of the respondent to distance itself from the homophobic and discriminative speech. It is also not important whether the speech was made by the director of the football club or the technical director of the team. The Court took the view that since the public considers the concerned person's speech as if it is the official view of the football club, the hate speech of the concerned person was considered attributable to the football club.

Following this judgment, the CJEU has rendered a judgment on a similar subject with some minor differences in the case of *NH v "Associazione Avvocatura per i diritti LGBTI - Rete Lenford"*.[39] This time the Court has explicitly commented on the freedom of expression aspect of hate speech concerning the pre-recruitment era. It should be noted that as long as the speech is made outside of the recruitment context, namely if the speech can be distinguished as if it does not constitute a pre-condition for recruitment policy, then it will not be viewed as discrimination in terms of 2000/78/EC.[40] On the other hand, ECtHR has stressed once that obligation to respect others and also not humiliate them exists and any contrary behavior might be

[34] Case C-81/12, para. 35.

[35] Case C-81/12, para.29.

[36] Article 17 Sanctions: "Member States shall lay down the rules on sanctions applicable to infringements of the national provisions adopted pursuant to this Directive and shall take all measures necessary to ensure that they are applied. The sanctions, which may comprise the payment of compensation to the victim, must be effective, proportionate and dissuasive. Member States shall notify those provisions to the Commission by 2 December 2003 at the latest and shall notify it without delay of any subsequent amendment affecting them."

[37] Case C-81/12, para.70.

[38] Case C-81/12., para. 69.

[39] Case C-507/18, Judgment of the Court (Grand Chamber) of 23 April 2020.

[40] Belavusau (2020), p. 1004. The author notes that discrimination, as well as the speech, must be avoided if they constitute "selection criteria" for the vacation, in the meaning of art.3 para.1 let. a of 2000/78/EC. Also, see the opinion of the Advocate General on *NH* case para.62. AG seems to require a link between hate speech and recruitment in light of the Directive. It is also equally important that the AG has acknowledged the jurisprudence of ECtHR concerning hate speech. See para.67. In order to support her stance where the interference made to freedom of speech in the context of 2000/78/EC, she considers such interference is necessary and proportionate to achieve the aim of the Directive.

unnecessary offensive in the given context.[41] In the context of freedom of expression, the CJEU has affirmed that especially homophobic expressions shall be considered in the ambit of freedom of expression and that freedom of expression shall be limited only to the extent 2000/78/EC requires so.[42] This means homophobic statements made by the employer or colleagues which do not constitute recruitment policy or selection criteria for the vacancy would not elevate to the violation of the Directive. Consequently, hate speech is not prohibited *per se* under CFR or 2000/78/EC.

As the owner of a law firm, Mr. N.H. has expressed his attitude towards homosexual people as he would never hire somebody who is homosexual and would not use the services provided by homosexual people. Even if this speech was made in a radio interview and there was no open vacancy at that time at the law firm, the speech of the employer inevitably would discourage potential employees in the future.[43] Consequently, this would hinder access to work and also discrimination on the basis of sexual orientation under Article 3 para.1 let. a of 2000/78 EC. Both the Advocate General and the CJEU have concluded in the same direction with the previous judgment "Asociația Accept" that this statement would fall into the ambit of the Equality Directive. Even if it is argued in legal doctrine whether there was a need for this judgment, especially as the *acte clair* comes into mind, the judgment however clarifies that the potential victim status would fall into the ambit of the Directive.[44] Furthermore, the CJEU opines that the statements made by the potential employer that negatively targets LGBTQ people are considered in the ambit of freedom of expression.[45]

---

[41] For the critics regarding the CJEU's silence on not to bow the jurisprudence of ECtHR on *Vejdeland and Others v. Sweden* Case see Belavusau (2020), p. 1016.

[42] Case C-507/18 para.51. See AG Opinion on Case C-507/18, para.62 and 66. On contrary, AG argues in her opinion that 2000/78/EC reflects the clear choice of the EU legislator for the sake of combatting discrimination against the enumerated grounds. For this reason, any speech that falls in the ambit of discrimination in terms of the Directive shall not be exonerated by arguing the freedom of speech. The AG is also of the opinion that the limitation to freedom of speech is already enshrined under 2000/78/EC.

[43] Case C-507/18 para.s 37, 39, 40, 43–44. The Court gives precedence to the broad interpretation of the term 'for access to employment or to occupation'. The Court also further notes that in the eye of the public such statements shall be comprehended as if the meaning that being non-LGBTQ is a pre-condition to be recruited at the concerned workplace.

[44] Case C-81/12, paras.36–37. Also, see Henrard (2019), p. 99.

[45] Case C-507/18, para. 46, 56–57.

4 Balancing Rights: Conflict Between Rights of the Employee and Employer

Regarding the above-mentioned cases on homophobic hate speech, it is explicit that States are under the obligation of protecting individuals against discriminatory behaviors from other persons. Furthermore, especially considering *Carl Johann Lilliendahl v. Iceland* judgment,[46] the ECtHR demonstrated a rather strong stance against homophobic speech and discriminatory behavior based on sexual orientation. Therefore, it is hard to envisage weighty enough reasons for justification of discrimination based on sexual orientation in the workplace, notwithstanding whether the employer is a private entity. As for the employers' rights such as the right to govern and establish policies, a balancing act would be needed. Indeed, the ECtHR has previously evaluated employers' right to project a certain corporate image and considered it as a legitimate aim.[47] However, considering the States' positive obligation regarding protection from discrimination, the domestic courts shall respect the protection of the rights of others. While the ECtHR provides States with a rather wide margin of appreciation when it comes to balancing competing Convention rights,[48] protection of the rights of sexual minorities constitutes a weighty aim in comparison to the protection of a certain image of a company.

In this direction, some may claim that protection from discrimination based on sexual orientation in the workplace can collide with the protection of the freedom of expression of the employer, and antidiscrimination regulations may cause excessive censorship.[49] Indeed, this argument is not completely unfounded, and the States' sanctions against private employers' discriminatory behavior should always be proportionate. It is clear that employers would also benefit from the right to freedom of expression as private persons. However, this does not mean that States should avoid intervening with private employers' governing decisions. Although ECtHR has not answered the question to what extent States can limit employers' operational decisions concerning discriminatory actions based on sexual orientation yet, one can make inferences based on the homophobic hate speech jurisprudence of the Court. In this direction, if an employer's action has the intention of securing a policy of non-discrimination within a workplace, the state authorities will benefit from a wide margin of appreciation when justifying the employer's action.[50] On the other hand, if the intention of the employer is just to protect a certain image that is not

[46] *Lilliendahl v. Iceland*, Application No. 29297/18, Judgment of 12 May 2020.

[47] *Eweida and Others v. The United Kingdom*, App. Nos. 48420/10, 36516/10, 51671/10, 59842/10, Judgment of 15 January2013, para. 94.

[48] *Eweida and Others* v. The United Kingdom, App. Nos. 48420/10, 36516/10, 51671/10, 59842/10, Judgment of 15 January 2013, para. 106.

[49] Miller (2020), p. 304.

[50] *Eweida and Others v. The United Kingdom*, App. Nos. 48420/10, 36516/10, 51671/10, 59842/10, Judgment of 15 January 2013, para. 109.

necessarily in line with Convention values, national authorities will have a rather narrow margin of appreciation for the justification of the employer's action.

By extension, the application of *Denis Viktorovich Oleynik against Russia*[51] can be interpreted by means of these explanations. In the application of Oleynik, which is a communicated case, the applicant uploaded his curriculum vitae to various headhunter websites. He was invited to participate in a Skype interview for a position. After the interview, the person in charge confirmed that the foundation was willing to hire the applicant as a training manager. During the communication, the applicant was asked whether he was gay, and it was specified that the foundation "adheres to traditional views" and that it would not hire a homosexual person. As the applicant confirmed that he was gay, he received an e-mail from the foundation confirming that he could not be employed by the foundation. No explicit reasons were given for the refusal to employ the applicant. After exhausting domestic remedies, the applicant complained under Article 14 in conjunction with Article 8 of the Convention that his denial of employment was of a discriminatory nature and that the domestic courts did not answer his arguments in this respect. Under the facts of the application, it is clear that the applicant was rejected by the employer solely on the ground of "protecting a certain image of the company". It is also evident that a hiring policy discriminatory against homosexuality is not in line with the values of ECHR, and therefore, Russian authorities have a narrow margin of appreciation regarding the justification of the employer's actions. While notifying the application to Russia, the Court also referred to the question of whether "the domestic courts offered effective protection against the alleged discrimination of the applicant by the employer company, on the ground of his sexual orientation". At this stage, we do not know the answer of Russian authorities to the Court's question. However, considering the facts of the case, the outcome of a violation for discrimination based on sexual orientation would not be surprising.

Consequently, under the ECtHR, employers' governing decisions regarding their business are not limitless. Although an employer may have a legitimate aim while taking certain operational decisions, the actions of the employer should be proportionate to the aim. Furthermore, considering States' positive obligations, States may and in some situations should intervene with private business owners' decisions.

When it comes to the CJEU, the stance of the court is closely linked to the legitimate interest pursued by the company regarding the discriminative behavior. Even if the Court has not delivered any judgment concerning any concrete sexual orientation based discrimination in the workplace, the Court has recently dealt with a headscarf ban in the workplace that directly targets female employees.[52] In this regard, two employees were given the notice to remove their headscarves.[53] The employers claimed to pursue the legitimate interest of being impartial towards their

[51] *Denis Viktorovich Oleynik v. Russia,* App. No. 4086/18, Communicated on 5 February 2020.

[52] *WABE eV* C-804/18 and *MJ* Case C-341/19 were rendered on 15 July 2021.

[53] The litigant did not cover her head at the beginning of recruitment but shortly after the recruitment.

enterprises. The Court mainly emphasized that there was no EU-wide consensus concerning wearing religious symbols at the workplace therefore, the Member States of the EU shall enjoy a wide margin of appreciation on the regulation concerning the social needs of their society. The legitimate aim pursued by the company on the other hand was also considered justifiable.[54]

The stance of the court was no different in a similar case when it was asked to interpret the Directive 2000/78 concerning the dismissal of an employee who covered her head while working at a kindergarten. However, this time, the legitimate interest of the defendant was based on the quality of the sector, which arguably required the employees to be neutral and not to influence the children in any manner concerning religious activities. In this case, it was once again affirmed by the CJEU that the customer groups' perception and expectation from the employer can be a legitimate aim and, therefore, any notification or dismissal of the employee on these grounds would not violate the EU law *per se.* Accordingly, considering the CJEU's case law regarding the extent of the governing decisions of employers, the legitimacy of such decision would solely depend on the legitimate interest of the employer.

Therefore, under such evaluations from the CJEU, any unequal interference with an employee's expressions in the workplace shall be evaluated considering the concrete case and the legitimate interest of the employer. However, even if it can be assumed that there can be a certain limitation of such expressions for specific sectors or job descriptions, such as for security personnel to wear pants so that they can run faster in case of emergency, this should be accorded to all employees regardless of their sex, sexual orientation, or gender identity.

5 The Burden of Proof and to Obtain Evidence Concerning the Anti-discrimination Claims in the Context of Sexual Orientation

Proving the existence of discrimination and harassment at the workplace might be hard for the victims since the perpetrators would hardly leave concrete footsteps behind.[55] In order to tackle procedural hurdles for the victims, 2000/78/ EC Directive reiterates the burden of proof level for the complainants, where the proof of *prima facie* case is deemed enough for the establishment of the discrimination as under the 2000/43/EC Directive.[56] It must be acknowledged that the decreased standard of burden of proof under the 2000/78 EC Directive is a noteworthy

[54] *WABE eV* Case, para.31 and *MJ Case*, para.63.

[55] Wladasch (2020), p. 235.

[56] Muir and de Witte (2017), p. 147. A similar provision concerning the burden of proof is enshrined under 2006/54/EC art. 19. On the other hand, criminal procedures and inquisitorial proceedings are exempted from the scope of the burden of proof under Directive 2000/78/EC, Article 10, para. 3.

development that aims to standardize and to avail the proof of discrimination. The purpose of diminishing the burden of proof also aims to support the complainants to prove their cases.[57] Even if the Directive 2000/78 has strengthened the victim's stance in terms of proof of the case, there are still some questions that should be answered for the proof of the case. For instance, the interpretation of the establishment of *prima facie* case is still not clear in the given context. As the statements of perpetrators have been made through public channels[58] in the analyzed cases, it was obvious that the hate speech already took place. On her opinion on "N.H." Case, AG Sharpston has developed four criteria for a speech to be considered as discrimination in the meaning of Directive. These criteria are (1) the status of the person making the statements being considered and the capacity in which he or she made them, (2) the nature and content of the statements concerned, and (3) the context in which the statements at issue were made.[59]

What if similar speeches were made in a recruitment process online or at the workplace where no recording is possible? Would the victim's (discriminated employee) mere statement be afforded to prove its case? The Employment Tribunal of the UK was confronted with the question of the proof of sexual orientation based discrimination in the workplace where the statements of the victim were accompanied by the former colleague's testimony. The Tribunal has considered both of the statements sufficient for the establishment of the case.[60] Since the jurisprudence of the CJEU with regard to sexual orientation-based discrimination is based on the applications of NGOs, we have no proof concerning the actual victims' hurdles to prove their cases when the discrimination takes place. The cases dealt with by the CJEU tackle the public statements of employers or people who have an influence on employment that is already reviewable by the judicial authorities.[61]

Furthermore, if the employer has made a public speech that negatively targets LGBTQ employees, it is considered that the burden of proof shifts to the respondent to prove that the expression of recruitment policy does not violate the principle of equal treatment.[62] Concerning the establishment of the case, the situation of the

---

[57] Muir and de Witte (2017), pp. 139, 147, 148.

[58] That the discriminative speech was made by means of public channels is of importance when taking into account whether or not the discrimination is established. On her opinion on "N.H." Case AG Sharpston has developed four criteria for a speech to be considered as discrimination in the meaning of Directive.

[59] See Opinion of Advocate General on Case C-507/18 paras. 44–46.

[60] *Mr D Robson v* NGP Utilites *Ltd*: 1805097/2019. Employment Tribunal decision rendered by HM Courts & Tribunals Service and Employment Tribunal on 16 June 2021.

[61] Henrard (2019), p. 99.

[62] Case C-54/07, Judgment of the Court (Second Chamber) of 10 July 2008. Feryn, C-54/07, para 31. Ellis and Watson (2012), p. 163. Even in that case, the respondent shall establish the actual recruitment practice of the undertaking which is corresponding with equal treatment, and the employee candidates and/or employees are not discriminated against on the basis of their race. On the other hand, the mere speech which is spread by social media channels might have a discriminatory impact on the potential candidates who are targeted in that speech.

victim (employee) should also be taken into account, especially where the employers (companies) are entitled not to disclose some information or statistics which might affect the outcome of the case as well as the establishment of the presumption, they possess.[63] Especially the reporting of discrimination is quite low amongst the LGBTQ community which is 10% according to the survey of European Union minorities and discrimination survey (EU-MIDIS). The hesitance of revealing sexual orientation (outing), concerns not to be taken into account seriously, lack of knowledge, bureaucracy, and time are one of the reasons for underreporting. To tackle this problem of access to justice, supporting judges as well as juridical personnel concerning the shift of the burden of proof, the unique characteristics of discrimination, and the hurdles that the victim face can improve the current backlash in the judiciary in terms of combatting against discrimination.[64] This would result in the failure of the establishment of the presumption.[65] On the other hand, the CJEU has most notably considered in the "CHEZ" Case that the defendant's avoidance not to disclose requested documents or information shall be taken into account by the national judge as to the establishment of the presumption.[66]

Therefore, continuous behaviors of co-workers or superiors of an employee towards the employee or their family members,[67] which have discriminatory characteristics in the sense of sexual orientation, shall be considered under the Directive 2000/78. Although in the "Colman" Case, the nexus between the mother and the child with disability was rather clear and the harassment made to the mother was obvious, it can be expected from the CJEU to answer further questions on whether a general hate speech at the workplace would elevate to the discrimination, especially if the concerned employees have LGBTQ acquaintances, friends, family members.[68] It is noteworthy to cite the Advocate General's remark regarding discriminator behavior. In his opinion, AG Maduro has rightly pointed out that the purpose of the Directive is to combat the discriminative behaviors on the enumerated grounds. It is, however, equally important that the concerned employee should be discriminated against on one of the grounds listed under 2000/78/EC art.1. There is also nothing

---

[63] CHEZ Case C-104/ CJEU, para.80.

[64] See Wladasch (2020), pp. 237, 243.

[65] Benoît-Rohmer (2017), p. 163.

[66] CHEZ Case C-104/ CJEU, para.80.

[67] Ellis and Watson (2012), p. 300. With regard to EC Directive 2006/54, 2000/78 and EC Directive 2000/43 even if the conduct is not directed to a specific employee, it is enough if there is a homophobic environment in the workplace. In this case, the conduct will be considered as harassment. Vinković et al. (2016), p. 7. Discrimination should not necessarily take place against the employee. CJEU has ruled once on Case C-303/06 Coleman that limiting the scope of the Directive's application only to the employees' status (in this case disability) would not be suitable for the purpose of combating discrimination at the workplace (para. 51). Additionally, the concerned employee is in charge of the daily needs of her disabled child. Therefore, discriminative behavior afforded to her makes her the victim of harassment at the workplace (para. 57).

[68] For further review of how far the victim status can be extended and harmful the discrimination can be on third persons. Waaldijk (2013), pp. 195–196.

under the Directive nor under its Recitals that limits the scope of application of discrimination to the employee's disability.

To take a step forward, would the mere fact that hate speech is made at the workplace be considered a form of discrimination by any means? As it can be seen from CJEU's jurisprudence so far, the Court has not dealt with these sorts of questions regarding victimization that should be clarified in future cases.[69] On the other hand, in the *"CHEZ" Case* CJEU has taken into consideration the applicant's status on discrimination where he was not amongst the discriminated group, namely Bulgarian people with Roma origin, but affected by the discrimination of Electricity Company in the territory.

Lastly, it should be pointed out concerning the actual recruitment policy that the means of evidence the respondent can use for the rebuttal of the burden of proof shall not violate the privacy rights of the current employees.[70] In other words, the respondent employee is not permitted to disclose the names of the LGBTQ employees to rebut the burden of proof to establish the company's actual practice. The CJEU, therefore, interprets the 2000/78/EC in light of the interests and rights of third persons as it does not allow for any further violations of third persons' privacy rights as well as the right to come out.[71] On the other hand, it can be argued that anonymized data concerning the sexual orientation of incumbent employees shall be used for the purpose of rebuttal along with other lawful evidence.[72]

As for the ECtHR, while applying Article 14 to the concrete cases, one significant problem would be proving the reason for the difference in treatment. Indeed, States or private entities may claim the reason for the different demeanor was not objectively discriminatory and the employee's sexual orientation was not relevant at all. It is important to point out that, as a result of the Court's interpretation of the Convention as a living instrument, differences based on sexual orientation require particularly weighty and serious reasons for their justification.[73] In fact, if the discriminatory behavior affects a particularly vulnerable group in society, in addition to the very weighty reasons requirement for justification, the States' margin of appreciation would also be reduced.[74]

Furthermore, if the reason for different treatment is solely based on sexual orientation, this difference in treatment would amount to a breach of Article 14.[75] Consequently, it is expected from States or private employers to hide their actual

---

[69] Muir and Waddington (2018), p. 544. See Case C-83/14 "CHEZ", para 50.

[70] Henrard (2019), p. 105. For further details concerning the right to come out, see Richter (2016), pp. 78–107. Also see Grote and Wenzel (2006), p. 1075. The difference between the freedom of expression and the expression of facts lies down in the limitation of these rights.

[71] C-81/12, para. 57.

[72] Wladasch (2020), p. 239. For instance, consistent evidence including the existence of Equal Opportunities on Recruitment Policy. See CHEZ Case C-104/ CJEU, para. 85.

[73] Harris et al. (2014), p. 803.

[74] Arnardóttir (2017), pp. 157–159.

[75] Johnson (2020), p. 24.

intention to discriminate because of sexual orientation since it would simply require stern justification. However, it is the States' positive obligation to investigate thoroughly any discrimination claim and private employers' genuine intentions. In this direction, any homophobic public statement from a state official or private employer might reasonably indicate that the decision-making process for the differential treatment in question was following a discriminatory rationale based on sexual orientation.[76]

6 A Room Left Open for the Discrimination: Exception of Churches

It is emphasized under Article 24 of the Recital of 2000/78/ EC as well as Article 4/2 that the employee candidate's belief or religion may play a role in the employment qualifications in regard to churches and other public or private organizations that the ethos of which is based on religion or belief. However, discrimination on other grounds is explicitly prohibited under the same provision's last sentence.

From this point of view, would the exception provided to the churches entail them discriminating against LGBTQ people for their application to any positions? If yes, are there any limitations to this entitlement of the churches? To take a step further, would the priest's preaching that comprises homophobic content elevate to a violation of the Directive and be considered hate speech? These questions might be answered in line with the European Parliaments' report on the proposal for the Directive. In this scope, the exception of the churches is justified as: "The intention is to widen the text to cover the wider 'social' activities of religious organizations while restricting it to personnel directly involved in ideological guidance (i.e., not

[76]In a case regarding the refusal of permission regarding organizing an assembly to draw attention to discrimination against minorities including LGBs, the refusal decision did not include any indication of discrimination based on sexual orientation or any other ground. However, according to the Court, "The Court cannot speculate on the existence of motives, other than those expressly articulated in the administrative decisions complained of, for the refusals to hold the assemblies concerned in the present case. However, it cannot overlook the fact that on 20 May 2005 an interview with the Mayor was published in which he stated that he would refuse permission to hold the assemblies... However, in the present case the Court considers that in the assessment of the case it cannot disregard the strong personal opinions publicly expressed by the Mayor on issues directly relevant to the decisions regarding the exercise of freedom of assembly. It observes that the decisions concerned were given by the municipal authorities acting on the Mayor's behalf after he had made known to the public his opinions regarding the exercise of freedom of assembly and "propaganda about homosexuality". It is further noted that the Mayor expressed these views when a request for permission to hold the assemblies was already pending before the municipal authorities. The Court is of the view that it may be reasonably surmised that his opinions could have affected the decision-making process in the present case and, as a result, impinged on the applicants' right to freedom of assembly in a discriminatory manner." Accordingly, the ECtHR found a violation of Article 14. See *Baczkowski v. Poland*, Application no. 1543/06, Judgment of 03 May 2007, paras. 97-100; Harris et al. (2014), p. 805.

receptionists or janitors). It also makes it clear that the dispensation will apply only to religious beliefs and not, for example, to sexual orientation."[77] Therefore, in the context of Art. 4/2, discrimination based on sexual orientation would not benefit from the exception afforded to the churches.

Regarding protection from discrimination where the employer is a church or other public, or private religious organization, the clash between the freedom of religion and the right to non-discrimination is evident. In this context, it is significant for States not to excessively intervene with the exercise of religious conscience, especially if the concerned religious organization is considered to be a religious minority.[78] However, on the other hand, religious beliefs may be a determent factor in shaping society's attitude towards homosexual behaviors and LGBTQ people.[79] Indeed, the religious practice might be the main source of intolerance towards various groups, including LGBTQ persons, and rather creates a non-affirming environment.[80] It is beyond doubt that this non-affirming environment contributes to the stigma, prejudice, and internalized homophobia amongst LGBTQ individuals.[81]

In this scope, concerning the recruitment of LGBTQ people at churches, it is hard to say that LGBTQ people's sexual orientation may be a determinant factor for the recruitment. First of all, as mentioned above, the Directive explicitly limits the exception provided to churches to the belief and religion of the concerned employees or employee candidates. Even if one might think that the churches' rules and dogma shall be a justification for the ethos they are based on, this rule should be interpreted together with the belief and religion of the concerned person.

When the employment court of Cardiff was once confronted with the implementation of Employment Equality Regulations 2003,[82] the Court has acknowledged that the employee's sexual orientation, including his past relationships, shall not be a

[77] European Parliment on the proposal for a Council directive establishing a general framework for equal treatment in employment and occupation (COM(1999) 565 – C5-0068/2000 – 1999/0225 (CNS), 23.

[78] Human Rights Watch (2018), p. 35.

[79] Doebler (2013), p. 24. "Traditional believers and fundamentalists in particular — those who believe that only their religion has any valid truth claim — were repeatedly found to be more homophobic than believers who are less traditionalist, and non-believers"

[80] Doebler (2013), pp. 24–25. Such as condemning same-sex behavior as sinful, barring LGBs from spiritual leadership positions (or requiring their celibacy in such positions), and refusing to sanction same-sex union ceremonies. See: Barnes and Meyer (2012).

[81] Barnes and Meyer (2012), p. 2.

[82] Employment Equality Regulation 2003 have come into force on the 26th of June, 2003 and prevents the employer's unfair discrimination of employees on the basis of sexual orientation. This secondary regulation however has been revoked by the Equality Act 2010.

justification for the employer to dismiss him from his occupation.[83] In addition, the concerned employee's past relationships also cannot be interpreted as an indicator of his future relationships.[84] However, priests' current civil status and affairs might play a role in their dismissal from the occupation based on the exception afforded to the churches.[85] When a lower court in Nottingham was confronted about whether or not the dismissal from the post based on same-sex marriage would elevate to discrimination,[86] the Court took into consideration that the churches are free to determine whether or not to accept same-sex marriage based on religious doctrine.[87] This decision was upheld by the Employment Appeal Tribunal, and the concerned case was not referred to the CJEU for clarification of any further questions regarding the interpretation of the EU law.[88]

7 Conclusion

Discrimination based on sexual orientation can occur in the workplace in many forms. Discrimination of LGBTQ individuals based on their sexual orientation stands as an absolute prohibition for the employer both in the context of the ECtHR and the CJEU. However, employers sometimes set some restrictions in the workplace that might be interpreted as discriminatory, and these restrictions can

[83] Legislation.Gov.UK (2003), Explanatory Note. These regulations transform 2000/78/EC Directive into the UK legal order. Therefore, the concerned case was closely linked to the implementation and interpretation of EU law. For the news related to this case see Personnel Today, "Gay Man Refused Job by Church of England Bishop Wins Case for Unlawful Discrimination". 2007. https://www.personneltoday.com/hr/gay-man-refused-job-by-church-of-england-bishop-wins-case-for-unlawful-discrimination/. Also see BBC, "Bishop Loses Employment Case". 2007. http://news.bbc.co.uk/2/hi/uk_news/wales/6904057.stm.

[84] BBC, "Bishop Loses Employment Case". 2007. http://news.bbc.co.uk/2/hi/uk_news/wales/6904057.stm.

[85] People Management, 'Gay Priest Barred From Working After Marriage Faces New Court of Appeal Ruling'. 2018. https://www.peoplemanagement.co.uk/news/articles/gay-priest-barred-marriage-court-of-appeal-ruling#gref.

[86] The Guardian, "Gay Priest Forced to Wait for Verdict in Church Discrimination Tribunal". 2015. https://www.theguardian.com/world/2015/sep/01/gay-priest-alleged-discrimination-church-of-england-employment-tribunal.

[87] The Guardian, "Gay Priest Forced to Wait for Verdict in Church Discrimination Tribunal". 2015. https://www.theguardian.com/world/2015/sep/01/gay-priest-alleged-discrimination-church-of-england-employment-tribunal. Deviation from the archaic perception concerning people in same-sex partnership can be seen in Case C-267/12 Hay v Crédit agricole mutuel de Charente-Maritime et des Deux-Sèvres as the civil partnership has been introduced in some Member States of EU since then. Concerning the comparability of registered partnership and marriage as regards equal treatment upon the payment of benefits see Case C-267/12 paras. 36-37, 45, 47.

[88] People Management, "Gay Priest Barred From Working After Marriage Faces New Court of Appeal Ruling". 2018. https://www.peoplemanagement.co.uk/news/articles/gay-priest-barred-marriage-court-of-appeal-ruling#gref.

pursue a legitimate interest for a commercial reason. It is accepted both by the ECtHR and the CJEU that the impartiality of the enterprise might be a justification for some discriminative rules. However, the obligation to conform to heteronormative social rules has not been considered a legitimate reason by any of the courts so far. The same conclusion is also valid for the hate speech of the employer that directly hinders LGBTQ individuals' access to work. Indeed, it is clear that hate speech can never be protected under the right to freedom of expression. Therefore, the arguments on the protection of the employer's freedom of expression are not valid in the context of homophobic speech. Consequently, according to the ECtHR's jurisprudence, employers' homophobic speech is not only a prohibited action in an employment relationship, but it can also give rise to the States' positive obligation.

When it comes to the procedural questions of proving discrimination at the workplace, the 2000/78 EC Directive is one of the most useful EU legislations that reduces the burden of proof of the victim to the establishment of a *prima facie* case. However, there are some questions left to be answered Europe-wide for the collection of the pieces of evidence, as well as the establishment of the *prima facie* case. For instance, it is still difficult to estimate the assessment of the CJEU concerning a rather private dispute, such as discrimination during job interviews or discrimination during the occupation, where the proofs and the facts are slightly blurred. Also, with this interpretation, the CJEU leaves the door open for likely hate speech based on any further convincing justification grounds.

In addition to this, it has not been clarified whether the sincere statements of the victim shall be sufficient for the *prima facie* case. However, the extent of victim status and the extent of *ratione personae* (by reason of the person) in terms of the 2000/78/ EC Directive remains open to be answered especially by the CJEU. With the aim of the Directive as well as with the recent trend of "No Tolerance for Homophobia", the victim status should be interpreted broadly. Even if the concerned person who feels discriminated against is not queer himself/ herself, having awareness and/or friends, members of a family LGBTQ, should be considered enough for the application of the Directive. Lastly, the exception afforded to the churches in many States in Europe, unfortunately, allows the homophobic dynamics to survive and remain in the part of the European society utilizing legislative acts. Nonetheless, interpretation of national courts, as well as current dynamics and trends in the field of human rights law, might hinder such odd exception.

References

Arnardóttir OM (2017) Vulnerability under Article 14 of the European Convention on Human Rights Innovation or Business as Usual? In: Bygrave LA, Strand VB, Ikdahl I (eds) Oslo Law Review. Scandinavian University Press, Oslo, pp 150–171

Barnes DM, Meyer IH (2012) Religious affiliation, internalized homophobia, and mental health in lesbians, gay men, and bisexuals. In: McLeigh JD, Spaulding W (eds) The American journal of

orthopsychiatry, vol 82(4). Global Alliance for Behavioral Health and Social Justice, Lenox, pp 505–515
Belavusau U (2020) The NH Case: On the "Wings of Words" in EU Anti-Discrimination Law. In: Barbou des Places S, Cannizzaro E, Davies G, Lazowski A, Vara JS, Thym D, Wessel RA (eds) A Journal on Law and Integration. European Papers, Italy, pp 1001–1020
Benoît-Rohmer F (2017) Lessons from the recent case law of the EU court of justice on the principle of non-discrimination. In: Lucia Rossi S, Casolar F (eds) The principle of equality in EU law. Springer International Publishing, Cham, pp 151–166
CoE (July, 2021a) Work-related Rights, from https://www.echr.coe.int/documents/fs_work_eng.pdf
CoE (2021b) A sexual orientation, gender identity or expression and sex characteristics approach, from https://rm.coe.int/diversity-in-the-workplace-a-sogiesc-approach/1680a477ce
Doebler S (2013) Religion, ethnic intolerance and homophobia in europe – a multilevel analysis across 47 countries, https://www.research.manchester.ac.uk/portal/files/54544421/FULL_TEXT.PDF
Ellis E, Watson P (2012) EU anti-discrimination law, 2nd edn. Oxford University Press, Oxford
European Union Agency for Fundamental Rights (2020) A long way to go for LGBTI equality, (14 May 2020), https://fra.europa.eu/en/publication/2020/eu-lgbti-survey-results
Grote R, Wenzel N (2006) Meinungsfreiheit. In: Dörr, Grote, Marauhn (eds) EMRK/GG Konkordanzkommentar zum europäischen und deutschen Grundrechtsschutz. Mohr Siebeck, Tübingen, pp 1050–1160
Harris DJ et al (2014) Law of the European Convention on Human Rights. Oxford University Press, Oxford
Henrard K (2019) The effective protection against discrimination and the burden of proof: evaluating the CJEU's guidance through the lens of race. In: Belavusau U, Henrard K (eds) EU anti-discrimination law beyond gender. Hart Publishing, Oxford, pp 95–118
Human Rights Watch (2018) Religious exemptions and discrimination against LGBT People in the United States, https://www.hrw.org/report/2018/02/19/all-we-want-equality/religious-exemptions-and-discrimination-against-lgbt-people
ILO (May, 2015) Discrimination at work on the basis of sexual orientation and gender identity: results of the ILO PRIDE project, https://www.ilo.org/gender/WCMS_368962/lang%2D%2Den/index.htm
Johnson P (2020) LGBT people, the Council of Europe and the European Court of Human Rights, https://doi.org/10.2139/ssrn.2927098
Legislation.Gov.UK (2003) Explanatory Note. https://www.legislation.gov.uk/nisr/2003/497/note/made
Miller J (2020) When workplace antidiscrimination law collides with freedom of expression: a delicate balancing Act. In: van der Heijden P, Warwas B (eds) International Labor Rights Case Law. Brill Publishing, Leiden, pp 300–304
Muir E, de Witte B (2017) The procedural and institutional dimension of EU anti-discrimination law. In: Rossi LS, Casolari F (eds) The principle of equality in EU law. Springer International Publishing, Cham, pp 133–149
Muir E, Waddington L (2018) Directive 2000/78/EC establishing a general framework for equal treatment in employment and occupation. In: Ales E, Bell M, Deinert O, Robin-Olivier S (eds) International and European labour law: article-by-article commentary, International and European business law. Nomos Verlagsgesellschaft ; co-published by Verlag C.H.Beck oHG, Hart Publishing, Baden-Baden, Germany: München, Germany: Oxford, pp 520–546
Mulder J (2017) EU non-discrimination law in the courts. Hart Publishing, New York
O'Connell R (2012) The Right to Work in the European Convention on Human Rights. In: Palmer S, Martin S, Hughes K (eds) European Human Rights Law Review. Sweet and Maxwell Limited, London, pp 176–190
Richter D (2016) Das Recht auf "Outing", in: "Sexuelle Orientierung" als Diskriminierungsgrund: Regelungsbedarf in Deutschland und Polen?'. In: Classen CD, Richter D, Łukańko B (eds)

'Sexuelle Orientierung' als Diskriminierungsgrund: Regelungsbedarf in Deutschland und Polen? Mohr Siebeck, Tübingen, pp 78–107

Tryfonidou A, Henrard K, Belavusau U (2018) The impact of the framework equality directive on the protection of LGB persons and same-sex couples from discrimination under EU law. In: EU anti-discrimination law beyond gender. Hart Publishing, London, pp 229–248

Tulkens F (2015, 7 July) When to say is to do freedom of expression and hate speech in the case-law of The European Court of Human Rights, http://www.ejtn.eu/Documents/Administrative%20Law%202015/5)%20ECtHR%20for%20Judicial%20Trainers/ECtHR%20and%20hate%20speech%20(paper).pdf

Vinković M et al (2016) Handbook of discrimination and mobbing in the workplace. Udruga za pomoć i edukaciju žrtava mobbinga, Zagreb

Waaldijk K (2013) The right to relate: a lecture on the importance of "Orientation" in comparative sexual orientation law. Duke J Comp Int Law 24:161–199

Weber A (2019, September) Manual on hate speech, http://icm.sk/subory/Manual_on_hate_speech.pdf

Wladasch K (2020) Making antidiscrimination law effective: burden of proof, remedies and sanctions in discrimination cases. In: Giegerich T (ed) The European Union as protector and promoter of equality, European Union and its neighbours in a globalized World. Springer International Publishing, Cham, pp 235–244

Alparslan Özaltug has completed his LLB (summa cum laude) at Istanbul University. After graduation, he has completed his legal internship at a law office and at the legal department of an international company. He has obtained his first master's degree from the Europa-Institut, with the thesis of "Interaction Between State Court and Arbitral Tribunal: A Comparison of German and Turkish Arbitration Law in light of UNCITRAL Principles". He is currently working as a compliance analyst in Germany and pursuing his second master's degree at Galatasaray University, Private Law Department with the subject of legal guardianship in private international law with one year at Tübingen University.

Berfu Yalcin obtained her LL.M from the Europa-Institut with the thesis of "Sexual Orientation Change Efforts and Their Compatibility with International and European Human Rights Protection". She specialized in European and International Protection of Human Rights and European Economic Law. She obtained her first LL.M from Istanbul University's Public Law Department with one year at Justus Liebig University Giessen with the thesis of "The Concept of Network Neutrality in the Scope of the ECHR". She completed her LL.B at Istanbul University. She is a Ph. D. candidate at Europa-Institut with the subject of artificial intelligence and human rights law. Currently, she is working as a lawyer in Istanbul.

A Gender-Sensitive Reading of the Obligation to Prevent War Crimes Under the Law of Armed Conflict

Rigmor Argren

Contents

Abstract The Law of Armed Conflict is an inherently male-normative branch under international law. Taking effect in situations of armed conflict, a context traditionally associated with masculinity, the law serves the purpose to: (a) set rules for conduct of warfare, and (b) ensure legal protection for those who are not taking actively part in the conflict. There are several distinct legal provisions that require States to take measures beforehand, that is, preventive measures, where the aim is to prevent future violations (including grave breaches) of the Law of Armed Conflict, should armed conflict erupt. The purpose of this paper is to explore what insights a feminist reading of the obligation to prevent war crimes might bring to the table. The analysis applies thoughts from feminist legal theory to the Law of Armed Conflict as a preventive legal regime. Furthermore, with regards to the preventive features, it is discussed how gender perspectives can purposefully be included in training and education for the civilian population and for members of the armed forces. In this paper, it is argued that a gender-sensitive reading of the law is required to ensure that war crimes are duly prevented. This would have to include war crimes other than acts of sexual violence, as arguably, the impact of certain war crimes, such as indiscriminate destruction of homes and the destruction of livelihoods may have an unduly heavy

R. Argren (✉)
School of Law, Psychology and Social Work, Örebro University, Örebro, Sweden
e-mail: Rigmor.Argren@oru.se

I. Krstić et al. (eds.), *Legal Issues of International Law from a Gender Perspective*, Gender Perspectives in Law 3, https://doi.org/10.1007/978-3-031-13459-3_5

impact on women, obscured by hegemonic masculine perceptions. Therefore, particular mechanisms that enable gender-sensitivity should be established beforehand, in order for a State to fully fulfill its obligation to prevent all war crimes.

1 Introduction

The Law of Armed Conflict (LOAC), consisting of Geneva Conventions I-IV[1] and Additional Protocols I and II,[2] is an inherently male-normative branch under international law. Taking effect in situations of armed conflict, a context traditionally associated with masculinity, the law serves the purpose of: (a) setting the rules for the conduct of warfare, and (b) ensuring legal protection for those who are not actively taking part in the conflict. There are several distinct legal provisions that require States to take measures *beforehand*, that is, *preventive* measures, where the aim is to prevent future violations (including grave breaches) of the LOAC, should armed conflict erupt. In this paper, it is argued that a refined understanding of gender perspectives and the LOAC could contribute to enhancing resilience and strengthening the overall respect for the LOAC, thus increasing the protection of *all* persons who find themselves in an armed conflict. The intention in this paper is not primarily to give women a voice, although that would be a familiar feature of feminist scholarship.[3] Rather, it's purpose is to explore what insights a feminist reading of the obligation to prevent war crimes might bring to the table. The analysis applies thoughts from feminist legal theory to the LOAC as a *preventive* legal regime. Therefore, aspects of feminist legal theory are first outlined in section two. Thereafter, in section three, the general preventive features of the LOAC are discussed and a gender lens is applied to the war crime of starvation. Finally, some conclusions are drawn.

---

[1] 1949 Geneva Convention for the Amelioration of the Condition of Wounded and Sick in Armed Forces in the Field of August 12, 1949, (1950) 75 UNTS 31–83 [Geneva Convention I]; 1949 Geneva Convention for the Amelioration of the Condition of Wounded, Sick and Shipwrecked Members of Armed Forces at Sea of August 12, 1949, (1950) 75 UNTS 85–133 [Geneva Convention II]; 1949 Geneva Convention Relative to the Treatment of Prisoners of War of August 12, 1949 (1950) 75 UNTS 135–285 [Geneva Convention III]; 1949 Geneva Convention Relative to the Protection of Civilian Persons in Time of War of August 12, 1949 (1950) 75 UNTS 287–417 [Geneva Convention IV].

[2] 1977 Protocol Additional to the Geneva Conventions of 12 August 1949, and Relating to the Protection of Victims of International Armed Conflicts and 1977 Protocol Additional to the Geneva Conventions of 12 August 1949, and Relating to the Protection of Victims of Non-International Armed Conflicts.

[3] Charlesworth et al. (1991), p. 615. For an argument that feminist legal scholarship in fact is much older than this, see Thomas (2021).

2 A Brief Note on Feminist Legal Theory and Public International Law

After some 40 years of research, feminist legal theory is by now considered a well established branch of legal scholarship.[4] This research area has had time to develop several diverse sub-branches. As a consequence, modern feminist jurisprudence cannot be categorized in a clear-cut way.[5] Despite the variation of voices, this field of research has experienced only "modest growth".[6] Furthermore, feminist legal scholarship has been slow to move beyond traditional concerns such as human rights (violence against women) and international criminal law. This paper seeks to adress the gap in research by applying a gender lens to the (civil) legal obligation States have to prevent war crimes in the first place, that is *before* they have been committed.[7] Applying a gender lens to the analysis, first requires that the gendered nature of public international law as a whole is discussed.

In the field of public international law, you may note an even steeper uphill start for feminist legal theory, in that central features in public international law such as the use of force, sovereignty and territory may at face value be perceived as neutral in terms of gender.[8] Thus, in the early days it was even seen as a novelty to "indicate the possibilities of feminist scholarship in international law".[9] But there can be no doubt that from both an historical as well as a contemporary perspective, the fundamental observation of international law as decidedly masculine still holds true, which can be evidenced in both organizational and normative terms.[10] The State may be seen as analogous to masculinity when it has "clear boundaries, strong government, and acts autonomously."[11] As Mégret has pointed out: "hegemonic masculinity [...] is embedded in the law itself."[12] It has been argued that in the arena of public international law, the private-public distinction is ever so present. The whole area of public international law has been described as gendered: the public being male, the private being female.[13] It follows that the State has been seen as intrinsically male.[14] Not only that, male dominance creates a privileged position for the dominant group, with one of the key mechanisms being that such privilege

---

[4]Davies and Munro (2013), p. 14.

[5]Davies and Munro (2013), p. 15.

[6]Rimmer and Ogg (2019), p. 12.

[7]Less central to the discussion in this paper is the observation that feminist discourse also lacks diversity perspectives such as race and sexuality. Rimmer and Ogg (2019), pp. 12–13.

[8]Charlesworth et al. (1991), p. 614.

[9]Charlesworth et al. (1991), p. 614.

[10]Charlesworth et al. (1991), p. 621.

[11]Chinkin and Charlesworth (2000), p. 137.

[12]Mégret (2018), p. 201.

[13]Charlesworth et al. (1991), pp. 625–626.

[14]Hooper (2001), p. 12.

becomes invisible; as in unexamined and taken for granted.[15] But such a distinction may be overly simplistic, in that it shapes the falsity of being a given (even natural?) distinction, instead of being socially constructed perceptions that ought to be scrutinized.[16] Furthermore, such a dichotomic description runs the risk of becoming entangled in the perception of the world as binary, a common approach in legal discourse.[17] Approaching a matter in mutually exclusive categories, is the very hallmark of the LOAC, which already at the point of being applicable is based on a binary distinction: *jus ad bellum* must at all times be kept categorically separate from *jus in bello,* the laws of war.[18] This is necessary for the best protection, but it does not mean that such a binary approach comes without a cost. There may well be circumstances when additional approaches should be sought, in order to seek to mitigate any adverse implications from having a strictly binary worldview. Two particular problems may be noted with a worldview predominantly consisting of two opposing parts. First, reducing the world around us to a question of either or; black or white; male or female is more often than not an oversimplification of realities. Second, when one of these aspects subsequently becomes the norm, this may result in such norms being seen as legitimate, even implicitly taken for granted, thus rendering the other aspect(s) invisible. These are the gender dynamics at play with regard to armed conflict and the LOAC.

Armed conflict and the legal regime that regulates it, the LOAC, have been termed as hyper-masculine.[19] It is further suggested that masculinity in a military setting is all-encompassing and reaches beyond biology. Female members of the armed forces uphold the institution and thus underpin patriarchal attitudes.[20] The application of the LOAC (once drafted by men)[21] follows on from the decision of the State(s) (generally perceived as male)[22] to engage in armed conflict (the archetype of masculine behaviour) against an adversary.[23] This legal regime has been characterized as a "static nature of underpinning treaties offering little opportunity for feminist influence".[24] When looking back at the progress feminist legal scholarship has achieved in particular with regard to the LOAC, Gardam notes with unease that scholarship on feminism and the LOAC in the early twenty-first century has been dominated "by the topic of sexual violence and its criminalization and

---

[15] Flood and Pease (2017), p. 122.

[16] Stern (2018), p. 90.

[17] Stern (2018), p. 89.

[18] *Jus ad bellum* refers to the lawful recourse to inter-State use of force. *Jus in bello*, on the other hand, applies primarily when the conflict is a fact and pertains to equal application of the legal norms to all Parties to the conflict. Dinstein (2016), p. 5.

[19] Mégret (2018), p. 204.

[20] Stern (2018), p. 94.

[21] Quataert (2018), p. 559.

[22] Charlesworth (1997), p. 253.

[23] Bianchi (2016), p. 187.

[24] Ng and Betancourt (2018), p. 147.

punishment."[25] Arguably, this has come at the expense of paying attention to more day-to-day challenges that have a different impact on women and men during armed conflict.[26] Let us be clear: There has been some remarkable progress in the area of prosecuting perpetrators of sexual violence with a war nexus, but such success in shaping the normative transformation may have come with the unintended consequence of putting the prosecution of war crimes at the centre stage of feminist scholarship in relation to the LOAC.[27] Gardam outlines three developmental stages. First, it was noted that the legal regime of IHL was indeed gendered, in that women and men are not treated equally by the law, neither implicitly (for instance in the perception of civilians) nor explicitly (in the provisions pertaining to women).[28] Second, legal feminists explored the protection of civilians.[29] Third, strong inroads were made into international criminal law, and the push for punishing sexual violence against women.[30] In order to provide a firm understanding of the progress achieved so far by applying a gender lens to the LOAC, and at the same time identifying where research gaps remain, the following section will recall the early stages of feminist readings. Thereafter, the notion of civil protection and feminist legal theory is discussed. Finally, the advancement in protecting women from sexual violence is highlighted.

2.1 The Early Stage of the Feminist Readings of the LOAC

Women, who are often subconsciously or explicitly perceived as making up the majority of the group civilians during an armed conflict, benefit from the general protection of civilians as outlined by the LOAC. Additionally, in the eyes of the LOAC, women are in need of (special) protection. Of all the provisions in the four Geneva Conventions and their two additional protocols, 42 provisions mention women, with 19 of these provisions dealing with reproductive aspects of women's lives, such as being pregnant or as nursing mothers.[31] As Gardam has pointed out, women appear in relation to, in this case, their (unborn) child, not in their individual right.[32] Bearing its mark of time, the archaic wording in the LOAC sets out for instance that female prisoners of war deserve "respect for their person and their

[25] Gardam (2013), p. 252.

[26] Davies and Munro (2013), p. 21.

[27] Gardam (2013), p. 254.

[28] Gardam (2013), p. 256.

[29] Gardam (2013), p. 256.

[30] Gardam (2013), p. 256.

[31] Gardam and Jarvis (2001), p. 93.

[32] Gardam (2013), p. 257.

honour".[33] As has been pointed out by Pictet in his commentaries to the Treaties, the notion of *honour* incapsulates protecting prisoners of war from rape.[34] Examining the special and general protection afforded to women in the LOAC, Stern contends that "[t]he fact that women are protected *while* they are pregnant, mothering or held as POWs, is not sufficient to conclude that women generally are adequately protected by the law. It is in its general protections that the law fails to provide adequate protection for women in conflict."[35] It stands to be examined in this paper whether there is additional scope for interpreting and understanding the existing provisions of general protection enshrined in the LOAC to better protect women during armed conflict. You may hold that in order to be capable of such novel analysis freed from binary prejudices deeply encapsulated in the discourse, a detached and external point of observation might be helpful.

In her piece on the alien who ponders over the deeper meaning of the LOAC, Gardam lets her alien be puzzled by the recognition that under the LOAC "all natural categories, except the state, appear to have 'honour' which must be protected, but exactly what this consists of is not clear."[36] This linkage between honour and rape paves the way for the basis of what Jarvis has termed '[t]he honour framework'[37] which according to her analysis has heavily tainted the perception of sexual violence held by ICTY prosecutors. Breaking free from the honour framework means to acknowledge that war brings monumental suffering, directly and indirectly, which is not limited to civilian women. But this should not obscure the fact that when the veil of victimhood is lifted from women in armed conflict, it is important to remember that wars have also become springboards particularly for women to gain access to the public domain, for example, as indispensable workers. This is readily illustrated by the American Government's call for women to work in industry after the men had left for the battlefields during the Second World War.[38] Furthermore, even long before the Second World War, armed conflict created an opportunity for women to expand their turf. Quataert has pointed out that in the late nineteenth century, female nurses driven by a desire to support the war effort also demonstrated "feminist determination to expand women's options in life."[39] It is well established in literature that armed conflict and similar turmoil may work as "windows of opportunity when gender norms sometimes relax in ways that give women more control and authority in their lives."[40] This is not to suggest that such windows of opportunity balance, or in some way 'make good' the suffering that people experience during

[33] 1949 Geneva Convention Relative to the Treatment of Prisoners of War of August 12, 1949 (1950) 75 UNTS 135–285, Article 14.

[34] Pictet (1960), p. 147.

[35] Stern (2018), p. 101.

[36] Gardam (1997), p. 239.

[37] Jarvis (2016), p. 113.

[38] Crowder (1943).

[39] Quataert (2018), p. 568.

[40] Petesch (2018), p. 343.

armed conflict.[41] If anything, it may serve as an indication that the effects of war are not limited to the actual conflict itself, but that the impact stretches into the future and may influence the social and economic settings of the post-conflict society. In other words, what is at stake in terms of space may be even more far-reaching than what first meets the eye.

Putting the post-conflict society aside, Gardam has underlined that the impact armed conflict has on the daily lives of women is fundamentally *different* from the impact men experience.[42] Aspects of social life that may differ considerably between men and women include "threats to safety and security; access to health care; family and community connections; and education and economic security."[43] That is not to say that men are immune to the negative effects of armed conflict.[44] What is suggested is that the destruction of housing, lack of clean water and food, diseases and forced displacement together with the loss of loved ones, have a different impact on men and women. In fact, the different experiences from armed conflict does not stop at gender: the impact of an armed conflict will also vary depending on "race, class, socioeconomic circumstances, urban or rural location, family situation, age, employment, sexuality and health."[45] Typical effects of armed conflict that may be particularly detrimental to women are, for instance, heightened economic insecurity and loss of livelihood.[46] You might say that these elements constitute the basic web of normal life—the life of civilians.[47] This civilian life, as we know it, sets out different conditions for men and women.

2.2 *Feminist Legal Theory and the LOAC Protection of Civilians*

The LOAC is to be applied without discrimination and "without any adverse distinction founded on race, colour, religion or faith, sex, birth or wealth, or any other similar criteria."[48] This provision of non-discrimination is a customary rule for

---

[41] The same intrinsicality of war time benefits has been discussed in relation to non-international armed conflicts. See, e.g. Fuest (2008), pp. 201–224, and Wood (2008), pp. 539–561.

[42] Gardam and Jarvis (2001), p. 19.

[43] Ng and Betancourt (2018), p. 354.

[44] For challenges researching war crimes against civilian men, see, *e.g.* Doolan (2018), pp. 86–102. Concerning how armed conflict affects men and masculinity in a given context see, *e.g.* El-Bushra and Gardner (2016), pp. 443–458.

[45] Charlesworth and Chinkin (2016), p. 173.

[46] Reynolds (2021), p. 196.

[47] It has been pointed out that since gender affects how armed conflict is experienced, it is essential that gender also informs research and policy. See in this regard Hoover Green (2018), pp. 316–325.

[48] Common Article 3, GC 1-IV. Similar provisions appear in GC I, Article 12; GC II Article 12; GC III Article 16; GC IV Article 13; AP I, Article 75(1) and AP II Article 4(1).

international armed conflict as well as non-international armed conflict.[49] The notion 'adverse distinction' points out that even if discrimination is not allowed on the given grounds, there may be a distinction, if required for and favourable to those most in need.[50] One of the reasons why civilian men and women may benefit differently from the protection of civilians as guaranteed by the LOAC is associated with the fact that women are often those seeking to provide for the survival not only of themselves, but also their families.[51] In this regard, damages or shortcomings in relation to food, housing, healthcare and psychosocial support are likely to be even more detrimental to women.[52] Several factors combine increasing the vulnerability of women; these include lower social status, particular expectations of womanhood including motherhood from their community and less access to resources, to mention a few.[53] The common cultural expectations of women as the ones providing food (albeit not necessarily officially acknowledged as breadwinners) and serving men first, means that women die of food insecurity at a disproportionate rate during armed conflict.[54] It is worth noting that when women rate gendered harms, some reportedly consider it more painful not to be able to feed their children than being exposed to sexual violence.[55] The risk of women suffering disproportionately from the effects of war may partly be explained by men's privileged position in society.

The notion of *agency*, may be defined as "the ability of an actor to exert influence, affect the outcome of a process or event, to make happen or prevent an event or action."[56] You may assume that any party that requires special protection, by law or otherwise, does not have full agency. Armed conflict often constitutes change, intended as well as unintended. Thus, the space for agency may shift rapidly as well as unpredictably. Again, this may well vary a great deal between men and women, with women suddenly having to take on the burden of wider responsibilities—and face up to the challenge of increased agency, whilst men might see their area of influence shrink. But for women, as a symbol of honour, as a symbol of the nation's culture, the space for their agency is likely to shrink even faster. It must also be borne in mind that there will often be an expectation that women should retreat back to their homebound duties as soon as a conflict has ended, the men have returned and life has supposedly gone back to 'normal' again.[57] In other words, there is an assumption, a request, that male dominance and privileges that are inherent to such dominance, should be restored when such an 'exceptional' period has come to an end. As Flood and Pease have explained, this is how privilege "is

[49] See Rule 88 in Henckaerts and Doswald-Beck (2005), p. 308.

[50] Henckaerts and Doswald-Beck (2005), p. 309.

[51] Lindsey (2001), p. 29.

[52] Hoover Green (2018), p. 317.

[53] Ng and Betancourt (2018), p. 354.

[54] Ng and Betancourt (2018), p. 356.

[55] Hoover Green (2018), p. 324.

[56] Sinclair (2020), p. 217.

[57] Lindsey (2001), p. 31.

institutionally produced and supported".[58] It is in this light Mégret's observation about the LOAC must be seen: even if it functions in the way it has been designed for and regulates means and methods of warfare to "protect civilians [the LOAC] could still empower masculinity".[59] The reason for this is, he explains, that restraint and control can be seen as intrinsically positive features of manliness.[60] This uplifted perception of manliness gives it authority, and creates the basis for a natural claim for power. Moreover, Mégret suggests that the 'duality of manliness'[61] composed of male violence and male restraint of violence is encapsulated in the LOAC, because of the "simultaneous authorisation and restriction of violence manifested in the laws of war."[62] Mégret concludes that rather than hoping that the LOAC would be "'civilising men'... one can surmise a vision of the laws of war 'masculinizing civilisation.'"[63] This analysis does not stop at glorifying masculinity that exerts restraint. Arguably, restraint does not come for free: in essence it constitutes domination. As Mégret points out: "The very definition of power, then, is not violence but the *possibility* of violence."[64] The dynamics of being protected through the restraints of masculine force causes two dynamics: (1) women end up being grateful for those who carry out control, and thus may well find themselves in a position of gratitude and caught in a situation that may lead to (involuntary) dependence. (2) This means that women, at least in a psychological sense, risk becoming indebted to those who restrain themselves, to those men that take up the role as protectors.[65] The double-edged reality, referred to as the protection racket, has been said to create a situation where someone is *protected from their protector by that very protector*."[66] A particular concern related to the protection racket, is when the protection is actually not for free, but rather takes on the form of sexual exploitation when female members of a community are required to 'pay' for the protection or resources with sexual services with the community accepting the practice.[67] Therefore, the question that may be posed is what preventive measures can be put in place to prevent the protection racket from appearing, or, in the event that it is already a fact, what can be done to remedy the situation?

---

[58] Flood and Pease (2017), p. 120.

[59] Mégret (2018), p. 204.

[60] Mégret (2018), p. 204.

[61] Mégret (2018), p. 209.

[62] Mégret (2018), p. 203.

[63] Mégret (2018), p. 211.

[64] Mégret (2018), p. 217.

[65] Mégret (2018), p. 217.

[66] Mégret (2018), p. 218. Emphasis in the original.

[67] Ng and Betancourt (2018), p. 361.

2.3 Sexual Violence As a War Crime

The issue of bringing perpetrators of sexual violence and rape to justice for committing war crimes has made significant progress in the last few decades through the work of international criminal tribunals such as the International Criminal Tribunal for Former Yugoslavia (ICTY)[68] and the International Criminal Tribunal for Rwanda (ICTR).[69] Against a historic backdrop where there was a lack of examples of prosecuting such conduct as war crimes,[70] these acts are now firmly incorporated and criminalised in the Statute of the International Criminal Court (ICC), regardless of whether the victim is male or female, or whether the act took place in an international armed conflict or a non-international armed conflict.[71] In the mid-1990s, when the ICTY started its work, there was a general perception that sexual violence had systematically been used for ethnic cleansing.[72] But the number of cases before the ICTY where the defendant was charged with giving express orders to his subordinates to commit sexual violence remained scarce.[73] What has been established by the ICTY, on the other hand, is that sexual violence was one of several elements in joint criminal enterprises (JCE).[74] Despite the success of prosecuting sexual violence before the ICTY, Engle has pointed out that there have also been unintended consequences such as the perpetuation of ethnic differences in the region. The strong emphasis on women as victims of sexual violence, downplayed the role women enjoyed in the political as well as the military spheres during the conflict, thereby effectively depleting women's agency.[75]

Some authors see systematic and widespread sexual violence against women as a means of deconstructing the adversary. Powers that seek to deconstruct another community might do so by "destroying social and cultural stability".[76] When female bodies are devalued into battlefields, sexual violence against women is "likely to destroy a nation's culture."[77] In a sense, this was already noted by Gardam's alien, who observed that "all states are in some way dependent on women and their sexual organs for their survival. Women thus become targets in warfare."[78] Perceiving

[68] 1993 Statute of the International Tribunal for Former Yugoslavia, UN Doc. S/25704 at 36, Annex.

[69] 1994 Statute of the International Tribunal for Rwanda, UN Doc. S/Res/955 Annex.

[70] Durham and O'Byrne (2010), p. 35.

[71] 1998 Rome Statute of the International Criminal Court, *entered into force* 1 July 2002; 2187 UNTS 90, Article 8(2)(b)(xxi).

[72] Jarvis (2016), p. 110.

[73] Jarvis (2016), p. 111.

[74] Jarvis (2016), p. 111. However, the sentences given for JCE are shorter in comparision with what is given for criminal acts not conducted jointly. Eboe-Osuji (2012), p. 114.

[75] Engle (2005), p. 810.

[76] Seifert (1996), p. 39.

[77] Seifert (1996), p. 39.

[78] Gardam (1997), p. 247.

women as the symbolic bearers of national or cultural identities, may exacerbate their vulnerability.[79] Furthermore, the female body is not only seen as symbolizing national identities, but extends to a commodity, an object of transaction between men; this makes rape of enemy civilians "proof of victory of one and loss and defeat for the other."[80] Perceiving women in a symbolic and objectified fashion may feed into the misconception that sexual violence is primarily an attack on the victim's honour (and thereby the honour of the adversary society) and not a ghastly physical and violent assault.[81] This would also be in line with the finding that war crimes are often spoken about in euphemisms by those who have committed them.[82] It should be pointed out that explaining sexual violence by assigning women the role of bearing a societies collective honour falls short of explaining sexual violence against men, which has since drawn more scholastic attention.[83] The heightened public attention to reports about sexual violence may also lead to a distorted perception of the reality. For instance, there is some evidence that sexual violence was not the most common harm suffered by women in Liberia, but instead it was forced displacement that was reported most frequently.[84]

In addition to feminist legal scholars discerning three distinctive stages to the LOAC, there are also two dominating schools of feminist thought favouring respective approaches for improvement. The 'enforcement school' holds that the LOAC in fact provides more protection for women than is currently being utilised—it is a matter of developing the enforcement of the law.[85] The revisionist school, on the other hand, argues that the lack of protection for women in armed conflict has to do with the misconception that the legal regime is neutral, when in fact it is masculine and thus intrinsically discriminatory.[86] Even so, revisionist scholars are acutely aware that reopening the LOAC treaties for discussion today would be a process dominated by men, and would thereby most likely remain within the hegemony of masculinity that brands public international law.[87] It was apparent at a rather early stage that the enforcement school could more easily be "entering mainstream discussions of IHL".[88] The progress on prosecuting perpetrators of sexual violence in the case law of the ICTY and the ICTR speak in favour of this effect, as does the project of revising the General Comments to the Geneva Conventions which is well underway.[89] In the following section, the path laid out by the enforcement school is

---

[79] Lindsey (2001), p. 28.

[80] Ericsson refers to Brownmiller in her writings. Ericsson (2011), p. 71.

[81] Jarvis (2016), p. 113.

[82] Muñoz-Rojas and Frésard (2004), p. 198.

[83] See, for instance Isaac and Jurasz (2018), pp. 853–882; Mouthaan, (2013), pp. 665–695.

[84] Hoover Green (2018), p. 323.

[85] Oosterveld (2009), p. 388.

[86] Oosterveld (2009), p. 389.

[87] Stern (2018), p. 225.

[88] Oosterveld (2009), p. 400.

[89] The revision was called for already in 1998. See Coomaraswamy (1998), para 95.

followed and the discussion turns to the scope of the preventive obligations under the LOAC, with indications of a gender-sensitive reading.

3 Gendering the Obligation to Prevent War Crimes Under the LOAC

This section is concerned with the basis of the obligation to prevent all war crimes in international armed conflict and what applying a gender lens to this particular obligation might entail. Under the LOAC an armed conflict is considered to be international when two or more High Contracting Parties to the Geneva Conventions,[90] that is States, take part on opposite sides in an armed conflict. There may also be groups other than States involved, such as in the recent airstrikes by Turkey, targetting Kurdistan Workers' Party PKK in Iraq without the consent of the Iraqi government.[91] First, a distinction must be made in this section between the preventive obligations of the parties to the conflict, and the more immediate preventive obligation of the commander, due to this person being (a) closer to information about the specific conditions at the given point in time, and (b) in possession of a certain amount of control over the situation and thereby having the power to decide on intervention.

Common Article 1 of all four Geneva Conventions[92] first of all provides that States have to abstain from committing war crimes. Additionally, there are indications that States are required to do more than limiting themselves to not committing war crimes. By virtue of this provision, the Contracting Parties "undertake to respect and ensure respect for the present Convention".[93] It seems that Contracting Parties have the twofold obligation (a) not to commit war crimes and (b) to ensure the respect of the provisions in the treaties; some form of additional positive action is implied.[94] As Article 1 applies to all the provisions in the Treaty, it must also apply to Common Article 3. This opens up the possibility that it applies in non-international armed conflict as well. And not only that, as it applies to *all* circumstances, a certain awareness about gender aspects may well be called for.[95] In the following section the argument that there is a general State obligation to

---

[90] See above, footnote 1 and 2.

[91] Al-Jazeera, 9 December 2021 Available at: https://www.aljazeera.com/news/2021/12/9/turkey-hits-pkk-targets-in-iraq-after-three-turkish-troops-killed. Al-Jazeera 2022, Available at: Available at: https://www.aljazeera.com/news/2022/2/2/turkish-air-raids-target-kurdish-groups-in-northern-syria-iraq.

[92] For a detailed analysis and drafting history of this Article, see Kalshoven (2007), pp. 665–727.

[93] Common Article 1 of the Geneva Conventions I-IV.

[94] Compare in this regard the discussion on the obligation to protect under human rights law. See generally van der Have (2018).

[95] Although the ICRC has insisted on the 'exclusion of "gendered power relations"' a pragmatic approach may still be acceptable. O'Rourke (2020), p. 305.

prevent all war crimes is presented. Thereafter, as an example, a gender lens is applied to the obligation to prevent starvation as a war crime that reasonably foreseeable unduly affects women.

3.1 The LOAC Obligation to Prevent War Crimes

A first indication that there may be a *general* obligation to prevent war crimes under the LOAC has its origins in the *raison d'être* of the Geneva Conventions. The purpose of these Conventions is to attenuate to the maximum extent possible the suffering of *all* victims of war. Presumably, women and men were expected to have the same level of protection by the LOAC. Gustave Moynier, the President of the International Committee of the Red Cross, identified and articulated the need to set out how States should implement the Treaties as early as in 1870.[96] He proposed "the establishment of an international jurisdiction for the *prevention* and repression of breaches of the Geneva Convention."[97] This idea was first captured in treaty law in the 1949 Geneva Conventions, which oblige States to "take measures necessary for the suppression of *all acts* contrary to the provisions".[98] The first issue to note is that this obligation is limited to the High Contracting Parties, it does not include parties to the conflict. Second, it must be noted that the law sets out a *general* objective which the States should meet.[99] Third, the notion of 'suppression' needs to be considered. It should be noted that the provision requires suppression of *all acts* contrary to the Conventions, the obligation is not limited to grave breaches, or even war crimes, it addresses *all acts* contrary to the Geneva Conventions.

Furthermore, to take all measures necessary for suppression of war crimes must be distinguished from punishing such crimes.[100] These are separate obligations, and therefore separate responses are necessary. As discussed in Sect. 2 above, progress has been made when it comes to punishing perpetrators of sexual violence in armed conflict to justice. Concerning a States obligation to *prevent all acts* contrary to the Treaties, it is unlikely that 'measures necessary for suppression' requires a State to criminalise all breaches. Administrative procedures, control mechanisms and reporting structures may well have the same result. In other words, the State has a

---

[96] Pictet (1952), p. 353.

[97] Pictet (1952), p. 354. (Emphasis added).

[98] Articles 49/50/129/146 in the Geneva Conventions respectively and Article 86 of Additional Protocol I. (Emphasis added).

[99] In contrast, when *grave breaches* have been committed, States are obliged "to search for persons alleged to have committed, or to have ordered to be committed, such grave breaches" (see Articles 49/50/129/146 respectively in the Geneva Conventions).

[100] Prosecuting those who have committed war crimes presumably has a deterrent effect on future perpetrators. Consequently, the implications of an obligation of enacting necessary measures is not limited to ending impunity, but is in fact also aimed at preventing future war crimes through deterrence.

broad range of options to comply with the provision that is general in nature. Some of these, it is argued here, could and should include a distinctive gender-sensitive reading of the LOAC.

If, as established in the previous section, there is a general obligation to prevent war crimes, it is reasonable to conclude that such an obligation applies irrespective of the form any violation takes. In other words, if certain war crimes have either particular gendered features, or disproportionally inflicts suffering on women, the State would have to act against such harm, not because of an obligation in relation to gender analysis as such, but because of the State's obligation to prevent the resultant war crime *for all*. Furthermore, due to the general nature of this obligation, it must arguably be wider in scope than having a primary focus on war crimes entailing sexual violence, only. In other words, attacks on housing, health facilities or the destruction of livelihoods at the level of war crimes might also constitute a breach of the State obligation to prevent war crimes. In practical terms this might mean that the State has an obligation to have in place a mechanism which can be activated in the case it is reasonably foreseeable that war crimes have significant and disproportionate gendered implications. This may include, but not be limited to, ensuring that appropriate and gender segregated data is reported, in systems that need to be put in place beforehand.

The strongest evidence of an obligation to prevent war crimes before they have been committed is to be found in the last part of Additional Protocol I. This part of the Treaty contains two sections, Section I being primarily concerned with "preparatory and preventive measures",[101] many of which have to be implemented *prior* to the outbreak of armed conflict. Typically, this includes providing national legal frameworks, training and rules of where combat material should be placed. Section II of Additional Protocol I deals with the prevention of breaches closer to the event; in other words, when an armed conflict is ongoing. Prevention during the course of events pertains to the conduct of and decisions made by key actors, given the factual circumstances at the given time and place.[102] At this point, the emphasis will be on human action.

Article 87 of Additional Protocol I outlines the State obligations concerning the duties of the commander, an idea already captured in the Geneva Conventions[103] and its predecessors. The provisions of the LOAC set out when in the course of events command responsibility may arise, namely, when a subordinate "was committing or was going to commit"[104] a prohibited act. The words "was going to commit" expressly show that the obligation arises prior to the event, subject to the commander's actual or presumed knowledge about the event and the possibility of

[101] Pilloud et al. (1987), p. 925, para 3280.

[102] The decisions made by the actors will also be influenced by their skills and the training they have received. Therefore, Parties are obliged to have legal advisors available "at all times" as well as "in time of armed conflict", Article 82, Additional Protocol I.

[103] Article 45 Geneva Convention I and Article 46 Geneva Convention II.

[104] Article 86, Additional Protocol I.

intervention. Given that these liabilities are set out in the LOAC (a body of law that is civil in nature), it must be understood as a concretization of the *State's* obligation to prevent war crimes. In other words, if an act is wrong when committed by an individual State agent as part of his duties, to the extent that individual criminal responsibility can be incurred, then it must be a civil wrong on the part of the State in question. This is the basis for the argument that there is indeed a general obligation to prevent war crimes.

Meting out punishments after a breach of the LOAC has been committed does not address the commander's responsibility to *prevent* the breach.[105] This is further underlined by Jarvis, when she calls this obligation 'command responsibility in real time'.[106] That is to say that when a war crime against women is almost certainly going to occur, there lies an obligation on particular actors with a nexus to the scene to supress the commission of such acts.

3.2 *Applying a Gender Lens to the Obligation to Prevent a War Crime*

As pointed out in Sect. 2, women are impacted in a different way than men when it comes to war crimes such as the destruction of civilian housing, denial of access to clean water and food, and forced displacement. The same events and the same context may be seen to put more strain and hardship on women, given that they often are the caretakers of children and the main food provider. Although discussing statistics falls outside of this papers purpose, it should be mentioned that by 2017, there were 16,2 million displaced women worldwide, whereas the same figure in 2009 was 10,6 million.[107] Presumably, displacements have to a large extent negatively impacted on their food security. When it comes to starvation, the LOAC is clear: "Starvation of civilians as a method of warfare is prohibited."[108] This prohibition is also considered to be a norm of customary international law.[109] It is further expanded by explicitly making it unlawful to "attack, destroy, remove or render useless objects indispensable to the survival of the civilian population".[110] Additionally, humanitarian aid has a central role when it comes to prevent or minimize conflict-induced food insecurity.[111] The obligation of belingerents to accept passage

[105] *Prosecutor v Blaškić* (Judgment [Trial Chamber I]) IT-95-14-T (3 March 2000), para 709.

[106] Jarvis (2016), p. 127.

[107] Bendavid et al. (2021), p. 524.

[108] Article 54(1), Additional Protocol I. The corresponding provision for NIAC is Article 14 in Additional Protocol II.

[109] See Rule 53, in Henckaerts and Doswald-Beck (2005), p. 186.

[110] Article 54(2), Additional Protocol I.

[111] Akande and Gillard (2019), p. 770.

of humanitarian aid is subject to consent by the parties to the conflict.[112] Nevertheless, arbitrarily denying such consent is unlawful.[113] In the area of providing assistance, applying a gender lens may be especially helpful, given the particular burden of being foodproviders many women have. In this regard, although not part of the LOAC, inspiration may be drawn from the Cluster Munition Treaty, which in Article 5 requires States to provide gender-sensitive assistance to victims.[114]

Even though it is clear in the law that willfull starvation is prohibited during warfare, no prosecutions for this war crime have so far taken place under international law.[115] One reason for this is that traditionally starvation during armed conflict has been perceived as an unfortunate consequence of warfare rather than a tactic applied by the parties to the conflict the conduct of which could give rise to criminal liabilities.[116] In this regard, it is informative to recall that starvation as a means or method of warfare is among the listed war crimes in the ICC Statute.[117] Furthermore, following an amendment of the ICC Statute on 6 December 2019, it is also considered a war crime in non-international armed conflict. A conduct which under specific circumstances may give rise to individual criminal responsibility for war crime under international law, clearly constitutes conduct for which there is simultaneously an obligation to prevent (or suppress) such conduct in the first place.[118]

It was established in Sect. 3.1 that there is a general obligation to prevent war crimes. Since this obligation is general in nature and applies to all war crimes, it must clearly also apply to the act of starvation as outlined above.[119] It is, therefore, fair to assume that applying the obligation to prevent war crimes to the crime of starvation could make substantial difference to a large group, if not the majority, of women affected by armed conflict. Thus, when one reasonably can assume that a war crime against women, such as conflict induced food insecurity, almost certainly is going to

---

112 Article 70(1) AP I states "... relief actions which are humanitarian and impartial in character and conducted without any adverse distinction shall be undertaken, subject to the agreement of the Parties concerned in such relief actions."

113 Akande and Gillard (2019), p. 770.

114 2008 Convention on Cluster Munitions, *entered into force* 1 August 2010, 2688 UNTS 39. As of 4 November, 2021, the Treaty has 110 Parties and 108 Signatories.

115 Prosecutions under national law for using starvation in non-international armed conflict have occurred. See D'Alessandra and Gillett (2019), p. 825.

116 Graham (2020), p. 268.

117 The provision of the 1998 ICC Statute reads "[i]ntentionally using starvation of civilians as a method of warfare by depriving them of objects indispensable to their survival, including wilfully impeding relief supplies as provided for under the Geneva Conventions" constitutes a war crime in international armed conflicts. 1998 Rome Statute of the International Criminal Court, *entered into force* 1 July 2002; UN Doc. A/Conf. 183/9, Article 8(2)(b)(xxv).

118 For a detailed analysis of the definition of starvation as a war crime and the elements of the crime, see Ventura (2019), pp. 781–814.

119 To prevent or at least mitigate conflict induced food insecurity, the consent given by parties to the conflict to permit relief operations also plays an important role. See further Akande and Gillard (2019), pp. 769–772.

occur, there lies an obligation on particular actors with a nexus to the scene to supress the commission of such acts. Additionally, there is also an obligation of the State to take measures well in advance of any armed conflict, that may be necessary to prevent the commission of such war crimes in the first place, should armed conflict occur.[120]

As noted above in Sect. 3.1, the State has several options at hand to fulfill this obligation of prevention, apart from criminalising war crimes in their national legislation. Training of military forces, administrative procedures, control mechanisms and reporting structures are some of the additional avenues that spring to mind. As for reporting and collecting data concerning the war crime of starvation (or war induced food-insecurity) reasonbly foreseeable to unduly affect women during armed conflict, there is clearly a lack of appropriately disagregated data. So far, this hampers a proper understanding of the scale and scope of the problem.[121] Although not a fresh suggestion, gender training of the military remains a central activity.[122] It can be added that such training should convey a two proned obligation, or an obligation with two distinct aspects. First, there is the normative obligation to abstain from applying starvation as a means of warfare. Second, there is an obligation to prevent, and therefore an obligation to *train how to prevent* the occurance of starvation during armed conflict also needs to be taken into account.[123] When it comes to control mechanisms, it is essential that they develop and apply gender-sensitive procedures and a gender-sensitive methodology.[124] Furthermore, fulfilling this preventive obligation may also require revision of military manuals and reviewing the planning of operations when the understanding of how certain war crimes unduly affects women evolves.[125] It must be considered beyond doubt that States have yet to explore and advance this category of preventive measures to the maximum extent possible. As captured by Prescott in his recent publication a considerable gap remains from the understanding of gender's operational relevance at high-level strategy all the way down to service-level doctrine.[126]

As pointed out above,[127] Additional Protocol I also spells out an obligation to prevent closer to the event; in other words, when an armed conflict is ongoing. Prevention at this stage pertains to the conduct of and decisions made by key actors, given the factual circumstances at the given time and place. This could include

[120] See above, footnote 94 and accompanying text.

[121] Bendavid et al. (2021), p. 530.

[122] Coomaraswamy (1998), para 107.

[123] This distinction aligns to the separation Prescott draws between education and training. Education is "in the military context to be primarily geared towards imparting information to students and fostering the development of general intellectual skills regarding its use, it sees training as being focused on specific skill development in the context of specific mission situations." Prescott (2019), p. 206.

[124] Coomaraswamy (1998), para 106.

[125] Coomaraswamy (1998), para 108.

[126] Prescott (2019), p. 198.

[127] See footnote 102 and accompanying text.

applying disciplinary measures towards subordinates that show inapproporate conduct. Additionally, in the spirit of preventing war crimes, it ought to include decisively addressing underlying attitudes of members of the forces which foreseeably lead to direct or indirect gender-insensitive action when operating in the field.[128]

4 Conclusions

It has been outlined that the LOAC must be seen as intrinsically masculine. To unveil such a hegemonic imbalance, it has been proposed that a gender-sensitive reading of the LOAC is required in general, but also to the particular obligation of preventing war crimes. Feminist readings have already contributed to the development of a gender-sensitive understanding and application of the LOAC in three stages. First, it was established that the LOAC was not gender neutral in its fabric. Second, feminist scholars pointed out that althoug the protection of civilians should apply equally and without discrimination to both men and women, the seemingly gender netural protection of civilians may not benefit women to the same extent as it benefits men. This is because women and men are affected by armed conflict in different ways. Women are not only fending for themselves; often they also have the burden of ensuring that their children are fed and supported. Third, a strong breakthrough in the enforcement of the LOAC was achieved when sexual violence during armed conflict was punished as a war crime under international law. Although prosecution is a measure that takes place after the event, (and therefore serious war crimes clearly have not been prevented in the first place) the prosecution of sexual violence as a war crime must be seen as a considerable progress in the enforcement of the LOAC. The ICTY and the ICTR have played significant roles in this development. But one further aspect needs to be kept in mind, notwithstanding the work of the Tribunals. The emphasis in this paper has been on the obligation to prevent, which refers to measures that should be taken to ensure that the war crime does not occur in the first place. This is a distinctivly separate obligation, in addition to the obligation to prosecute for war crimes after they have occured. Therefore, these two separate obligations each require their own separate response.

It has here been argued that the fulfillment of the obligation to *prevent* war crimes may benefit women to a higher degree than men. After establishing that there is indeed a general State obligation to prevent all war crimes, it has therefore been argued in this paper that this requires a gender-sensitive reading of the LOAC to ensure that war crimes are duly prevented, including war crimes that disproportionally impact women. This would include war crimes such as indiscriminate destruction of homes and the destruction of livelihoods. There is clearly an obligation on States to prevent the occurance of such war crimes in the first place.

[128] Coomaraswamy (1998), para 106.

Therefore, States have the obligation to take certain measures beforehand. This could mean that mechanisms, which enable gender-sensitivity should be established beforehand, in order for a State to fully fulfill its preventive obligations under the LOAC. In addition to this first level of preventive obligations, the LOAC also establishes obligations to prevent the occurance of war crimes closer to the events, that is when armed conflict has errupted. At this stage, command responsibility may arise if a commander or superior has failed to prevent a war crime perpetration he had actual or presumed knowledge about. The duty to suppress such acts means first that systems of disciplinary measures need to be in place, and second, that they must be made use of, not least when the victims of a war crime to a disproportionat extent are women.

It is clear from the discussion above that the two-proned general obligation to prevent war crimes (beforehand, and closer to the event) provides protection under the LOAC that would particularly benefit women. But these two-proned obligation to prevent war crimes is currently not being utilized to its fullest potential. This author alignes herself with the so called enforcement school, supporting the continued work based on the current LOAC, rather than proposing treaty revisions to alleviate and prevent suffering of women during armed conflict. In this regard, the still ongoing project of revising the General Comments to the Geneva Conventions must be seen as a decisive step forward. It has brought new understandings and increazed clarification to several areas, not least when it comes to applying a gender lens to the application of the LOAC. Bearing in mind that the obligation to prevent all war crimes, requires States to take measures beforehand, there ought now to be an onus on States to examine and revise State practices by applying a gender lens to their military manuals and rules of engagement. It has been argued that undertaking such activities is not only an integral but also an essential part of fulfilling the general obligation to take appropriate measures beforehand to prevent all war crimes, also those that disproportionally cause harm and suffering of women.

References

1949 Geneva Convention for the Amelioration of the Condition of Wounded and Sick in Armed Forces in the Field of August 12, 1949, (1950) 75 UNTS 31–83

1949 Geneva Convention for the Amelioration of the Condition of Wounded, Sick and Shipwrecked Members of Armed Forces at Sea of August 12, 1949, (1950) 75 UNTS 85–133

1949 Geneva Convention Relative to the Protection of Civilian Persons in Time of War of August 12, 1949 (1950) 75 UNTS 287–417

1949 Geneva Convention Relative to the Treatment of Prisoners of War of August 12, 1949 (1950) 75 UNTS 135–285

1977 Protocol Additional to the Geneva Conventions of 12 August 1949, and Relating to the Protection of Victims of International Armed Conflicts

1977 Protocol Additional to the Geneva Conventions of 12 August 1949, and Relating to the Protection of Victims of Non-International Armed Conflicts

1998 Rome Statute of the International Criminal Court, *entered into force* 1 July 2002, 2187 UNTS 90

2008 Convention on Cluster Munitions, *entered into force* 1 August 2010, 2688 UNTS 39
Akande D, Gillard E-C (2019) Conflict-induced food insecurity and the war crime of starvation of civilians as a method of warfare. J Int Criminal Justice 17:753–779
Al-Jazeera, 9 December 2021., https://www.aljazeera.com/news/2021/12/9/turkey-hits-pkk-targets-in-iraq-after-three-turkish-troops-killed
Al-Jazeera, 2 February, 2022., https://www.aljazeera.com/news/2022/2/2/turkish-air-raids-target-kurdish-groups-in-northern-syria-iraq
Bendavid Eran, Ties Boerma, Nadia Akseer, Ana Langer, Espoir Bwenge Malembaka, Emelda A Okiro, Paul H Wise, Sam Heft-Neal, Robert E Black, Zulfiqar A Bhutta and the BRANCH Consortium Steering Committee. 2021. The effects of armed conflict on the Health of Women and Children. The Lancet 397: 522–532.
Bianchi A (2016) International law theories: an inquiry into different ways of thinking. Oxford University Press, Oxford
Charlesworth H (1997) The sex of the state in International Law. In: Naffine N, Owens RJ (eds) Sexing the subject of law. Sweet & Maxwell, London, pp 251–268
Charlesworth H, Chinkin C (2016) An Aliens review of women and armed conflict. In: Dale S, Babie P (eds) Imagining law. University of Adelaide Press, Adelaide, pp 171–194
Charlesworth H, Chinkin C, Wright S (1991) Feminist approaches to International Law. Am J Int Law 85(4):613–645
Chinkin C, Charlesworth H (2000) The boundaries of international law: a feminist analysis. Manchester University Press, Manchester
Coomaraswamy R (1998) Report of the special rapporteur on violence against women, its causes and consequences E/CN.4/1998/54, 26 January 1998
Crowder MP (1943) Choosing women for war-industry jobs. U.S. Govt Print. Off, Washington, D.C
D'Alessandra F, Gillett M (2019) The war crime of starvation in non-international armed conflict. J Int Criminal Justice 17:815–847
Davies M, Munro VE (2013) Editors' introduction. In: Davies M, Munro VE (eds) The ashgate research companion to feminist legal theory. Routledge, London, pp 14–24
Dinstein Y (2016) The conduct of hostilities under the law of International Armed Conflict. Cambridge University Press, Cambridge
Doolan C (2018) Victims who are men. In: Aoláin FN, Cahn N, Haynes DF, Valji N (eds) The Oxford handbook of gender and conflict. Oxford University Press, Oxford, pp 86–102
Durham H, O'Byrne K (2010) The dialogue of difference: gender perspectives on International Humanitarian Law. International Review of the Red Cross 92:31–52
Eboe-Osuji C (2012) Superior responsibility for the rape of women during armed conflict. Martinus Nijehoff, Leiden
El-Bushra J, Gardner J (2016) The impact of war on Somali men: feminist analysis of masculinities and gender relations in a fragile context. Gender Dev 24:443–458
Engle K (2005) Feminism and It's (Dis)Contents. Am J Int Law 99:778–816
Ericsson K (2011) Rape, love and war – personal or political? Theoretical Criminol 15:67–82
Flood M, Pease B (2017) Undoing Men's Privilege and Advancing Gender Equality in Public Sector Institutions. Policy Soc 24:119–138
Fuest V (2008) 'This Is the Time to Get in Front': changing roles and opportunities for women in Liberia. Afr Aff 107:201–224
Gardam J (1997) An Alien's encounter with the law of armed conflict. In: Naffine N, Owens RJ (eds) Sexing the subject of law. Sweet & Maxwell, London, pp 233–250
Gardam J (2013) A new frontline for feminism and International Humanitarian Law. In: Davies M, Munro VE (eds) The Ashgate research companion to feminist legal theory. Routledge, London, pp 252–269
Gardam J, Jarvis MJ (2001) Women, armed conflict and International Law. Kluwer Law International, The Hague

Graham L (2020) Prosecuting starvation crimes in Yemen's Civil War. Case Western Reserve J Int Law 52:267–286

Henckaerts J-M, Doswald-Beck L (2005) Customary International Humanitarian Law, vol I. Cambridge University Press, Cambridge

Hooper C (2001) Manly states: masculinities, international relations, and gender politics. Columbia University Press, New York

Hoover Green A (2018) "Mind the Gap": measuring and understanding gendered conflict experiences. In: Aoláin FN, Cahn N, Haynes DF, Valji N (eds) The Oxford handbook of gender and conflict. Oxford University Press, Oxford, pp 316–325

Isaac M, Jurasz O (2018) Towards an intersectional understanding of conflict-related sexual violence: gender, sexuality, and ethnicity at the ICTY. Int Criminal Law Rev 18:853–882

Jarvis MJ (2016) Prosecuting conflict-related sexual violence crimes: how far have we progressed and where do we go from here? Some thougths based on ICTY experience. In: Dale S, Babie P (eds) Imagining international law, conversations with gardam. University of Adelaide Press, Adelaide, pp 105–132

Kalshoven F (2007) The undertaking to respect and ensure respect in all circumstances: from tiny seed to ripening fruit. In: Kalshoven F (ed) Reflections on the law of war: collected essays. Martinus Nijhoff Publishers, Leiden, pp 665–727

Lindsey C (2001) Women facing war. International Committee of the Red Cross, Geneva

Mégret F (2018) The laws of war and the structure of masculine power. Melb J Int Law 19:200–226

Mouthaan S (2013) Sexual violence against men and international law – criminalising the unmentionable. Int Criminal Law Rev 13:665–695

Muñoz-Rojas D, Frésard J-J (2004) The roots of behaviour in war: understanding and preventing IHL violations. International Committee of the Red Cross, Geneva

Ng LC, Betancourt TS (2018) Risk and resilience: the physical and mental health of female civilians during war. In: Aoláin FN, Cahn N, Haynes DF, Valji N (eds) The Oxford handbook of gender and conflict. Oxford University Press, Oxford, pp 354–364

O'Rourke C (2020) Women's rights in armed conflict under International Law. Cambridge University Press, Cambridge

Oosterveld V (2009) Feminist debates on civilian women and International Humanitarian Law. Windsor Yearb Access Justice 27(2):385–402

Petesch P (2018) Agency and gender norms in war economies. In: Aoláin FN, Cahn N, Haynes DF, Valji N (eds) The Oxford handbook of gender and conflict. Oxford University Press, Oxford, pp 343–352

Pictet JS (1952) The Geneva Conventions of 12 August 1949: commentary Vol I. International Committee of the Red Cross, Geneva

Pictet JS (1960) The Geneva Conventions of 12 August 1949: commentary Vol III. International Committee of the Red Cross, Geneva

Pilloud C, Sandoz Y, Swinarski C, Zimmerman B, with the collaboration of Jean Pictet (1987) Commentary on the additional protocols of 8 June 1977 to the Geneva Conventions of 12 August 1949. M. Nijhoff, The Hague

Prescott JM (2019) Armed conflict, women and climate change. Routledge, London/New York, p 2019

Prosecutor v Blaškić (Judgment [Trial Chamber I]) IT-95-14-T (3 March 2000)

Quataert JH (2018) A new look at International Law. Human Rights Q 40(3):547–569

Reynolds AN (2021) Women at work and war: integrating gender and conflict into impact assessment. Impact Assessment Project Appraisal 39:196–205

Rimmer SH, Ogg K (2019) Introduction to the research handbook on feminist engagement with International Law. In: Rimmer SH, Ogg K (eds) Research Handbook on Feminist Engagement with International Law. Edward Elgar Publisher, Cheltenham, pp 1–16

Seifert R (1996) The second front: the logic of sexual violence in wars. Women's Stud Int Forum 19:35–43

Sinclair A (2020) Why we should see International Law as a structure: unpicking international law's ontology and agency. Int Relations 35:216–235

Stern OM (2018) Gender, conflict and international humanitarian law: a critique of the 'Principle of Distinction'. Routledge, London

Thomas TA (2021) 'The Long History of Feminist Legal Theory', https://ssrn.com/abstract=3740082 or https://doi.org/10.2139/ssrn.3740082

van der Have N (2018) The prevention of gross Human Rights violations under International Human Rights Law. T.M.C. Asser Press, The Hague

Ventura MJ (2019) Prosecuting starvation under International Criminal Law. J Int Criminal Justice 17:781–814

Wood EJ (2008) The social processes of civil war: the wartime transformation of social networks. Ann Rev Political Sci 11:539–561

Rigmor Argren is a Senior Lecturer of Public International Law and International Humanitarian Law at Örebro University. She has a Ph.D. in International Human Rights Law from Essex University (2012) and holds an LL.M. degree in International Human Rights Law from Essex University (2003) as well as a Master of Communications from Örebro University (2004). She also holds a Diploma in Humanitarian Leadership from the Centre for Humanitarian Leadership at the Deakin University (2014), where she has remained a visiting faculty member for the Humanitarian Leadership Programme. She teaches International Humanitarian Law, Law and Digitalisation at Örebro University and coaches on the Humanitarian Leadership Programme at Deakin University. She has published in Swedish and English, and has recently focussed on pedagogics and collegial learning, as well as contributing in the tradition of Scholarship of Teaching and Learning (SoTL), with a focus on new teaching techniques and International Humanitarian Law. Other recent publications are in the field of sustainability concerning the use of human rights courts for environmental litigations.

The Recognition of Refugee Women in International Law

Ivana Krstić

Contents

Abstract According to the UN Refugee Agency (UNHCR), around 80 million people have been forced into displacement, with more than half of them being women and girls. In addition to marginalization, poverty, and other challenges that all refugees face, women are exposed to gender discrimination and persecution. Despite this, refugee protection is based on the 1951 Convention and its 1967 Protocol, both of which are gender-neutral and do not recognize "gender" as a ground for persecution.

This paper examines a number of human rights instruments that provide women refugees with complementary protection. The author argues that the 1951 Convention protects women either as a "social group" or when gender-related claims intersect with other recognized grounds of prosecution, such as race, nationality, ethnicity, or religion. Gender-based persecution takes very specific forms and it

I. Krstić (✉)
University of Belgrade, Faculty of Law, Belgrade, Serbia
e-mail: ikrstic@ius.bg.ac.rs

I. Krstić et al. (eds.), *Legal Issues of International Law from a Gender Perspective*, Gender Perspectives in Law 3, https://doi.org/10.1007/978-3-031-13459-3_6

needs to be recognized in national legislation and understood by public authorities, in order to provide proper protection to women refugees. However, even if these preconditions are met, the author underlines that an asylum procedure must be gender-sensitive, as this allows for the submission of an asylum claim, the proper conduct of an interview, and the assessment of case evidence, all of which lead to a successful recognition of refugee status.

1 Introduction

Last year, the international community marked the 70th anniversary since the adoption of the Convention on the Status of Refugees (the 1951 Convention). That is significantly more than the traditional age for retirement in many countries, to reference Julian M. Lehmann.[1] This international instrument is a cornerstone of refugee protection, defining refugees and their rights and obligations, as well as the responsibilities of States Parties to protect persons in need. The Convention was adopted after the Second World War, and was designed to resolve the refugee crisis that occurred as a consequence of this global conflict, subjecting it to temporal and geographical limitations. As a result, it referred only to Europeans who became refugees before 1951, and was regarded a Eurocentric post-world war instrument, as it did not include refugees from China, the Korean War, Palestinians, and others at the time.[2] This limitation was eventually lifted for countries that ratified the 1967 Protocol. Nevertheless, it did not become universally applicable as it continued to be "rooted in Western political thought" and hardly relevant to the non-European context.[3] This was, among other things, visible in the fact that certain types of harm that primarily affect women, such as rape and circumcision, were not recognized as forms of persecution.[4]

The Convention contains a very limited definition of a "refugee," which is based on the well-founded fear of being persecuted for five recognized grounds: race, religion, nationality, political opinion, or membership in a particular social group. In other words, sex/gender is not expressly recognized as a ground for persecution, despite the fact that in many States, women face systemic and massive human rights violations as well as gender discrimination. The first international instrument that introduced a catalog of women's rights—the Convention on the Elimination of All Forms of Discrimination Against Women (CEDAW), adopted on a UN level in 1979—does not include the issue of migration and refugee status. However, the Committee on the Elimination of Discrimination Against Women (CEDAW Committee) has addressed this problem in some recent general statements. Another

[1] Lehmann (2019), pp. 2–15.
[2] Mayblin (2010), p. 1.
[3] Hathaway (1990), p. 141.
[4] Kelley (2001), pp. 559–568.

regional instrument, the 2011 Istanbul Convention Action against violence against women and domestic violence (Istanbul Convention), highlights this link and includes several provisions important for women in migration.

In this paper, the development of an international legal framework concerning refugee women will be presented. Following that, three main arguments will be developed. First, it will be argued that, even though the 1951 Refugee Convention must have been interpreted in a gender-inclusive and gender-sensitive manner, only after many years has the Convention been interpreted to include "gender." Gender inclusion in the Convention can be done in two ways. First, "gender" can fall into the category of "particular social group." In addition, other grounds of persecution need to be interpreted from a gender perspective, and a woman can be recognized as a refugee based on her religious or political beliefs. Second, it is essential to recognize gender-related forms of persecution as their form and purpose are very specific. Finally, despite this recognition, women will not be recognized as refugees unless a gender-sensitive asylum procedure is introduced, allowing access to asylum procedures and a proper assessment of gender-related asylum claims.

2 International Legal Framework

2.1 General Refugee Framework

2.1.1 The Refugee Convention

As already underlined, the main legal framework for refugee protection is provided by the 1951 Convention.[5] With this Convention, a definition of "refugee" was included for the first time in international law. According to this instrument, a refugee is a person who "owing to a well-founded fear of being persecuted for reasons of race, religion, nationality, membership of a particular social group or political opinion, is outside the country of his nationality and is unable or, owing to such fear, is unwilling to avail himself of the protection of that country; or who, not having a nationality and being outside the country of his former habitual residence as a result of such events, is unable or, owing to such fear, is unwilling to return to it."[6] This definition has several elements that need to be cumulatively met in each specific case for a person to be considered a refugee. These elements are the following: (1) a person needs to be outside the country of nationality or habitual residence in case of statelessness; (2) there must be a real threat in their country, with regard to which the person has subjective fear and there are objective circumstances; (3) a person was subjected to persecution or there is a serious threat to their life and integrity; (4) a person is persecuted by the state authorities or by private entities, but the state

[5]Convention related to the Status of Refugees (1951), p. 137.

[6]Article A 2) of the 1951 Convention.

deprives them of assistance and protection; (5) a person belongs to one of the five groups referred to in the Convention, such as race, religion, nationality, social group or political opinion.

A refugee is obliged to conform to the laws and regulations of the country that granted them the refugee status and to the measures aimed at maintaining public peace and order. Refugees enjoy a series of rights guaranteed by the Convention, such as non-discrimination, freedom of confession (religion), acquisition of property, right to free access to courts, right to housing, access to education, and employment and social insurance rights. However, the Convention makes no reference to sex/gender, or women, although the UN Charter and Universal Declaration on Human Rights (UDHR) affirms "the principle that human beings shall enjoy fundamental rights and freedoms without discrimination,"[7] as stated in its Preamble. Furthermore, the non-discrimination clause in Article 3 recognizes only "race, religion, or country of origin" as prohibited grounds. The *travaux préparatoires* showed that "gender" was barely discussed among the delegates. The Yugoslav delegation first proposed to include the additional words "or for other reason" in the provision, which would provide a basis to recognize "sex" as well, but this proposal was rejected. [8] The Yugoslav delegation also proposed to include the term "sex," but several delegations opposed this proposal and it was withdrawn.[9] Other provisions are also gender-neutral, and no specific provision applies to women only or recognizes their special status.

Two other regional refugee instruments do not specifically mention "gender," but their definitions are broader than the 1951 Convention, allowing for women refugees to be recognized as such. For example, the Convention governing the specific aspects of refugee problems in Africa from 1969, defines "refugee" as "every person who, owing to external aggression, occupation, foreign domination or events seriously disturbing public order in either part of the whole of his country of origin or nationality, is compelled to leave his place of habitual residence in order to seek refuge in another place outside his country of origin or nationality."[10] Also, the Cartagena Declaration on Refugees, in addition to the elements of the 1951 Convention, recognizes that refugees are "persons who have fled their country because their lives, safety or freedom have been threatened by generalized violence, foreign aggression, internal conflicts, massive violation of human rights or other circumstances which have seriously disturbed public order."[11] Therefore, these two definitions do not exclude gender from their definition, limiting it to some specific grounds for persecution.

---

[7]The UN Charter in Article 1 (3) expressly prohibits, among other grounds, discrimination based on sex.

[8]Weis (1951).

[9]The representatives from Austria, Colombia, Italy Switzerland, Turkey, the UK, and the U.-S. rejected the proposal.

[10]Article I (2) of the OAU Convention.

[11]Section III (3) of the Cartagena Declaration.

2.1.2 European Convention on Human Rights

The European Convention on Human Rights was not primarily designed to provide protection to refugees, but it does have an extensive jurisprudence in relation to Article 3, specifically the assessment of the *non-refoulement* principle. In addition, its non-discrimination clause (Article 14) identifies several prohibited grounds, including "sex." As a result, the European Court of Human Rights (ECtHR) dealt with many cases where women's claims concerned the risk of ill-treatment if sent back to their countries of origin. However, the majority of them have been determined to be either manifestly ill-founded and declared inadmissible, or rejected on credibility grounds,[12] which must be criticized as the Court's restrictive approach. Another reason for the large number of unsuccessful applications is that the Court's evaluation in most cases was that the information provided was not detailed, that the persecution was not well documented, or that the evidence was inconsistent. This information shows that the case was not properly handled by the national asylum authorities. Furthermore, women are persecuted by private actors in the majority of cases, which brings to the table the public/private divide and understanding that acts of persecution are not necessarily inflicted by state agents.[13] Finally, in some cases, the Court explores the existence of legal prohibitions of certain forms of persecution, but does not assess if domestic laws are appropriately applied in practice, even if the case involves a very serious form of gender-based violence (e.g. female genital mutilation,[14] forced prostitution ring,[15] etc.).

On rare occasions, substantive assessments of claims revealed violations of Article 3. For example, in *N. v. Sweden*, an applicant from Afghanistan submitted an asylum claim based on the husband's political activities and her activities in educating women being persecuted.[16] As she intended to divorce and was in an extramarital relationship, she was criticized as a "bad woman" and feared being stoned for adultery. She claimed that by separating from her husband, she would not be able to obtain a divorce in her country of origin, and that she had dishonored both their families. Her family had disowned her, and she stated that because she would not be able to find work and had no children, she would be considered a social outcast in her home country. Despite these arguments, her application was rejected in Sweden. The ECtHR considers that "women are at particular risk of ill-treatment in Afghanistan if perceived as not conforming to the gender roles ascribed to them by society, tradition and even the legal system."[17] According to UNHCR reports, those women are exposed to domestic violence and other forms of gender-based violence,

---

[12] Peroni (2018), p. 350.

[13] Peroni (2018), p. 351.

[14] See, e.g. *Collins and Akaziebie v. Sweden*, 2007; *Izevbekhai v. Ireland*, 2011; *R.B.A.B. and Others v. The Netherlands*, 2016.

[15] *V.F. v. France*, 2011; *F.A. v. the United Kingdom*, 2013.

[16] *N. v. Sweden*, 2010.

[17] *N. v. Sweden*, 55.

such as isolation, stigmatization, and honor crimes, which leads to the conclusion that by returning to Afghanistan, she will be exposed to ill-treatment.

In another case, an applicant from Guinea applied for asylum in France. Her claim was based on the fact that she was subjected to different forms of violence from her Muslim father and brothers because her husband was Christian.[18] The forms of violence were threats to kill her, beatings, and tying her to a tree due to which she lost a pregnancy. The Court also took into account that the Guinean authorities did nothing to prevent harm inflicted on the applicant, which was contrary to Article 3 of the European Convention on Human Rights.[19]

2.2 Gender-Specific Human Rights Instruments

2.2.1 Convention on the Elimination of All Forms of Discrimination Against Women

As it was said, the CEDAW did not explicitly cover women's migration and refugee status. Only Article 6 prescribes that States are obliged to "take all appropriate measures, including legislation, to suppress all forms of traffic in women and exploitation of prostitution of women." However, although this provision is broad in scope, human trafficking and exploitation of women are not explicitly mentioned in the context of migration *per se*. It took some time for the Committee to recognize this link.

The first general recommendation that addressed this issue was General recommendation no. 24 from 1999 dealing with health.[20] By this recommendation, the Committee required special attention to be given to the health needs and rights of migrant and refugee women.[21] It also emphasized that adequate protection and health services need to be provided to them, including trauma treatment and counseling.[22] In addition, the Committee addressed a particular group of women migrants, such as older women, as deserving of special attention, since they often face discrimination, neglect, and abuse. They usually suffer from post-traumatic stress disorder that is not always recognized by health workers. Despite this, they are sometimes denied health care as they lack legal status or legal documents.[23] For the first time, it was emphasized that States need to pay attention to the situation of older women while addressing sexual violence, as well as the conditions of refugees

[18] *R.D. v. France*, 2016.
[19] *R.D. v. France*, 40-41.
[20] General recommendation No. 24 (1999).
[21] General recommendation No. 24 (1999), 6.
[22] General recommendation No. 24 (1999), 16.
[23] General recommendation No. 24 (1999), 16.

during armed conflict.[24] Moreover, the Committee called States to introduce gender and age-sensitive laws and procedures to protect older women refugees.[25] The Committee also recognized that all rights guaranteed by the Convention apply to refugees and that women are rights-bearers, with emphasis on the most marginalized groups of women.[26]

In 2013, the Committee emphasized for the first time that the Convention *reinforces and complements* the refugee regime, especially "because explicit gender equality provisions are absent from relevant international agreements," referring to the 1951 Convention and its 1967 Protocol.[27] Therefore, the Committee acknowledged that the Convention has no explicit provision mentioning women refugees. A year later, a special recommendation dedicated to the gender-related dimensions of refugee status was issued.[28] The Committee underlined that "the Convention provides a gender-sensitive interpretation of human rights law and protects women from sex- and gender-based discrimination."[29] The Committee acknowledges the specific position of women asylum seekers and refugees, and requires that States, first and foremost, protect women from any violence while on their territory (as they can be exposed to trafficking, forced prostitution, etc.),[30] refrain from any measures that can discriminate against women and investigate acts of discrimination if they occur.[31] Therefore, the risk of violence and different forms of exploitation appear not only in a country of origin, but are also often present in a destination country as a result of "increased border control, refusal of entry, pushbacks, expulsion or detention."[32]

Importantly, the Committee notes that gender-related persecution is not explicitly mentioned in the 1951 Refugee Convention, but that States need to apply the gender perspective when they interpret grounds covered by this instrument.[33] In addition, the Committee founds that gender-related claims can also intersect with other prohibited grounds, such as race, ethnicity, religion, etc.[34] For example, persecution based on race or ethnicity may take different forms for men and women, and include sexual violence for the latter.[35] When women disobey certain social norms, that can be perceived as evidence of unacceptable political views[36] or demonstration of religious conviction, as in the case of Afghan women who adopted a Western

[24] General recommendation No. 24 (1999), 38.
[25] General recommendation No. 24 (1999), 50.
[26] General recommendation No. 28 (2010), 26.
[27] General recommendation No. 30 (2013), 22.
[28] General recommendation No. 32 (2014).
[29] General recommendation No. 32 (2014), 5.
[30] General recommendation No. 32 (2014), 7,14.
[31] General recommendation No. 32 (2014), 8.
[32] General recommendation no. 38 (2020), 24.
[33] General recommendation no. 38 (2020), 13.
[34] General recommendation no. 38 (2020), 16.
[35] Australian Department of Immigration and Multi-Cultural Affairs (1996), 4.29.
[36] Canadian Immigration and Refugee Board (1996), p. 5.

lifestyle.[37] Women can also face specific forms of persecution based on nationality or ethnicity, such as denial of citizenship after divorce or marriage to a foreigner, or sexual violence as an act of ethnic "cleansing."[38] The Committee, therefore, criticizes that women's asylum claims are regularly classified under the social group ground, as this demonstrates "stereotyped notions of women as dependent victims."[39] In the opinion of the Committee, it creates standards that are based on preconceived notions of gender-based violence and persecution, while women can be persecuted as political leaders, journalists, human rights defenders, etc.[40] However, although this is true, it is important to acknowledge that women can be recognized as a social group if no other ground for persecution exists.

In 2010, the Committee underlined that gender-related forms of persecution are defined,[41] and that gender is also important in deciding whether or not to grant international status to a person who fears death or torture if returned to the country of origin (so-called subsidiary protection).[42] This rule also encompasses the *non-refoulment* principle, which is a cornerstone of refugee protection and prohibits extradition, deportation, or expulsion of a person to a country where there is a substantial ground for believing that their physical and psychological integrity are threatened. However, this principle has not been recognized in the CEDAW, and it is critical that the Committee underlines that this principle is well established in international conventional and customary law.

However, when it comes to the jurisprudence of the CEDAW Committee in relation to *non-refoulement* cases, it must be determined that the majority of applications were inadmissible, as it was not found that the States failed to give the asylum claims sufficient consideration, or that the asylum procedure had serious defects.[43] Also, in some cases, the CEDAW Committee found that the applicant did not demonstrate "a real, personal and foreseeable risk of serious form of gender-based violence," despite the factual situation in country of origin.[44] The argument was that the applicant was discriminated against in terms of their right to access to justice, as more female than male asylum seekers are denied asylum by the authorities under the "manifestly unfounded" procedure. However, this argument was not considered at all. Furthermore, the procedure before the Committee has recently been discontinued in several cases due to various reasons such as the applicant no longer residing in the country and no longer being at risk of deportation,[45] loss of

[37] Hooper (2019), p. 29.
[38] Hooper (2019), p. 30.
[39] General recommendation No. 32 (2014), 31.
[40] General recommendation No. 32 (2014), 31.
[41] General recommendation No. 32 (2014), 15.
[42] General recommendation No. 32 (2014), 13.
[43] *S.J.A. v. Denmark*, 2017; *H.D. v. Denmark*, 2018; *S.O. v. Canada*, 2014; *A.S. v. Denmark*, 2018.
[44] *Y.W. v. Denmark*, 2015.
[45] *X. v. Denmark*, 2018.

contact with the applicant,[46] or the residence permit being granted and the risk of non-refoulement disappearing.[47] The first two situations raise serious concerns about the whereabouts of the female applicants and whether the rejection of asylum claims on a national level put them at risk of gender violence.

2.2.2 Istanbul Convention Action Against Violence Against Women and Domestic Violence

The Istanbul Convention, a regional instrument of the Council of Europe, was adopted in 2011, with the aim of protecting women against all forms of violence, and preventing, prosecuting and eliminating violence against women and domestic violence.[48] In its Preamble, the Convention recognizes "the structural nature of violence against women as gender-based violence," which is "one of the crucial social mechanisms by which women are forced into a subordinate position compared with men." The Convention recognizes all forms of violence against women and defines the terms "violence against women" and "domestic violence." It prescribes that the provisions must be implemented without any discrimination based on, among other things, migrant or refugee status.[49] Chapter 7 is dedicated to migration and asylum, as women migrants and asylum seekers are recognized as particularly vulnerable to gender-based violence.[50] Despite the fact that migrant women leave their country of origin voluntarily while women asylum seekers are forced to flee, both experience violence and face similar difficulties and structural barriers.[51]

Chapter 7 contains three provisions. Article 59 relates to the residence status and requires States to ensure an autonomous residence permit of limited validity to victims whose status depends on the status of their spouse or partner as defined by internal law, such as to stay in a marriage or relationship for a certain period, before granting them an autonomous residence status.[52] This provision is critical as losing a residence status, for example in case of divorce, is used by perpetrators to prevent the victim from seeking help or from leaving them.[53] This permit should be granted if particularly difficult circumstances exist, such as violence committed by a spouse or partner, which can be documented by court conviction, restriction order, medical evidence, etc.[54] This autonomous permit should be granted regardless of the length of the marriage or partnership and must be realistic and sensitive to women's unique

---

[46] *X. v. Austria*, 2018; *J.O. v. Switzerland*, 2018; *O.D.A. v. Denmark*, 2019.

[47] *H.S. v. Denmark*, 2018; *N.S. v. Denmark*, 2019; *Y. v. Ecuador*, 2018.

[48] Article 1 a) of the Istanbul Convention.

[49] Article 4 (3) of the Istanbul Convention.

[50] Explanatory report (2011), 298.

[51] Explanatory report (2011), 298.

[52] Article 59 (1) of the Istanbul Convention.

[53] Explanatory report (2011), 301.

[54] Explanatory report (2011), 303.

situations. Moreover, victims should request a suspension of expulsion proceedings in relation to a residence status dependent on that of their spouse or partner.[55] This issue arises if spouses or partners are granted family reunification, but face expulsion due to the violence they committed.[56] This provision is particularly relevant in situations where spouses or partners will be deported to the country of origin with a poor record of prevention, protection, and prosecution for acts that are considered gender-based violence.[57] Therefore, this provision allows the victim to request suspension of expulsion and to apply for residence on humanitarian grounds. The residence status can be renewed if the competent authority believes it is necessary that victims remain on their territory due to their personal situation, or for their cooperation in the investigation or criminal proceedings.[58] Finally, victims of forced marriages can reclaim this status if they were brought into another country for the purpose of the marriage and if they lost their residence status in the country where they normally reside, due to the dissolution or annulment of the marriage.[59]

When it comes to the implementation of this obligation, the GREVIO finds that Portugal and Spain have aligned their legislation with Article 59, and applauded Italy for being the first to grant an autonomous residence permit to a migrant woman who are victims of domestic violence, by order of the Tribunal of Bari in January 2021.[60] Albania and Andorra, on the other hand, did not implement measures to secure an autonomous residence permit.[61] At the same time, Denmark, France, the Netherlands, and Sweden need to continue their efforts to protect victims of domestic violence from revoking the residence permit granted on the basis of family reunification.[62] Some countries, such as Austria and Turkey, deny this permit to some women based on their nationality or that of their spouse/partner, which is considered discriminatory.[63] There are also certain practices that make this provision illusory, such as imposing an 385 euros application fee in Belgium, or concentrating on the fact that the relationship had ended due to "serious" violence in Sweden, or violence that posed a "real and present danger" in Italy.[64] Moreover, Montenegro and Serbia need to take into account the isolation, language barriers, and dependency of migrant women when assessing their case and to inform them about the possibility to grant an autonomous residence permit.[65]

[55] Article 59 (2) of the Istanbul Convention.
[56] Explanatory report (2011), 306.
[57] Explanatory report (2011), 306.
[58] Article 59 (3) of the Istanbul Convention.
[59] Article 59 (4) of the Istanbul Convention; Explanatory report (2011, 308).
[60] GREVIO (2022), p. 515.
[61] GREVIO (2022), p. 517.
[62] GREVIO (2022), p. 517.
[63] GREVIO (2022), p. 518.
[64] GREVIO (2022), pp. 520–521.
[65] GREVIO (2022), pp. 521–522.

Article 60 further requires that gender-based violence be recognized as a form of persecution, and it can be used a basis for granting refugee or subsidiary protection status. Moreover, all five grounds covered by the 1951 Refugee Convention must be interpreted in a gender-sensitive manner by domestic authorities. Acts of sexual violence and reproduction control can be present in situations of ethnic "cleansing," for example.[66] Also, tactical rape can be used in armed conflicts as a deliberate strategy to attack the enemy.[67] However, in order to properly assess these asylum claims, it is necessary to develop gender-sensitive reception procedures, support services for asylum seekers, issue gender guidelines, and introduce gender-sensitive procedures. This provision is extremely important as gender neutrality in asylum procedures leads to the non-recognition of gender-based violence in refugee protection.[68]

Finally, Article 61 imposes an obligation to respect the non-refoulment principle and to apply this principle regardless of the victim's status of residence. In other words, it means to provide protection to women asylum seekers and refugees, as well as to women who did not apply for asylum or whose request has been rejected, but are at risk in their country of origin.[69] This principle also protects women from indirect *refoulement*, or from returning to the country which might further send them to another state where that risk exists.[70] Finally, it must be interpreted in such a way to prevent state officials from denying women asylum seekers access to the territory. These two elements are critical as many States, such as Malta, Italy, and Turkey, impose entry restrictions and do not assess the risks of indirect *refoulement*,.[71] Some States, such as Belgium and Spain, lack adequate identification procedures, and accelerated procedures are especially vulnerable to rash decisions.[72]

3 Women Refugees

3.1 Gender As a Social Group

As previously stated, the 1951 Convention recognizes five grounds for persecution, but does not explicitly mention "gender." Despite this fact, gender-based groups can fall within the category of membership of a particular social group.[73] This was recognized in 1985 in a case involving women asylum seekers due to their

[66] Explanatory report (2011), 313.
[67] Fitzpatrick (2016), p. 5.
[68] Explanatory report (2011), 310.
[69] Explanatory report (2011), 322.
[70] EASO (2018), p. 28.
[71] GREVIO (2022), pp. 572–575.
[72] GREVIO (2022), p. 577.
[73] Hathaway (1991), p. 162.

vulnerable position and frequent exposure to "physical violence, sexual abuse, and discrimination."[74]

There are two approaches to the examination of the existence of social groups: the "protected characteristics" approach and the "social perception" approach.[75] The first examines whether a group's characteristics are so immutable or fundamental that a person cannot abandon them.[76] These characteristics can be innate or unalterable as a result of historical circumstances, for example. The second approach explores whether a group shares common feature which make it identifiable in a society.[77] These two elements very often intersect as a group can have common immutable or fundamental characteristics and be perceived as a particular group in society. However, this does not imply that members associate with one another, only that they have common characteristics.

There is no enumerated list of groups that may be regarded "a specific social group," which allows the 1951 Convention to be applied to different groups, including those that are recognized as such from the perspective of evolving human rights norms.[78] Therefore, women can be recognized as a special group, having innate and immutable characteristics, and being differently treated by men.[79] Due to their characteristics, women are identified as a special group that is subjected to discrimination and different standards in many societies. However, several authors are arguing that the vulnerability of women "to ill-treatment is institutionally and societally shaped and not an innate characteristic of certain groups."[80] While this is true, recognizing women as a "social group" allows national authorities to apply the 1951 Convention and recognize women as refugees if no other ground exists in the case.

Some national courts accept that "gender" can be regarded as a "particular social group." For example, in one case, "Guatemalan women" were recognized after Ms. Perdomo left her home country of Guatemala at the age of 15 to join her mother in the United States.[81] She submitted an asylum claim on the basis of the systemic human rights violations toward women. The U.S. court found that "women in a particular country (...) could constitute a particular social group."[82] It stated that women suffer from an "overwhelming incidence of gender violence committed with impunity" in Guatemala and that there is an increasingly high rate of violence, femicide committed with brutality, and impunity for male perpetrators.[83] Therefore,

[74] UNHCR Executive Committee (1985, d).

[75] UNHCR Guidelines (2002), 2-3.

[76] UNHCR Guidelines (2002), 29.

[77] UNHCR Guidelines (2002), 7.

[78] UNHCR Guidelines (2002), 3.

[79] UNHCR Guidelines (2002), 30.

[80] Peroni (2018), p. 370.

[81] *Perdomo v. Holder* (2010).

[82] *Perdomo v. Holder* (2010), 667. See for more Lieberan (2010) and Elias (2010).

[83] Center for Refugees and Gender studies (2011), p. 2.

in this case, a special group were "Guatemalan women who try to escape systemic and severe violence but who are unable to receive official protection." Young women from the Tchamba-Kunsuntu Tribe of Northern Togo, who oppose the practice of female genital mutilation, have also been recognized as a "particular social group."[84] Members of a "particular social group" are also "married women in Guatemala who are unable to leave their relationship."[85] The same can be said for women who are lesbian, bisexual, or transgender, who may also face certain forms of gender-related persecution.[86]

However, it must be noted that judges have in some cases expressed objections to recognizing "women" as a social group as it "encompasses a large number of people" and opens "floodgates to a large number of women" seeking asylum.[87] An illustrative case is when UK authorities rejected to recognize Pakistani women who were subjected to domestic violence, claiming that being women does not make them a social group.[88] The common feature recognized in this case was domestic violence within marriage, which is persecution in and of itself, and not an unchangeable characteristic of a group. This example also shows that establishing that gender represents a "particular social group" is more difficult than establishing any other ground of persecution, and this higher threshold would be avoided if the 1951 Convention recognized gender as a form of persecution.

3.2 *Gender-Related Forms of Persecution*

Although "gender" is not expressly included in a refugee definition, it can influence or dictate the type of persecution, which must be recognized as such in practice.[89] There is no universally accepted definition of persecution. This notion has not been defined by the 1951 Convention, although it is a central concept to a refugee definition—a refugee is a person that has a well-founded fear of "being persecuted." This term requires identification of the serious harm in a country of origin and assessment that the State is not able or willing to provide protection.[90] It also needs to be interpreted taking into account "developments within the broad field of human rights."[91]

Some argue that the concept was either so obvious in 1951 that there was no need to define it, or that drafters wanted to introduce a flexible concept that can be

[84] *In re Fauziya KASINGA*, 1996.

[85] *Matter of A-R-C-G- et al., Respondents* (2014).

[86] *Minister voor Immigratie en Asiel v X and Y and Z v Minister voor Immigratie en Asiel* (2013).

[87] See, e.g. *Da Silva v. Attorney General* (2012); *Safaie v. INS* (1994).

[88] The UK Immigration Appeal tribunal (1996).

[89] UNHCR Guidelines (2002), 6.

[90] Hathaway (1991), p. 125.

[91] Goodwin-Gill (1996), p. 67.

applicable to a variety of acts.[92] Whatever is reason may be, States need further guidelines on how to interpret the term "persecution." It is useful to look into different legal dictionaries, which underline four elements of persecution: (1) it is inflicted by person(s); (2) it is unjust/discriminatory; (3) it is cruel or serious; and (4) it is persistent.[93] Further guidelines are provided by EU law, specifically Directive 2011/95/EU,[94] which does not define the term, but prescribes actors of persecution (Article 6) and acts of protection (Article 7). Importantly, it defines acts of persecution in Article 9 as acts that are "sufficiently serious by its nature or repetition as to constitute a severe violation of basic human rights" and are "accumulation of various measures," including human rights violations that are sufficiently severe. Among the enlisted acts of persecution are: (1) acts of physical or mental violence, including *acts of sexual violence*; (2) prosecution or punishment which is disproportionate or discriminatory; (3) denial of judicial redress resulting in a disproportionate or discriminatory punishment; (4) prosecution or punishment for refusal to perform military service in a conflict; and (5) acts of a *gender-specific* or child-specific nature. The Directive, therefore, explicitly recognizes gender-related forms of persecution. Discrimination is particularly interesting, as it also can amount to persecution when the consequences are sufficiently severe, such as access to employment and education, access to the public sphere, dress codes, etc.[95]

Gender-related persecution can take four different forms. First form is when the method of persecution is gender-related, such as when sexual violence has a disproportionate effect on women.[96] Since 1987, many States have granted international protection to women who have been victims of sexual violence.[97] The second form is when women face persecution as punishment for disobeying certain social and cultural norms, such as refusal of forced marriage.[98] The third form takes place when a law, policy, or practice severely restricts the rights and freedoms of women, such as the practice of genital mutilation.[99] This form also occurs when the law prohibits certain behavior, but state officials fail to put this legislation into practice.[100] Finally, the fourth form takes place when practices or methods of implementing the law are persecutory, like in the case of forced abortion and forced sterilization.[101] All of these forms of persecution must be recognized as such, and it is thus important to understand and be aware of all of them.

---

[92] Grahl-Madsen (1966), p. 193.

[93] Maiani (2008), p. 7.

[94] Directive 2011/95/EU (recast).

[95] Louise Hooper (2019), pp. 22–23. See also UNHCR Gender Guidelines No. 1 and UNHCR Handbook (2019), 54–55.

[96] Gender-Related Persecution: An Analysis of Recent Trends (1997), pp. 84–85.

[97] Gender-Related Persecution: An Analysis of Recent Trends (1997), pp. 84–85.

[98] Gender-Related Persecution: An Analysis of Recent Trends (1997), pp. 91–92.

[99] Gender-Related Persecution: An Analysis of Recent Trends (1997), pp. 96–97.

[100] See, e.g., *Talpis v. Italy (*2017).

[101] Gender-Related Persecution: An Analysis of Recent Trends (1997), p. 100.

This obligation also stems from Article 60, para. 1 of the Istanbul Convention, as mentioned above. The GREVIO expressed satisfaction with the fact that out of the 17 States evaluated thus far in relation to this provision, only Albania does not specifically define gender-based violence as a form of persecution.[102] The majority of States explicitly mention this form of violence.[103] While many women refugees are fleeing a particular form of persecution that is not gender-specific, some are fleeing persecution that targets them as women. Gender-related forms of persecution are defined as those that "are directed against a woman because she is a woman or (...) affect women disproportionately."[104] In other words, a woman is persecuted due to her gender, "because of her identity and status as a woman."[105] There is a common consensus that rape, genital mutilation, forced sterilization, dowry-related violence, serious domestic violence, or trafficking are gender-related forms of persecution.[106] Also, that violence against women must be understood as "physical, sexual and psychological violence" occurring in the family or within the general community. Domestic violence includes "battering, sexual abuse of female children in the household, dowry-related violence, marital rape, female genital mutilation and other traditional practices harmful to women, non-spousal violence, and violence related to exploitation," while the general violence includes "rape, sexual abuse, sexual harassment, and intimidation at work, in educational institutions and elsewhere, trafficking in women, and forced prostitution."[107]

It is also important to underline that a particular feature of gender-specific forms of persecution is that they are usually perpetrated by private individuals. In this case, it is usually a partner, ex-partner, husband, family member, etc. Directive 2011/95/EU defines that actors of persecution can also be non-State actors, if it can be demonstrated that the State is unable or unwilling to provide protection (Article 6).

In this specific context, it means that the State is unable or unwilling to provide protection for women who want to avoid a certain practice. For example, a State can introduce laws that prohibit female genital mutilation, but continue to tolerate this practice, which is done by close relatives.

---

[102] GREVIO (2022), p. 535.

[103] For example, Finland, Sweden, and Serbia. GREVIO (2022), p. 536. See also Gender Related Asylum Claims in Europe (2012), p. 45.

[104] Gender Related Asylum Claims in Europe (2012), p. 15.

[105] Explanatory report, 310; Haines (2003), p. 326.

[106] Explanatory report, 310.

[107] UN GA 'Declaration on the Elimination of Violence Against Women (1994), Article 2; UNHCR Position Paper (2000), 4-5.

4 Gender-Sensitive Asylum Procedure

Even if a State provides a strong legal foundation for determining women as refugees, protection will not be granted if there is no gender-sensitive asylum procedure. This argument is supported by the majority of cases rejected by the ECtHR and the CEDAW Committee because the case was not well-established and the real risk of ill-treatment was not demonstrated. The reasons for this can be found in the inability of state officials to obtain proper information, but also in women's difficulties to explain their asylum claims, which is the result of deeply rooted cultural norms and patterns. As a result, the Istanbul Convention requires in Article 60 that States Parties introduce gender-sensitive asylum procedures. What exactly does this mean? It does not mean that women are to be subject to different asylum procedures than man, but that their specific position is recognized and that some phases in the procedure are designed to remove obstacles to their access to asylum and an efficient and just procedure.

First and foremost, all women must have access to asylum procedures. Not only should information on their rights and the procedure be available and in a language that women can understand (Article 19 of the Istanbul Convention), but they should also be explained using a gender-sensitive language.[108] It should also include free legal aid, as prescribed by Article 57 of the Istanbul Convention. The procedure must be carried out without undue delay and in an effective manner, as required by Article 49 of the Istanbul Convention.

Second, if a woman travels with a male companion who is her husband, partner, or other family member, she must be able to submit her asylum claim separately in order to properly disclose all facts of the case.[109] At the very least, she should have the possibility to be interviewed individually. This opportunity also stems from Article 56 of the Istanbul Convention, which requires allowing victims to testify without the presence of the alleged perpetrator.

Furthermore, it is critical that an interview be conducted by female officials and interpreters, because otherwise, the woman asylum seeker may be embarrassed to share her story, or may perceive a "hostile" atmosphere, making her unwilling to reveal what had happened to her. An interview should be conducted by officials who understand the forms of gender-related persecution, are trained to ask relevant questions, avoid secondary victimization, and build a relationship of trust during the interview. This also means that the interview is conducted in a pleasant environment, with breaks provided if needed.

When assessing the facts of the case, the asylum officials must be trained to recognize specific forms of gender-based violence, evaluate all the evidence, and take a proactive role, meaning that they do not rely solely upon facts provided by a woman asylum seeker. This requirement stems from Article 55 of the Istanbul Convention, but also from UNHCR reports on refugee situations in specific

[108] Hooper (2019), p. 34.
[109] UNHCR (2000).

countries, which need to be consulted. Many other reports of respective international and national NGOs, as well as reports from UN human rights bodies, must be taken into account while assessing the risk of ill-treatment in a country of origin. As this assessment requires time, women asylum seekers should not be subjected to accelerated procedures.[110]

After the decision is made, a women asylum seeker must have the right to an accessible and effective legal remedy. During this phase, free legal aid is given by providers who are trained in gender-related persecution and are familiar with relevant international standards. Usually, the best providers of free legal aid are lawyers engaged in NGOs. Therefore, the legislation on free legal aid should recognize diverse providers and not limit the participation of NGOs, as is the case in many Balkan countries.

5 Conclusion

The refugee law was gender-neutral and did not recognize the different forms and reasons for persecution related to gender. "Sex" was not a recognized ground for persecution in the 1951 Convention, but it has become accepted over time that women can be granted a refugee status by recognizing that they belong to a "particular social group" in a certain country. Also, some regional asylum regimes, such as the EU, recognized gender-related forms of persecution, and gender issues moved "from the margins to the center" of refugee law.[111] This tendency was supported by international human rights law, which gradually started providing protection for women in the form of the *non-refoulement* principle, autonomous residence permits, or requests for gender-sensitive asylum procedures. Apart from gender-sensitive procedures, in order to properly assess women's asylum claims, it is necessary to develop gender-sensitive reception procedures, support services for asylum seekers, and issue gender guidelines. This does not mean that women are subject to different asylum procedures, but that their specific position is recognized and that some phases in the procedure are designed to overcome obstacles to their access to asylum and an efficient and just procedure.

However, despite these positive tendencies, there are still many difficulties in a refugee regime for women. First, recognizing women as a social group imposes stereotypical views that women are not prosecuted for reasons other than their gender, such as religious or political beliefs. Second, despite the introduction of gender-sensitive asylum procedures, it takes time to truly understand the different forms of gender-based violence, its consequences for women's well-being, and to consider how stereotypes may affect an objective assessment of asylum claims. It is not enough to assess if a country outlaws a certain form of persecution, but also how

[110] Hooper (2019), p. 39.

[111] Arbel et al. (2014), p. 11.

the law is implemented in practice, while not putting the burden of proof solely on the asylum applicant. This problem is particularly obvious in the jurisprudence of the ECtHR and the CEDAW Committee, as the majority of cases concerning the *non-refoulement* principle of women asylum seekers are rejected as ill-founded. Finally, the existing jurisprudence illustrates that the division between public/private still exists and that it is much harder to accept that persecution comes from private individuals than from public authorities. Moreover, refugee claims cannot be assessed using the traditional and familiar circumstances of male refugees. As a result of this problem, many refugee women's asylum claims are rejected on the grounds that they can obtain "sufficient" or "effective" protection from the authorities, that the evidence is not credible, or that private individuals are not recognized as actors of prosecution. In other words, the quality of the refugee status determination for refugee women needs to be improved. Therefore, it is fair to say that despite its great progress, the refugee law is still "not there" in terms of providing full recognition and protection for women.[112]

References

Arbel E, Dauvergne C, Millbank J (2014) Introduction. In: Dauvergne E, Millbank C, Jenni (eds) Gender in refugee law: from the margins to the centre. Routledge, London

Australian Department of Immigration and Multi-Cultural Affairs (1996) Guidelines on gender issues for decision-makers, 4.29

Canadian Immigration and Refugee Board (1996) Guidelines on women refugee claimants fearing gender-related persecution

Center for Refugees and Gender Studies (2011) Amicus brief in support of respondent

EASO (2018) Judicial analysis: Asylum procedures and the principle of non-refoulment

Elias P (2010) Federal court opens door for Guatemalan asylum claims. Associated Press, New York

Fitzpatrick B (2016) Tactical rape in war and conflict: International recognition and response. Policy Press, Great Britain

Foster M (2014) Why we are not there yet: the particular challenge of "Particular Social Group". In: Arbel E, Dauvergne C, Millbank J (eds) Gender in refugee law: from the margins to the centre. Routledge, London

Gender-Related Persecution: An Analysis of Recent Trends (1997) International Journal of Refugee Law: 9 (Special Issue), 79–113

Gender-Related Asylum Claims in Europe (2012) European Parliament

Goodwin-Gill GS (1996) The refugee in International Law. Clarendon Press, Oxford

Grahl-Madsen A (1966) The status of refugees in International Law. A.W. Sijithoff, Leyden

GREVIO (2022) Mid-term horizontal review of Grevio baseline evaluation reports

Haines QCR (2003) Gender-related persecution. In: Feller E, Türrk V, Nicholson F (eds) Refugee protection in international law: UNHCR's global consultations on International Protection. Cambridge University Press, Cambridge, pp 129–184

Hathaway JC (1990) A reconsideration of the underlying premise of refugee law. Harv Int Law J 31(1):129–184

[112] Michelle Foster (2014), p. 17.

Hathaway JC (1991) Law of refugee status. Butterworths, Toronto
Hooper L (2019) Gender-based asylum claims and non-refoulement: Articles 60 and 61 of the Istanbul Convention. Council of Europe, Strasbourg
Kelley N (2001) The Convention refugee definition and gender-based persecution: a decade's progress. Int J Refugee Law 13(4):559–568
Lehmann JM (2019) At the crossroads: The 1951 Geneva Convention Today in Satvinder Singh Juss. In: Research handbook on International Refugee Law. Edward Elgar, Cheltenham, pp 2–15
Lieberan A (2010) Appeals case gives hope to Guatemalan refugees, Women's E-News
Maiani F (2008) The concept of "Persecution" in refugee law: indeterminacy, context-sensitivity, and the quest for a principled approach, OpenEdition Journals
Mayblin L (2010) Historically European, morally universal? The 1951 Geneva Convention on the Status of Refugees, E-International Relations
Peroni L (2018) The protection of women Asylum Seekers under the European Convention on Human Rights: unearthing the gendered roots of harm. Human Rights Law Rev 18:347–370
UNHCR Executive Committee (1985) Refugee Women and International Protection no. 39
UNHCR (2000) Position paper on gender-related persecution
Weiss P (1951) The refugee convention, 1951

Legal Documents and Cases

Directive 2011/95/EU of the European Parliament and of the Council of the European Union of 13 December 2011 on standards for the qualification of third-country nationals or stateless persons as beneficiaries of international protection, for a uniform status for refugees or for persons eligible for subsidiary protection, and for the content of the protection granted (recast)
Convention related to the Status of Refugees, Geneva 28 July 1951, United Nations, Treaty Series, vol. 189, 137
The Refugee Convention, 1951: The Travaux préparatoires analysed with a Commentary by Dr. Paul Weis, available at: https://www.unhcr.org/protection/travaux/4ca34be29/refugee-convention-1951-travaux-preparatoires-analysed-commentary-dr-paul.html.
Collins and Akaziebie v. Sweden, Application no. 23944/05, Decision from 8 March 2007
Izevbekhai v. Ireland, Application no. 43408/08, Decision from 17 May 2011
R.B.A.B. and Others v. The Netherlands, Application no. 7211/06, Decision from 7 June 2016
V.F. v. France, Application no., 7196/10, Decision from 29 November 2011
F.A. v. the United Kingdom, Application no. 20658/11, Decision from 10 September 2013
N. v. Sweden, Application No. 23505/09, Judgment from 20 July 2010
R.D. v. France, Application No. 34648/14, Judgment from 16 June 2016
General recommendation No. 24: Article 12 of the Convention (women and health), 1999
General recommendation No. 28 on the core obligations of States parties under article 2 of the Convention on the Elimination of All Forms of Discrimination against Women, 2010
General recommendation No. 30 on women in conflict prevention, conflict and post-conflict situations, 2013
General recommendation No. 32 on the gender-related dimensions of refugee status, asylum, nationality and statelessness of women, 2014
General recommendation no. 38 on trafficking of women and girls in the context of global migration, 2020
S.J.A. v. Denmark, Communication no. 79/2014, Decision from 6 November 2017
H.D. v. Denmark, Communication no. 76/2014, Decision from 9 July 2018
S.O. v. Canada, Communication no. 49/2013, Decision from 27 October 2014
A.S. v. Denmark, Communication no. 80/2015, Decision from 26 February 2018

Y.W. v. Denmark, Communication no. 51/2013, Decision from 2 March 2015
X. v. Denmark, Communication no. 73/2014, Decision from 29 October 2018
X. v. Austria, Communication no. 112/2017, Decision from 29 October 2018
J.O. v. Switzerland, Communication no. 115/2017, Decision from 9 July 2018
O.D.A. v. Denmark, Communication no. 84/2015, Decision from 15 July 2019
H.S. v. Denmark, Communication no. 113/2017, Decision from 9 July 2018
N.S. v. Denmark, Communication no. 109/2016, Decision from 15 July 2019
Y. v. Ecuador, Communication no. 83/2015, Decision from 29 October 2018
Perdomo v. Holder, 611 F.3d 662 (9th Cir. 2010)
In re Fauziya KASINGA, U.S. Department of Justice, Executive Office for Immigration Review, Board of Immigration Appeals, 13 June 1996
Matter of A-R-C-G- et al., Respondents, U.S. Department of Justice, Executive Office for Immigration Review, Board of Immigration Appeals, 26 August 2014
Minister voor Immigratie en Asiel v X and Y and Z v Minister voor Immigratie en Asiel C-199/12 to C-201/12, Judgment from 7 November 2013
Da Silva v. Attorney General, 459 F. App'x 838, 841 (11th Cir. 2012)
Talpis v. Italy, Application no. 41237/14, Judgment from 2 March 2017
Safaie v. INS, 25 F.3d 636, 640 (8th Cir. 1994)
The UK Immigration Appeal tribunal, TH/23443/93 (13956), 2 October 1996.
UN General Assembly, 'Declaration on the Elimination of Violence Against Women', 20 Dec. 1993, UN doc. A/RES/48/104, 23 Feb. 1994.

Ivana Krstić is Professor of International Human Rights Law and Director of the Human Rights Centre at the University of Belgrade, Faculty of Law. She obtained her LLM (2003) at the School of Law, University of Pittsburgh (USA), along with an LLM (2004) and Ph.D. (2008) at the University of Belgrade, Faculty of Law. In the academic year 2006/2007, she was a Chevening Scholar working on her Ph.D. research at Exeter College, Oxford University. She teaches several courses, including the European Immigration Law and Policy, Non-Discrimination, Gender Equality, and Minority Rights. She is also a member of several governmental bodies, including the Republic Commission for Transgender Persons. As a leading Serbian expert in human rights, she is engaged in many projects run by various international organizations and agencies. She has published monographs and textbooks, around 20 handbooks, and more than 60 articles in international human rights law, international refugee law, and international public law.

Screening International Environmental Law Through Gender Lenses: Already Gender-Sensitive, Still Not Gender-Responsive?

Bojana Čučković

Contents

Abstract The article explores gender perspectives of landmark hard law and soft law international instruments for the protection of the environment, from the early stage of the development of international environmental law up to the most recent ones. The analysis focuses on two main hypotheses. Firstly, it is argued that an important evolution has occurred with regard to taking a gender-sensitive approach to drafting States' international duties in protecting the environment. As opposed to an initial silence on the matter, international instruments that were adopted in the 1990s onward seem to have first acknowledged the influence that environmental degradation has on women and the role women play in addressing it, whereas subsequently adopted international instruments started to include gender equality not only as a proclamatory goal but an integral part of the prescribed treaty

B. Čučković (✉)
University of Belgrade, Faculty of Law, Department of International Law and International Relations, Belgrade, Serbia
e-mail: cuckovic@ius.bg.ac.rs

I. Krstić et al. (eds.), *Legal Issues of International Law from a Gender Perspective*, Gender Perspectives in Law 3, https://doi.org/10.1007/978-3-031-13459-3_7

commitments. Secondly, the author challenges the practical implications of gender-sensitive provisions contained in international environmental instruments and the potentials of achieving concrete results. An attempt is therefore made to assess the existing solutions and their capability to enhance the prospects of a more successful implementation of gender-responsive international environmental commitments.

1 Introduction

International environmental law (IEL) appears to be more gender-sensitive than other branches of public international law. A number of important international environmental instruments have either acknowledged the vital role that women have in environmental management and the importance of their full participation in achieving sustainable development goals[1] or required contracting parties to consider gender-responsiveness of specific measures that they are taking when implementing commitments stipulated by international environmental treaties.[2]

Authors offer different interpretations for such development, but their common characteristic lies in the specific link that exists between women and the environment. While Hughes, Abuiyada and Abebe focus on the objectification and subordination of both women and the environment and the tendency to perceive them as something "made to serve the needs" of others,[3] Cole and Castaneda et al. move away from the victim role of women and ascertain their strengths and advantages that may be used for the benefit of protecting the environment, especially concerning negotiations and ratification of international environmental treaties.[4] Although the reasoning differs, neither the doctrine nor the texts of international environmental treaties seem to dispute the twofold relationship between gender and environmental degradation. On the one hand, environmental degradation is deepening gender inequality, whereas on the other hand gender does indeed influence the level of vulnerability to pollution. The two aspects of the relationship between gender and the environment appear to be two sides of the same coin, thus making their interconnection a vicious circle. Due to their different socially constructed roles, environmental degradation does not impact women and men in the same manner, while being particularly detrimental for certain categories of women. Although

[1]Principle 20 of the Rio Declaration on Environment and Development, General Assembly, A/CONF.151/26 (Vol. I), 12 August 1992. Similar formulation, although targeting the specific role that women have in the conservation and sustainable use of biological diversity and combating deforestation is contained in the Preamble to the 1992 Convention on Biological Diversity (United Nations, *Treaty Series*, vol. 1760, 79) and the Preamble of the Convention to Combat Desertification in those Countries Experiencing Serious Drought and/or Desertification, particularly in Africa (A/RES/53/191 of 18 February 1999).

[2]Articles 7(5) and 11(2) of the Paris Agreement, 17 March 2016.

[3]Hughes (1995), p. 504; Abuiyada (2017), p. 1; Abebe (2014), p. 125.

[4]Cole (2014), pp. 26–28; Castaneda et al. (2013), p. 680.

"gender roles and responsibilities women retain are parallel with their lack of access and control over resources",[5] another important factor lies in the lack of their participation in environmental decision making. If a vulnerability is perceived as sensitivity to certain impacts and capacity to adapt and react, gender roles are indeed among factors that determine and enhance women's exposure to negative effects of pollution and their ability to minimize them. The essential interconnection between gender equality and environmental issues has also been recognized in the context of the United Nations Millenium Development Goals. Authors acknowledge gender equality not only as one of the eight goals but also as a "cross-cutting issue" that "needs to be mainstreamed in all the other MDGs, including the one on environmental sustainability".[6]

As eloquently put by Hayes, the women's rights movement and the environmental movement aspire to achieve changes in today's society that overlap at some points since the former seeks "to change the way in which the two halves of the species related to each other in terms of equity and justice" whereas the latter is concerned with "how the entire species related to the planet as a whole".[7] Only by combining their respective tools, instruments and mechanisms would it be possible to root out or at least minimize the consequences of the above-mentioned two-fold mutual influence between gender and environmental degradation.

Instead of outlining and analyzing instrument per instrument, the paper will focus on several common and differentiating traits of engendering IEL. The analysis is divided into three parts. It will firstly focus on the evolution of engendering IEL by tracing the origins and the reasons for the shift from the focus on women's role towards introducing gender considerations in international environmental instruments and treaties, as well as by detecting the rationale behind the tendency to unevenly apply gender-sensitive approach across various sectors of environmental protection. The analysis will next closely consider the nature and content of engendering IEL. Four different aspects are the subject matter of the analysis in the content-oriented part of the paper. Firstly, gender balance in IEL will be opposed to gender equality in IEL provisions. Secondly, international environmental instruments are distinguished from the perspective of the criterion of permanency of gender issues on the agenda of relevant international bodies that supervise their implementation. Thirdly, international environmental treaties are analyzed from the standpoint of the strong vs weak approach to introducing gender. Finally, this part of the paper will accentuate the necessity to perceive gender as a multilayer issue and assess the width of engendering IEL in the sense of the level of its presence within various elements of a specific international environmental treaty. Before concluding remarks, the analysis will delve into the future prospects of engendering IEL and reflect on how it may be improved and intensified. Namely, it will be explained that gender issues need to be addressed by taking into account other relevant criteria for

[5] Abebe (2014), p. 115.

[6] Kameri-Mbote (2013), p. 325.

[7] Hayes (2001), pp. 657–658.

differentiation. In addition, the necessity to shift from gender-sensitive towards gender-responsive IEL will be explained through the assessment of gender dimensions of national action plans as key instruments for the implementation of international environmental regimes.

2 The Origins and Evolution of Introducing Women and Gender Issues in IEL

If origins and subsequent evolution of engendering IEL are compared, two tendencies may be discerned. On the one hand, the initial focus on women was later either replaced or complemented by gender considerations. On the other hand, the initial approach consisting in making IEL women and/or gender-sensitive across all sectors of environmental protection was subsequently replaced by particularization and further development within only a few specific environmental protection regimes.

2.1 From Focusing on Women to Introducing Gender into IEL

As opposed to the 1972 Stockholm Declaration of the United Nations Conference on the Human Environment that refers exclusively to the man as the bearer of both rights and responsibilities concerning the protection of the environment,[8] the Rio Declaration adopted 20 years later did come as a promising change. Except for Principle 20 that explicitly recognized "the empowerment of women and,

[8]The word 'man' is used fifteen times throughout the document. In addition to paragraph 1 of the Preamble to the Stockholm Declaration that provides that "man is both creature and moulder of his environment" and that "both aspects of man's environment, the natural and the man-made, are essential to his well-being", specific principles of the Declaration also refer exclusively to the man. Principle 1 states that "man has the fundamental right to freedom, equality and adequate conditions of life, in an environment of a quality that permits a life of dignity and well-being", Principle 4 stresses that "man has a special responsibility to safeguard and wisely manage the heritage of wildlife and its habitat", Principle 8 provides that "economic and social development is essential for ensuring a favorable living and working environment for man", whereas Principle 26 proclaims that „man and his environment must be spared the effects of nuclear weapons and all other means of mass destruction". UN General Assembly, United Nations Conference on the Human Environment, 15 December 1972, A/RES/2994. Whereas Ituarte-Lima considers that "women and girls were subsumed within the category of "man" and that the reason for such a formulation did not consist in the lack of women's "agency in drafting the declaration", gender equality still not being perceived as a priority for the environmental agenda back in 1972 would appear to be a more logical explanation. Ituarte-Lima, Claudia. 2022. Women's Rights in Environmental Law from 1972 to today. Global Issues – Gender. Climate Diplomacy, https://climate-diplomacy.org/magazine/cooperation/womens-rights-environmental-law-1972-today.

specifically, their ability to effectively participate in their countries' economic and social processes as an essential condition for sustainable development",[9] the Rio Declaration, instead of using the word 'man', solely referred to the 'human' environment, 'human' beings and 'human' health.[10] Other instruments produced at the 1992 conference or adopted as its follow-up,[11] took different approaches to integrate women's rights and gender issues into the international environmental legal framework. Agenda 21 abundantly stressed both the significance of empowering women through full participation in decision making as one of the major disadvantaged groups identified and introduced the relevance of gender-specific programmes, of using gender-disaggregated data and gender-relevant knowledge, as well as the necessity to develop and include gender-impact analyses as an integral part of monitoring environmental policies and programmes.[12] On the contrary, the Convention on Biological Diversity (CBD) simply restated the formulation contained in the Rio Declaration, although making it biodiversity-specific, and chose to stick to the focus on women approach,[13] whereas the United Nations Framework Convention on Climate Change (UNFCCC) kept silent on the matter and failed to use either the focus on women or the gender equality approach.[14] Except for UNFCCC, it may be noticed that the nature of the instrument in question may have influenced the way environmental protection would become engendered. Agenda 21, as an instrument of soft law, opted for interchangeably using both approaches, whereas the Convention on Biological Diversity, although being hard law, decided on the restrictive focus on women approach. At this point of evolution of IEL, it may be concluded that the intensity and the level of engendering IEL were inversely proportional to the hardness of the particular legal instrument and that relevant proclamations were restricted to the essentially non-binding, preambular part of international treaties.

A qualitative step forward came with the adoption of the 1999 United Nations Convention to Combat Desertification (UNCCD) that, although not including gender-specific language, introduced two significant novelties. In addition to stressing the important role of women in its Preamble, it recognized the importance of ensuring „the full participation of both men and women at all levels in programmes to combat desertification" and introduced women's rights considerations in the operative part of the treaty.[15] Not focusing exclusively on women might be considered as a first step in the direction of distinguishing between sex and

[9] Tuohy (2019), p. 32.

[10] General Assembly, Rio Declaration on Environment and Development, A/CONF.151/26 (Vol. I), 12 August 1992.

[11] Brown Weiss (2011), p. 11.

[12] United Nations Conference on Environment and Development, Agenda 21, A/CONF.151/26, vol.II.

[13] Convention on Biological Diversity, United Nations, *Treaty Series*, vol. 1760.

[14] UN General Assembly, United Nations Framework Convention on Climate Change: resolution / adopted by the General Assembly, 20 January 1994, A/RES/48/189.

[15] Convention to Combat Desertification in those Countries Experiencing Serious Drought and/or Desertification, particularly in Africa, A/RES/53/191 of 18 February 1999.

gender, at least at the level of international environmental treaties. More importantly, consideration of women's needs and their specific status became an integral part of obligations of affected country Parties (Article 5), their National Action Plans (Article 10), and measures stipulated to raise public awareness and ensure proper capacity building (Article 19).[16]

The path proposed by Agenda 21 awaited for 24 years to be officially and explicitly applied in a hard environmental law instrument. The 2016 Paris Agreement introduced gender equality as a wider and less limiting concept as opposed to the focus on women's role approach that dominated the IEL instruments up to that point. It also used stronger formulations in the very provisions of the treaty. Namely, Article 7 of the Agreement provides that „Parties acknowledge that adaptation action should follow a country-driven, gender-responsive, participatory and fully transparent approach, taking into consideration vulnerable groups, communities and ecosystems", whereas in Article 11 it is stipulated that „capacity-building should be guided by lessons learned, (...) and should be an effective, iterative process that is participatory, cross-cutting and gender-responsive".[17]

Introducing gender equality as an integral component of the international environmental legal framework has been stressed by Castaneda et al. as crucial, and the focus should shift from women to gender.[18] It is only by differentiating between the biological and physical differences between men and women on the one side and their socially constructed roles on the other,[19] that truly gender-sensitive and gender-responsive IEL will be able to emerge. For two reasons. Firstly, solely focusing on women, their role and vulnerability when faced with environmental degradation is an oversimplification of the matter. Instead, as rightly noticed by Grant Bowman, these concerns should be situated „in the historical and social relationships of gender, such as differential access to resources, household division of labor, and participation in decisionmaking".[20] Secondly, gender inequality actually represents a major contributor to the enhanced vulnerability of women to environmental harm.[21] In other words, women are not vulnerable because of their sex, but because of their gender and gender issues thus cannot be limited to women's issues.[22]

Judging by the recent developments concerning engendering IEL, it appears that it has finally started to be acknowledged that „women are not vulnerable because

[16] Similar approach is applied in the Nagoya Protocol on on Access to Genetic Resources and the Fair and Equitable Sharing of Benefits to the Convention on Biological Diversity, adopted in 2010. Provisions relevant for the topic of this paper are contained in Articles 12, 22 and 25 of the Nagoya Protocol. UNEP/CBD/COP/DEC/X/1 of 29 October 2010. See also the Preamble of the 2001 Stockholm Convention on Persistent Organic Pollutants, as well as its articles 7 and 10. United Nations, *Treaty Series*, vol. 2256, 119.

[17] Paris Agreement, 17 March 2016.

[18] Castaneda et al. (2013), pp. 680–681.

[19] Abuiyada (2017), p. 2.

[20] Grant Bowman (2013), p. 645.

[21] Pratiwi et al. (2016), p. 11.

[22] Broeckhoven (2014), pp. 24–25.

they are naturally weaker“ but due to their limited access to physical, financial, social and natural assets over which they lack control owing to their socially constructed roles.[23] Yet, proclamations relating to the relevance of women's empowerment appear to persist and stand hand in hand with reference to gender equality even in the most advanced hard law international environmental instrument in terms of the level and intensity of gender inclusion—the Paris Agreement. The Preamble to the Paris Agreement acknowledges that "Parties should, when taking action to address climate change, respect, promote and consider (...) gender equality, empowerment of women and intergenerational equity". This seems to certify the argument brought up by Fisher and Mohun that "while gender equality is not a 'women's issue', it is typically women who are disadvantaged in terms of control of and access to resources or decision making where gender inequality exists".[24] It appears that the approach that focuses on women is here to stay, although in a slightly different context and as an important element aiming to achieve gender-responsive IEL.

2.2 *From Generalizing Towards Compartmentalizing Gender Issues in IEL*

Another feature of engendering IEL stems from the above analysis. It is unevenly spread across international environmental instruments. Whereas the first international environmental instruments, such as the Rio Declaration and Agenda 21, advanced the importance of women and/or gender in all segments of environmental protection, women and/or gender considerations were subsequently introduced and further developed in only a limited number of environmental treaties that target at specific areas of environmental protection—biodiversity, combating desertification, persistent organic pollutants and climate change. Several aspects of gender mainstreaming development in IEL may be noticed. Firstly, it was introduced and deepened in very significant, but only a few areas of IEL. This suggests that, as opposed to an initial tendency to conceptualize women/gender issues as issues of general nature that apply across IEL, compartmentalization of engendering IEL occurred. Secondly and paradoxically, gender sensitiveness has been achieved to the greatest extent in the area of climate change although UNFCCC was the only 1992 international environmental instrument that was completely silent on the matter. It, therefore, appears that the engendering of IEL is not necessarily dependent on the presence of women/gender issues within the basic instrument, but may instead evolve through subsequent practices and treaties. Thirdly, it should also be stressed that in such cases soft law instruments appear to play a significant role and that they influence further specialization of gender issues in a particular sector of environmental protection. Taking climate change as an example, UNFCCC's initial silence

[23] Smyth (2009), p. 800.

[24] Fisher and Mohun (2015), p. 12.

on the matter was broken in 2001 in Marrakesh and further developed at the 2012 Conference of the Parties (COP) held in Doha.[25] Other gender-relevant COPs ensued with concrete soft law instruments as a result, such as the Programme of Action on Gender adopted in 2014 in Lima,[26] significantly influencing the introduction of gender issues in the Paris Agreement in 2016. Soft law instruments had a significant role in those regimes that did possess a gender element from the very beginning as well. Numerous COPs to the Convention on Biological Diversity influenced how engendering within this particular regime evolved, and whether it was perceived as a gender balance or a gender-equality issue.[27] This appears to suggest that the influence of soft law instruments within a specific regime is not limited to the origin and evolution aspect of engendering IEL, but is also present as regards its contents. Finally, the compartmentalized engendering of IEL did not occur due to perceiving gender issues as issues that divert attention from other, more significant environmental protection elements. As proposed by some authors, the focus on universal issues during difficult negotiations and the crisis atmosphere that existed at the time of drafting the Kyoto Protocol can be considered as a crucial reason for not including gender considerations into this particular environmental instrument.[28] However, the negotiations to conclude the Paris Agreement were neither easy nor free from serious tensions and, yet, gender issues were introduced into the text of this Agreement in the most developed manner so far accepted within an international environmental treaty. The approach consisting in developing gender sensibilization and gender responsiveness within particular environmental regimes should instead be understood as an attempt to make them more focused and effective, taking into account the characteristics, mechanisms and aims of the regime in question. It remains to be seen whether other areas of IEL will follow the path of this limited number of international environmental instruments and develop their gender dimensions in the near future.

3 Identifying the Nature and Content of Gender Issues Within IEL

This part of the paper will focus on the nature and content of engendering IEL, i.e. on how and with regard to which issues gender considerations are integrated into international instruments mentioned above. Differences between international environmental treaties, and relevant soft law instruments that accompany them, exist at various levels. Gender considerations may thus be distinguished as issues of gender balance or gender equality. They may be included as standing or an *ad hoc* issue. In

[25] Mukhopadhyay and Das (2019), p. 82.
[26] Lima work programme on gender, Decision 18/CP.20, FCCC/CP/2014/10/Add.3.
[27] Broeckhoven (2014), pp. 27–29.
[28] Hemmati and Röhr (2009), p. 29.

addition, weak as opposed to the strong engendering of international environmental regimes may be discerned, whereas gender issues may be present concerning a single or multiple elements of the particular environmental regime.

3.1 Gender-Balanced IEL or Gender Equality in IEL

Gender balance is focused on participatory issues, whereas gender equality is a wider concept that includes, but is not limited to balancing the participation of women and men in negotiations, decision-making processes and membership within relevant international bodies established for monitoring respective international environmental treaties.[29] Although the tendency to achieve gender balance is of high significance and represents a common feature of all the above-mentioned gender-sensitive environmental regimes, in order to become truly gender-responsive those regimes need to detach from simply counting women and develop other gender issues that are encompassed within the concept of gender equality. The biodiversity and climate change regimes may serve as examples of different approaches to the issue depending on whether they focus more on gender balance or gender equality.

The climate change regime has been criticized for having "concentrated more on enhancing women's participation and promoting gender balance in negotiating bodies than on addressing the bigger issue of gender equality".[30] Identified as important at the early stage and even without explicit reference in the texts of respective hard law instrument, gender composition was attached particular relevance at COP 18 in Doha in 2012 by further developing methods for achieving equal participation of women and their representation "in all aspects of the UNFCCC process, including through membership of their national delegations and the chairing and facilitation of formal and informal negotiating groups".[31] During the COP 20 held in Lima in 2014, the Lima Work Programme on Gender was adopted that decided that "additional efforts needed to be made by Parties to improve the participation of women in their delegations and in all bodies established under the Convention", but in addition invited "Parties to advance gender balance, promote gender sensitivity in developing and implementing climate policy, and achieve

[29] According to Tenzing, Andrei and Gama, "gender balance refers to the ratio of women to men in any given situation" and it is achieved "when there are approximately equal numbers of men and women present or participating". Tenzing et al. (2015), p. 3. On the other hand, Fisher and Mohun identify gender equality as "a normative position" that is "associated with not only the relationships between men and women, but also the social construction of gender and gender roles". Fisher and Mohun (2015), p. 12.

[30] Tenzing et al. (2015), p. 1.

[31] Promoting gender balance and improving the participation of women in UNFCCC negotiations and in the representation of Parties in bodies established pursuant to the Convention or the Kyoto Protocol, Decision 23/CP.18, FCCC/CP/2012/8/Add.3, 47.

gender-responsive climate policy in all relevant activities under the Convention".[32] The approach consisting in combining efforts to achieve both the gender balance and gender equality within the climate change regime persisted and was applied in the decisions adopted at subsequent COPs. This is particularly evident from the decision taken at COP 22 held in Marrakech in 2016. Namely, the Secretariat was requested "to continue to prepare an annual report on gender composition" and "to undertake research and analysis on challenges to the full and equal participation of women in climate-related processes and activities and to prepare a technical paper on achieving the goal of gender balance", whereas both the Secretariat and the Parties were encouraged and invited to take other relevant steps and measures to achieve gender equality and gender-responsiveness in other aspects of the climate change regime such as appointing the national gender focal point, mainstreaming „a gender perspective in the enhancement of climate technology development and transfer", etc.[33] Both the numbers[34] and the latest Decision adopted within COP 25 held in 2019, certify that the international community is still struggling not only with achieving a gender-responsive climate change regime, but also a gender-balanced one. The Decision took note of the report on gender composition that stressed „the persistent lack of progress in and the urgent need for improving the representation of women in Party delegations and constituted bodies".[35] Notwithstanding the efforts made and the time passed since the introduction of the issue of gender balance on the agenda of the COP to UNFCCC, it appears that gender balance is still an unresolved issue within the climate change regime and a goal that is yet to be achieved, thus making true gender equality within IEL even further away.

On the other hand, the CBD regime did attach significance to the participation of women in relevant bodies but appears to have focused more on integrating gender equality. As noted by Broeckhoven, gender language appearing in the COP decisions before 2008 focused mainly on „participatory issues such as affirming the need for women's participation and calling for mechanisms to allow increased participation" and „did not directly deal with the promotion of gender equality as such".[36] However, subsequent COP decisions opted for the approach that focused on gender equality rather than gender balance. At COP 10 held in Nagoya in 2010, the COP requested the Secretary "to enhance efforts to fully implement the Plan of Action in order to mainstream gender considerations in all aspects of the work under the Convention and formulate clear indicators to monitor progress".[37] Such a wide approach that targets "all aspects of the work under the Convention" was further

[32] Lima work programme on gender, Decision 18/CP.20, FCCC/CP/2014/10/Add.3, 35.

[33] Gender and climate change, Decision 21/CP.22, FCCC/CP/2016/10/Add.2, 17-20.

[34] Kimura (2017), p. 201.

[35] Enhanced Lima work programme on gender and its gender action plan, Decision 3/CP.25, FCCC/CP/2019/13/Add.1, 6-8.

[36] Broeckhoven (2014), pp. 27–29.

[37] Decision adopted by the Conference of the Parties to the Convention on Biological Diversity at its tenth meeting, UNEP/CBD/COP/DEC/X/19, 29 October 2010.

affirmed in COP decisions that ensued. In fact, in 2014, at COP 12, the 2015-2020 Gender Plan of Action under the Convention on Biological Diversity was adopted that explicitly referred to promoting gender equality as one of the strategic objectives of the Convention. What is more, gender equality is referred to within the Gender Plan of Action both as regards institutional capacities and organizational sphere and as regards specific activities and policies taken within the CBD regime,[38] thus perceiving participation of women as only an aspect of the overall aim of reaching gender equality and not an aim in itself.

3.2 Gender As an Ad Hoc *or a Standing Issue*

A common feature of the three most gender-developed environmental regimes consists in the evolution of gender considerations from an *ad hoc* towards an issue that is permanently on the agenda of respective administrative and supervisory bodies. Such a development can be considered as crucial from the standpoint of the content and nature of gender considerations within IEL.

Gender became a standing issue in the UNFCCC regime at COP 18 held in 2012 in Doha. Decision 23/CP.18 on Promoting gender balance and improving the participation of women in UNFCCC negotiations and in the representation of Parties in bodies established pursuant to the Convention or the Kyoto Protocol added "the issue of gender and climate change as a standing item on the agenda of sessions of the Conference of the Parties".[39] A similar development occurred within the CBD regime. After the adoption of the Gender Action Plan by COP 9 in 2008,[40] gender mainstreaming was on the agenda of all COPs that were held in the following years, most often resulting in the adoption of a specific decision on the matter.[41] In addition, the UNCCD regime made gender mainstreaming a standing issue quite early—at COP 11 held in 2012. According to the Overview of gender mainstreaming in the implementation of the Convention: 1998–2018, it was Decision 9/COP.11 that

[38] Decision adopted by the Conference of the Parties to the Convention on Biological Diversity, UNEP/CBD/COP/DEC/XII/7, 17 October 2014.

[39] Decision 23/CP.18 on Promoting gender balance and improving the participation of women in UNFCCC negotiations and in the representation of Parties in bodies established pursuant to the Convention or the Kyoto Protocol, FCCC/CP/2012/8/Add.3, 48.

[40] Decision adopted by the Conference of the Parties to the Convention on Biological Diversity at its ninth meeting, UNEP/CBD/COP/DEC/IX/24, 9 October 2008.

[41] The only COP not resulting in a special decision was the Cancun COP 13 held in 2016. However, gender mainstreaming was among the issues discussed during the meeting. These discussions contributed to the assessment of progress on the Gender Plan of Action adopted at the next COP held in 2018. Decision adopted by the Conference of the Parties to the Convention on Biological Diversity, CBD/COP/DEC/14/18 30 November 2018.

requested "the secretariat to regularly report to the Conference of the Parties (COP) on the implementation of the gender policy advocacy framework".[42]

It may be concluded that making gender a standing issue on the agenda of respective COPs occurred almost simultaneously and that it took contracting parties between 13 and 20 years since the regimes were established to realize the significance of transforming gender from an *ad hoc* to a permanently discussed issue. Such a transformation enabled gender mainstreaming to be regularly discussed during COP meetings, thus not only confirming the significance of the mutual influence between gender and environment but also contributing to the level of integrating gender considerations within IEL, as well as their further deepening.

3.3 Weak vs Strong Engendering of IEL

Gender-relevant provisions contained in environmental treaties appear to suffer from the same weaknesses as the treaties themselves. Another common feature of the three environmental regimes discussed above, therefore, consists in the weak character of both their primary rules in general and those provisions that aim at accentuating their gender dimensions. As stressed by Kimura, gender or women are mentioned only in "basic documents or preambles of the conventions, and there are no mandatory characteristics or specific obligations based on protocols".[43] However, the analysis provided so far seems to point to another tendency that has been occurring in recent years. Soft law instruments, such as decisions of COPs and gender action plans and programmes, offer added value and try to compensate for the lack of clarity and accuracy of provisions that are contained in hard law. It appears that the weak and ineffective provisions stipulated in international environmental treaties are slowly gaining precision and specification through various instruments of soft character. However, this positive impact of soft law for engendering IEL currently appears to be limited to defining the contents of gender issues within environmental regimes, both in terms of their comprehensiveness and intersectionality. On the other hand, the ability of soft law instruments to enhance the level and intensity of engendering IEL, i.e. to shift from gender-sensitive to gender-responsive IEL remains to be tested in practice.

[42] Overview of gender mainstreaming in the implementation of the Convention: 1998–2018, ICCD/COP(13)/CRP.1, 7 September 2017, 1.

[43] Kimura (2017), p. 195.

3.4 *Gender As a Multilayer Issue in IEL*

To be truly gender-responsive, it does not suffice that a particular environmental regime addresses gender considerations from a general point of view. Instead, gender issues need to be integrated into every specific element and aspect of a particular environmental regime. In other words, gender equality should be taken into account when the composition of relevant delegations and bodies is concerned, at the level of designing adequate policies, programmes and measures to address environmental degradation, with regard to capacity building, but also concerning any other aspect of the environmental regime in question. Soft law instruments seem to have contributed to such a specialization of gender issues as well.

Within the climate change regime, the Paris Agreement explicitly acknowledges this concerning adaptation action[44] and capacity building.[45] However, the relevance of integrating gender into other aspects of the climate change regime has been asserted through COP decisions and other instruments. For example, the latest COP decision on the matter stressed "the continuing need for gender mainstreaming through all relevant targets and goals in activities under the Convention as an important contribution to increasing their effectiveness, fairness and sustainability",[46] whereas the enhanced Lima work programme on gender identified five priority areas: capacity building, knowledge management and communication; participation of women; coherence with the relevant activities of other UN entities and stakeholders; implementation and means of implementation; and monitoring and reporting.[47] More specifically, a number of activities were identified within a particular priority area, thus providing guidance "on how states and other entities can practice the creation and maintenance, across all policy sectors, of equitable gender standards".[48] Such activities include, but are not limited to gender-responsive policies, plans and programmes on adaptation, mitigation, capacity-building, technology and finance.

A slightly different approach was adopted within the CBD regime. The CBD Gender Plan of Action identified four strategic objectives consisting in (a) mainstreaming a gender perspective into the implementation of the Convention, (b) promoting gender equality in achieving objectives of the Convention, (c) demonstrating the benefits of gender mainstreaming in measures towards the conservation of biodiversity and (d) increasing the effectiveness of the work under the Convention.[49] As opposed to the climate change regime, the CBD Gender Plan

---

[44] Article 7 of the Paris Agreement.

[45] Article 11 of the Paris Agreement.

[46] Decision 3/CP.25, Enhanced Lima work programme on gender and its gender action plan, FCCC/CP/2019/13/Add.1, 6.

[47] Decision 3/CP.23, Establishment of a gender action plan, FCCC/CP/2017/11/Add.1, 15-16.

[48] Tuohy (2019), pp. 38–39.

[49] Decision adopted by the Conference of the Parties to the Convention on Biological Diversity, UNEP/CBD/COP/DEC/XII/7, 17 October 2014, 2.

of Action differentiated between actions to be taken by the Parties and the Secretariat, formulating the first category of policy actions in more loose wording, obviously being aware of the limited possibilities to steer Parties into acting in line with the proposal.

4 Future Prospects for Engendering IEL

A relatively adequate current position of gender issues and their integration within analyzed environmental regimes, at least on paper, does not mean that further progress is not expected and welcome. On the contrary. Not only are there additional aspects that should be included in the process of engendering IEL, there is also ample space for improvement which is best perceived through the survey and critique of the level of gender-inclusiveness into national action plans.

4.1 Taking into Account the Diversity of Women As a Constituency in Environmental Protection

Although women have been acknowledged as a constituency within the environmental regimes analyzed so far, their diversity, both in terms of vulnerability and as regards their potential role of actors of change, does not seem to have been sufficiently taken into account. Therefore, to be truly gender-responsive, IEL needs to become sensitive to specific categories of women. Namely, certain environmentally harmful events have shown that not all women became equally exposed to the consequences of such events. As noted by Verchick, single mothers that lived in poverty and lacked childcare support were less mobile and unable to respond to evacuation warnings in a timely manner with hurricane Katrina approaching in 2005.[50] Prescott stressed three factors of enhanced gender-based vulnerability for rural women when it comes to climate change consisting of their "unequal access to resources; unequal opportunities to change and improve their livelihoods; and exclusion from decision-making".[51] Samy adds that not only exposure to the consequences of climate change but also post-disaster recovery would be more difficult for certain categories of women.[52] In other words, not all women will be equally exposed to environmental accidents and degradation of the environment since not all women are vulnerable to the same extent. However, and this is of crucial importance, differentiating between women as a constituency concerning environmental issues cannot be reduced to a simple division between rich and poor or those

[50] Verchick (2008), p. 796.

[51] Prescott (2014), p. 774.

[52] Samy (2011), p. 100.

living in rural or urban areas. Things are much more complex. There are rich societies with strong patriarchal values that influence the position of women and their ability to be involved in environmental decision making, and there are poor societies in which their position does not necessarily depend on whether women live in urban or rural areas and in which women are included in decision making. Such an argument suggests that more factors determine the level of not only environmental vulnerability of women in a particular society but also their ability to act as actors of change and that each environmental regime should include solutions that address both gender in general and solutions tailored in accordance to the needs of sub-groups that are particularly sensitive to the environmental threat in question.

Turning to the three environmental regimes analyzed in the paper, it may be concluded that the initial "insistence on women's universal vulnerability"[53] and "homogeneity of women as a group"[54] has in the meantime been replaced by a focus on different levels of environmental vulnerability of particular groups of women. However, it should also be stressed that the shift to particular instead of universal vulnerability has only been partial and that it is mainly limited to factors such as wealth, differentiation between women living in rural and urban areas, as well as indigenous women as a particularly sensitive sub-group. Other factors need to be taken into account as well and mitigation and adaptation measures should be tailored accordingly. These factors include but are not limited to, disability, age, health, religion, minority status, migration, family considerations and level of dependence.

The UNFCCC regime does not address these issues in detail, but instead, it simply recognizes the multidimensionality of factors that lead to current gender inequalities since climate change effects "can be more pronounced in developing countries and for local communities and indigenous peoples".[55] The Gender Action Plan, in a similar way, briefly touches upon the necessity to consider multidimensional factors "to better inform gender-responsive climate policies, plans, strategies and action", but only regarding activity D.7 within priority area D dealing with gender-responsive implementation.[56] The Gender Plan of Action adopted under the CBD regime makes a step further and, by proposing possible actions for Parties, it urges them to "review relevant policies to identify gender differences, including policies related to tenure and use rights, employment, education, health, local governance and decision-making and access to financial resources, and consider steps to address these".[57] However, throughout the document, the focus appears to be only on two criteria for differentiation—age and indigeneity. Last but

[53] Kameri-Mbote (2013), p. 324.

[54] Broeckhoven (2014), p. 25.

[55] Decision 3/CP.25, Enhanced Lima work programme on gender and its gender action plan, FCCC/CP/2019/13/Add.1, 1.

[56] Decision 3/CP.25, 10.

[57] Decision adopted by the Conference of the Parties to the Convention on Biological Diversity, UNEP/CBD/COP/DEC/XII/7, 17 October 2014, 3.

not least, the UNCCD regime appears to focus on poverty and life in rural areas as the most relevant factors for making the response to desertification gender-responsive.[58]

It may be concluded that, at least for the moment, the intersectional approach to considering gender in environmental regimes is still in its rudimentary phase. Firstly, it is reduced to mere proclamations. Secondly, only a limited number of factors such as age, poverty, indigeneity and life in rural areas are to a certain extent recognized as relevant within the respective gender action plans. Thirdly, even regarding factors that are acknowledged, the shift from simple recognition to true integration within environmental policies and measures, both at national and international levels, still needs to be achieved, thus being one of the preconditions for truly gender-responsive IEL.

4.2 From Gender-Sensitive to Gender-Responsive IEL: National Action Plans As a Mirror of the Current Level of Gender Mainstreaming

To shift from gender-sensitive to truly gender-responsive regimes, the activities, policies and measures identified and recommended at international levels need to be transposed to national levels and become an integral part of national policies and measures intended to address climate change, biodiversity and desertification. The only available means of analyzing the level of inclusion of gender considerations at national levels consists in reviewing parties' reports submitted to relevant treaty bodies as key instruments to implement the respective conventions, such as the National Adaptation Plans (NAPs) within the UNFCCC regime and Nationally Determined Contributions (NDCs) within the Paris Agreement, the National Biodiversity Strategies and Action Plans (NBSAPs) within the CBD regime and National Action Programmes (NAPs) within the UNCCD regime.

Whereas previous analysis shows that "mainstreaming gender into NAPs remains the exception rather than the rule",[59] the most recent Synthesis report on nationally determined contributions under the Paris Agreement prepared by the Secretariat based on information from the 164 latest available NDCs indicates a higher level of gender mainstreaming present in NDCs.[60] According to the 2021 Report "many Parties provided information related to gender in their NDCs and many affirmed that they will take gender into account in implementing them".[61] Translated into specific

[58] 2018 UNCCD Gender Action Plan. https://www.unccd.int/sites/default/files/documents/2018-01/GAP%20ENG%20%20low%20res_0.pdf.

[59] Castaneda et al. (2013), p. 674.

[60] Nationally determined contributions under the Paris Agreement—Synthesis report by the secretariat, FCCC/PA/CMA/2021/8, 17 September 2021.

[61] Nationally determined contributions under the Paris Agreement, par. 106.

percentages, this statement shows that there is still plenty of room for further improvement. Namely, the majority of NDC reports do not refer to gender at all (71% in previous NDCs and 15% in new or updated NDCs), whereas among those that do refer to gender, in most cases it is not clear to which specific issues gender mainstreaming actually relates.[62] Parties that referred to gender in a specific manner, either "treated it as a cross-cutting issue to be addressed across adaptation and mitigation", or "considered gender exclusively in the context of adaptation".[63] Since most NDC reports that mainstreamed gender used the approach that focuses on women and their vulnerability, whereas only a few Parties explicitly referred to other genders,[64] it is obvious that the gender equality approach discussed earlier has still not permeated the climate change regime. Although it may be concluded that there is an increase in the number of Parties that consider gender in their NDCs when previous and new NDCs are compared, as well as an increase in the share of Parties that address gender in a more elaborative manner, these trends are occurring at a rather slow pace and it still needs to be taken into account that real-life practice usually drastically differs from what is written in reports.

Similarly, if previous and most recent reports on integrating gender within NBSAPs are compared, there is a fairly modest improvement that can be noticed. The Secretariat of the CBD reported in 2008 that out of 166 NBSAPs submitted, only 78 included reference to women or gender, with only a few addressing gender issues in more detail, still "in a very fragmented and *ad hoc* manner".[65] Research conducted in 2017 has shown that out of 254 NBSAPs from 174 Parties, 143 reports

[62] Nationally determined contributions under the Paris Agreement, para. 22, figure 6.

[63] Nationally determined contributions under the Paris Agreement, para. 108.

[64] Nationally determined contributions under the Paris Agreement, para. 111. For example, the NDC submitted by Canada in 2021 refers to non-binary people. Reflecting on fairness and equity considerations, Canada invokes its latest climate plan informed by a „gender-based analysis plus (GBA+), which assesses how diverse groups of women, men and non-binary people may experience policies, programs and initiatives". Although the Canadian NDC also mentions transgender, queer, questioning, intersex and asexual people at one point, it does that in a way which is not relevant for climate change considerations. Canada's 2021 Nationally Determined Contribution under the Paris Agreement, 22 available at: https://www4.unfccc.int/sites/ndcstaging/PublishedDocuments/Canada%20First/Canadas%20Enhanced%20NDC%20Submission1_FINAL%20EN.pdf. On the other hand, Iceland in its 2021 Update of the Nationally Determined Contribution invoked, in the context of priorities acknowledged when joining the Paris Agreement, its intention to "create and maintain equal rights and opportunities for all genders in all aspects of the community". Update of the Nationally Determined Contribution of Iceland, Communicated to the UNFCCC on February 18, 2021, 7. https://www4.unfccc.int/sites/ndcstaging/PublishedDocuments/Iceland%20First/Iceland_updated_NDC_Submission_Feb_2021.pdf. Taking into account that only two NDCs appear to open the floor for the approach that includes other genders within the climate change regime, and that both do it in a rather limited and dubious manner, it is still early to consider the gender-climate change link in the context of other genders.

[65] Castaneda et al. (2013), 674.

from 107 countries included reference to women and gender.[66] However, the percentage of reports that qualify empowerment of women and/or gender equality as guiding principles is rather low (14%), whereas most recent NBSAPs refer to specific activities aimed to "advance gender equality".[67] Though this may appear to be promising, splitting it into narrower categories certifies that much is yet to be achieved. Namely, according to the analysis, only 9% of Parties "dedicated budget allocated to gender or women-focused activities", whereas 7 Parties expressed the intention to conduct gender analysis, a precondition to design and plan activities aimed at proactively contributing to making CBD regime truly gender-responsive.[68]

5 Conclusion

The analysis suggests that IEL may currently be qualified as gender-sensitive but that it is far from being gender-responsive. If we consider gender-sensitiveness and gender-responsiveness as two levels of including gender aspects within a particular international environmental regime, the former may be characterized as antecedent, proclamatory and followed by insufficient transposition to the national level, whereas the latter may be qualified as appearing later in time, being more precise and targeting specific national activities and measures.[69]

Three imperatives should guide further engendering of IEL if it is to become truly gender-responsive. It should be specified, implemented and measurable. Firstly, not only national action plans but also other monitoring and reporting instruments adopted within the three environmental regimes, such as national strategies or reports addressing particular issues (for example NDCs within the climate change regime), lack specificity when it comes to gender-related matters. If they wish to continue being considered as the most advanced regimes when it comes to engendering IEL, major improvements need to take place. To use the words of Grant Bowman, "instead of running on parallel tracks", gender and environmental protection need to truly intersect, permeate and integrate.[70] To achieve this, all the different layers of gender need to be recognized and every single aspect of environmental protection that may raise gender issues should be addressed. Not only through plain

[66] IUCN. 2017. Gender and biodiversity: Analysis of women and gender equality considerations in National Biodiversity Strategies and Action Plans (NBSAPs). https://www.cbd.int/gender/doc/gender-biodiversity-nbsaps-report-final.pdf, 11.

[67] IUCN. 2017, 25.

[68] IUCN. 2017, 25.

[69] Other authors suggest additional criteria for differentiating between gender-sensitiveness and gender-responsiveness. Ihlainen et al. understand gender sensitivity as "being mindful of gender differences", whereas gender-responsiveness "systematically addresses gender gaps" in specific responses to environmental degradation. Ihalainen et al. (2017), p. 2.

[70] Grant Bowman (2013), p. 646.

words, but through very specific measures and activities that produce concrete outcomes. At the moment only two international environmental regimes acknowledge the importance of adopting the intersectional approach to dealing with gender. Though taking account of intersectionality within the climate change and biodiversity regimes is to be praised, it remains to be seen how effective such an approach will turn out to be. Especially if one considers that the two regimes are not identical in this regard. While the climate change regime focuses on priority areas that are further divided into specific activities, the CBD regime is less specific. It identifies no more than four objectives of strategic character and, in addition, it differentiates between the duties of states parties and the Secretariat to apply the intersectional approach, the former being formulated using rather loose wording. Secondly, measures and activities intended to attain gender equality have to actually be implemented. In other words, gender action plans and national action plans are not enough anymore. They should be taken a step further and 'action plans' translated to 'action'. Action may consist in transposing relevant gender-responsive provisions in national environmental legislation, allocating specific funds for gender-inclusive measures taken at the national level, or undertaking other proactive measures aimed at enhancing the level of gender- responsiveness of national environmental practices. Finally, the outcomes reached through the action have to be measurable and indicators need to be developed for assessing the actual level of integration of gender considerations within environmental regimes. Much has been done but there is still a long road to cross. Both in terms of the gender-responsiveness of IEL and its general effectiveness. The more ambitious and effective IEL is, the more gender-responsive it will surely be.

References

Abebe M (2014) Climate change, gender inequality and migration in East Africa. Washington J Environ Law Policy 4:104–140

Abuiyada R (2017) Gender, poverty elimination and environmental protection: three key paths to sustainable rural development. Int J Soc Stud 5:1–6

Broeckhoven N (2014) Loss and climate change: gender issues in international law and policy. J Diversity Gender Stud 1:23–38

Brown Weiss E (2011) The evolution of International Environmental Law. Jpn Yearb Int Law 54:1–27

Castaneda I, Aguilar C, Rand A (2013) Measurement and reporting: important elements of gender mainstreaming in environmental policies. Cornell J Law Public Policy 22:667–684

Cole M (2014) Gender disparities in environmental negotiations. J Alternative Dispute Resolution 4:17–32

Fisher S, Mohun R (2015) Low carbon resilient development and gender equality in the least developed countries. International Institute for Environment and Development, London

Grant Bowman C (2013) The path from feminist legal theory to environmental law and policy. Cornell J Law Public Policy 22(3):641–648

Hayes B (2001) Gender, specific knowledge, and attitudes toward the environment: a cross-national analysis. Political Res Q 54:657–671

Hemmati M, Röhr U (2009) Engendering the climate-change negotiations: experiences, challenges and steps forward. Gender Dev 17:19–32
Hughes E (1995) Fishwives and other tails: ecofeminism and environmental law. Can J Women Law 8:502–530
Ihalainen M, Basnett BS, Larson A, Duchelle A, Djoudi H (2017) What should be included in the Green Climate Fund's new Gender Policy and Action Plan?: lessons from CIFOR's research and analyses. Center for International Forestry Research, Bogor
Kameri-Mbote P (2013) climate change and gender justice: international policy and legal responses. In: Ruppel O, Roschmann C, Ruppel-Schlichting K (eds) Climate change: International Law and Global Governance. Nomos Verlagsgesellschaft mbH, Baden-Baden, pp 323–348
Kimura H (2017) Gender justice in International Environmental Law. In: Daniels J (ed) Advances in environmental research. Nova Science Publishers, New York, pp 195–210
Mukhopadhyay K, Das N (2019) The discourse of climate change and women's health: some insights on gender mainstreaming. J Soc Sci Humanities 2:79–86
Pratiwi NA, Rahmawati YD, Setiono I (2016) Mainstreaming gender in climate change adaptation: A case study from Cirebon, Indonesia. International Institute for Environment and Development, London
Prescott J (2014) Climate change, gender, and rethinking military operations. Vermont J Environ Law 15:766–802
Samy K (2011) Women and climate change: an opportunity to address gender inequality. Yale J Int Aff 6:99–101
Smyth I (2009) Gender in climate change and disaster risk reduction. Dev Practice 19:799–802
Tenzing J, Andrei S, Gama S (2015) Advancing gender equality in the post-2020 climate regime. International Institute for Environment and Development, London
Tuohy H (2019) Where gender equality and environmental law meet: appointing a gender focal point for Ireland. Univ College Dublin Law Rev 19:29–45
Verchick R (2008) Katrina, feminism, and environmental justice. Cardozo J Law Gender 13:791–800

Bojana Čučković is an Associate Professor of Public International Law and Human Rights Law at the University of Belgrade Faculty of Law. She has a Ph.D. in Public International Law from the University of Belgrade Faculty of Law (2012) and holds an LL.M. degree in International Law and International Organizations from Paris 1 Panthéon-Sorbonne University (2006). She teaches a number of courses at various levels of studies (undergraduate, master, and doctoral studies): Public International Law, Human Rights Law, Legal Clinic, EU Environmental Law and Policy, EU Immigration and Asylum Law and Policy, and International Environmental Law. She has taken part in several European, international and national scientific projects, both as a research team member and in the capacity of the head of the research team. She has published books and articles in Serbian and English on various topics of general international law, international protection of the environment, asylum law and international human rights.

Putting Women's Rights to Work: The Participation of Women on Company Boards As a Human Rights Law Issue

Linde Verhoeven and Alexandra Timmer

Contents

Abstract Most of the legal scholarship on the participation of women on company boards focuses on European Union (EU) law and/or national law. In this chapter we take a novel approach by offering a critical reflection on the question to what extent international human rights law mandates the use of positive measures to improve the participation of women on company boards, and what obligations this entails on the state and on companies themselves.

We thereby use the Convention on the Elimination of All Forms of Discrimination against Women (CEDAW) Committee's multi-layered conception of equality—consisting of formal, substantive and transformative equality—as framework to assess and critique human rights law.

This chapter shows that the proper implementation of CEDAW indeed requires States Parties adopt measures to tackle the underrepresentation of women in top

L. Verhoeven (✉)
Utrecht University, Utrecht, The Netherlands

A. Timmer
Netherlands Institute of Human Rights (SIM), Utrecht University, Utrecht, The Netherlands
e-mail: A.S.H.Timmer@uu.nl

I. Krstić et al. (eds.), *Legal Issues of International Law from a Gender Perspective*, Gender Perspectives in Law 3, https://doi.org/10.1007/978-3-031-13459-3_8

corporate positions, though there is considerable discretion as to the content of these measures. Also under the United Nations Guiding Principles on Business and Human Rights (UNGPs) states should take an active stance towards the private sector on this topic. Responsibilities for companies are based on the UNGPs' corporate responsibility to respect. We argue that promoting the participation of women on company boards falls into the scope of what is currently expected from companies.

1 Introduction

Women filled only 16% of board positions in the world's largest Multinational Enterprises in 2020.[1] In Europe, 34% of all board positions in the largest listed companies were occupied by women and 17% of all leaders at the executive level were women in 2020.[2] These low numbers are caused by a complex set of factors—including the persistence of gender role stereotypes, horizontal sex segregation in the labor market (segregation according to occupation), vertical segregation (the lack of promotion of women throughout the ranks), the uneven distribution of care tasks among men and women, and other factors.[3]

In the past two decades, the female presence on company boards has been taken up by a broad array of social organizations and individual campaigners,[4] who have succeeded in putting the issue prominently on the agenda of national governments, as well as regional and international organizations. The first country to adopt a law introducing gender quotas on company boards was Norway, in 2003. From Norway there was a 'snowball' effect towards other European countries.[5] The result is that there is currently a variety of both regulatory and enforcement approaches at the national level to remedy the scarcity of women on corporate boards.[6] These range from no action, to self-regulation by companies, to soft public law with soft targets, to hard public law with binding quota's.[7] The European Commission put forward a proposal for a directive on 'improving the gender balance among non-executive directors of companies listed on stock exchanges' in 2012,[8]

[1] OECD, 'What big data can tell us about women on boards' (2020). https://www.oecd.org/gender/data/what-big-data-can-tell-us-about-women-on-boards.htm.

[2] EWOB (2020). https://europeanwomenonboards.eu/portfolio/gender-diversity-index-2020/. See for an overview of measures and corporate boards in Europe: Oppenheimer (2019), pp. 87–97.

[3] See Raday (2019), pp. 45–60.

[4] E.g. Initiatives such as the 50/50 Women on Boards (2020), https://www.5050wob.com; EWOB (2022), https://www.europeanwomenonboards.eu.

[5] Machold (2013).

[6] Senden (2014), pp. 51–66.

[7] Senden (2014), pp. 51–66.

[8] European Commission (2012).

which—after negotiations stretching out over 10 years—will enter into force soon.[9]

This chapter aims to provide a critical reflection on the research question to what extent international human rights law mandates the use of positive measures to improve the participation of women on company boards, and what obligations this entails on the state and on companies themselves. We focus on two aspects in particular: first, what conceptions of equality underly human rights law's support of positive measures to create gender balanced company boards, and, second, what obligations human rights law envisages for the state and for corporations in this respect. We thereby use CEDAW's multi-layered conception of equality—consisting of formal, substantive and transformative equality—as framework to assess and critique human rights law.

The chapter employs legal doctrinal research as method, understood as appraising the validity, coherence and applicability of legal arguments.[10] Our main primary sources are the CEDAW Convention and the interpretation of the Convention by the CEDAW Commitee. We examined all CEDAW's General Recommendations, as well as all Concluding Observations from 2015 to the present. We systematically searched for the key words 'board', 'enterprise', 'representation', 'management' and 'corporate', to find relevant statements regarding women on boards. This time span provides the most recent results and is sufficiently broad to get a clear view of the Committee's interpretation of the Convention on this topic.

In terms of exisiting scholarship, we note that the EU's efforts to increase the participation of women on company boards has been analyzed extensively,[11] but the position of international human rights law on this topic less so.[12] There is no human right as such to become a company board member (if only!) so perhaps that already explains why there is not much scholarship—nor much activity from human rights bodies on the topic of the underrepresentation of women on company boards, as this chapter will show later. Perhaps many in the human rights community also do not consider the issue grave enough. Unlike, say, violence against women, it does not directly affect a large group of women. What is more, the women who stand to gain directly from positive measures to improve gender balance on company boards, are already privileged.

Critical human rights scholars and activists have identified fundamental contradictions between the notion of universal and indivisible human rights on the one hand, and global competitive capitalism on the other hand, which is characterized by

[9]European Parliament, 'Legislative Train Schedule. Area of Justice and Fundamental Rights. Gender Balance on Boards'. https://www.europarl.europa.eu/legislative-train/theme-area-of-justice-and-fundamental-rights/file-gender-balance-on-boards.

[10]Roux (2014), p. 178.

[11]Elomäki (2018), pp. 53–68; European network of legal experts in gender equality and non-discrimination (2018); Havelková (2019), pp. 187–216; Szydlo (2015), pp. 97–115; Senden (2016).

[12]See Tobler (2007); Meyersfeld (2013), p. 208; Raday (2019), pp. 45–60.

the commodification of human life.[13] At the same time, however, scholars also warn that human rights have been co-opted by neoliberal politicians.[14] Against this background, we agree with Grosser that the economic and political power of corporations 'means that the ways in which they do or do not address gender equality have become increasingly important with respect to feminist agendas, and increasingly worthy of investigation'.[15]

Before proceeding further, two caveats are in order. The first concerns the terminology. Various terms have been used to refer to greater female participation on company boards, including 'equal participation', 'gender balance', 'gender diversity' and 'parity'.[16] While these terms signal differences in content, in this chapter we use these terms interchangeably, as international human rights law documents also do not consistently prefer one term over the other. We seek to capture all forms of positive measures to promote the participation of women on company boards. The second caveat concerns the gender binary (male/female). As far as the authors are aware, most existing national and international instruments that seek to enhance women's participation on company boards do not explicitly challenge the gender binary, California being an exception.[17] These instruments are based on an essentialization, namely that there are only two sexes; male and female.[18] This paper will not further explore in depth whether that is problematic in the context of company boards,[19] except to say that transwomen—and minority women more generally—are grossly underrepresented in company boards.[20] Whether transwomen can benefit from measures proactively seeking to increase the number of women on company boards could depend on the national legal context regarding gender recognition. Under international human rights law transwomen are included in the category of 'women', which means that this should be so according to the international standard.

In what follows, in order to set the scene we first outline various considerations that have been invoked to take action on the low number of women on boards (Sect. 2). Second, we turn to the question to what extent CEDAW entails an obligation for

---

[13] See Catalan (2021) and Moyn (2018).

[14] See Whyte (2019).

[15] Grosser (2021), pp. 1626–1627.

[16] See also Lépinard and Rubio-Marín (2018b), p. 1; Rubio-Marín (2018), p. 74.

[17] An exception is Californian Law AB 979 of 2020, which stipulates that 'California-headquartered public companies have at least one director on their boards who is from an underrepresented community, defined as "an individual who self-identifies as Black, African American, Hispanic, Latino, Asian, Pacific Islander, Native American, Native Hawaiian, or Alaska Native, or who self-identifies as gay, lesbian, bisexual, or transgender."' See Bell et al. (2020).

[18] See also Rosenblum (2008), p. 2886.

[19] Legal instruments that are based on the gender binary tend to exclude people who do not identify as either male or female, and therefore tend to be problematic. On the other hand, it is hard to completely avoid essentialism in the quest for social transformation. See Carbado and Harris (2019).

[20] See e.g. Haridasani Gupta (2021).

states to ensure women's participation on company boards. As mentioned above, we use the CEDAW Committee's tripartite conception of equality to analyse these obligations. We include the UN Guiding Principles on Business and Human Rights (UNGPS) in our discussion (Sect. 3). Third, we briefly analyze the responsibilities of companies under human rights law to increase the number of women on company boards (Sect. 4), and then we conclude (Sect. 5).

2 Justifying More Participation of Women on Boards: Equality and the Business Case

In order to set the scene for the human rights law analysis, we will first outline the different considerations that have led to taking action on the issue of women's underrepresentation on corporate boards. The use of gender quota's and other measures to increase women's participation in decision-making has a longer history in the realm of politics than in the realm of economic governance.[21] The movement to include gender quotas or other measures to promote the presence of women on company boards to some extent grew out of efforts to enhance women's participation in political life, but is also distinct from it. Comparative research by Lépinard and Rubio-Marín has shown that 'the adoption of corporate board quotas... rarely spark[s] mobilization from the traditional actors in the women's movement. Nor is the cause often framed as a matter of equality or equal rights. Rather, [company board quotas] have often been encouraged by businesswomen... often in the name of women's specific abilities in governance (i.e. risk averse attitudes) or in the name of diversity (the business case for diversity).'[22]

The business case is founded on the belief that gender diversity on company boards ultimately improves profitability and increases shareholder value as it enhances productivity and innovation.[23] Significant research has found a positive link between women on boards and corporate financial performance, although the evidence is not conclusive.[24] Put bluntly, 'there is money at stake' for gender diversity in boardrooms.[25] This corresponds to a broader perspective on gender equality; that greater gender equality enhances societal economic prosperity and improves (sustainable) development outcomes.[26] Argued the other way around, 'misallocating women's skills and talent comes at a large (and rising) economic

[21] See also Lépinard and Rubio-Marín (2018b), p. 6. For more of the history see Krook (2009).

[22] See also Lépinard and Rubio-Marín (2018a), p. 447.

[23] See Gómez Ansón (2012), p. 25; Seierstad et al. (2017), p. 31; Binder et al. (2019), pp. 290–291; Morehead Dworkin and Schipani (2018), p. 105.

[24] See for an overview of research that is done e.g. Galbreath (2018), pp. 853–864.

[25] Hirsch (2021).

[26] See World Bank (2011); UN General Assembly (2015), para. 20.

cost'.[27] The business case for women on company boards has therefore frequently had the upper hand, for example in the initial reasoning behind the EU's draft directive on gender balanced company boards.[28] The business case is not necessarily formulated in terms of purely financial goals, however. The current EU Gender Equality Strategy 2020–2025, for example, stresses quality of decision-making and innovation: 'Having both women and men represented is crucial for successful leadership. Inclusive and diverse leadership is needed to solve the complex challenges that decision-makers face today. More inclusion and more diversity is essential to bring forward new ideas and innovative approaches that better serve a dynamic and flourishing EU society.'[29]

Not surprisingly, the business case for gender diversity on corporate boards is also popular in the private sector itself. The topic is sometimes part of companies' voluntarily adopted Corporate Social Responsibility (CSR) policy. These CSR-policies rely strongly on business case arguments.[30] Having a CSR-policy in place as enterprise, however, is not equivalent to respecting human rights.[31] This is also true for gender equality initiatives, including those related to corporate leadership. To begin with, having a policy in place on paper does not guarantee that human rights are protected in practice (otherwise human rights would be reduced to a tick-the-box exercise). The notions of CSR and of business respecting human rights (BHR) overlap to some extent as both strive towards socially beneficial action by business beyond merely profit-maximization and increasing wealth,[32] but the fundamental difference is that 'rather than a privatization of human rights, a BHR perspective demands a politicization of corporate responsibility.'[33]

Several scholars have argued that building upon the business case argument, without involving a normative rationale, may ultimately undermine equality outcomes.[34] An example of a corporate leadership initiative that has been criticized for its sole reliance on the business case argument, is the UN initiative entitled 'Women's Empowerment Principles' (WEPs).[35] The WEPs provide guidance to companies, amongst others, on the underrepresentation of women in business leadership roles.[36] Subtitled 'Equality means Business', the WEPs

[27] World Bank (2011), p. 3.

[28] Szydlo (2015), pp. 97–115.

[29] European Commission (2020), p. 13.

[30] Wettstein (2020), p. 23.

[31] Wettstein (2020), p. 23.

[32] Wettstein (2020), p. 33.

[33] Wettstein (2020), p. 39. See for the differences between these two notions also e.g. Ramasastry (2015).

[34] See Fisher (2017), p. 393; Ramasastry (2015), p. 237; Roberts (2015), pp. 213–214.

[35] UN Women and the UN Global Compact (2017); See e.g. Ramasastry (2015), p. 237; Roberts (2015), pp. 213–214.

[36] UN Women and the UN Global Compact (2017), principle 1.

emphasize that the business case for promoting gender equality is financially compelling.[37]

In human rights documents addressing the participation of women on company boards different rationales prevail. The low share of women among economic decision-makers was already addressed in the 1995 Declaration and Platform for Action that were adopted at the UN Beijing Fourth World Conference of Women. Stakeholders were convinced that '[w]omen's empowerment and their full participation on the basis of equality in all spheres of society, including participation in the decision-making process and access to power, are fundamental for the achievement of equality, development and peace'.[38] As such, they agreed that the low proportion of women among economic decision-makers reflects 'structural and attitudinal barriers that *need* to be addressed through positive measures'.[39] Affirmative action was seen as necessary cure to these barriers.[40] The Platform for Action proposed such affirmative measures to governments and the private sector, for instance to recruit more women in strategic decision-making positions and to create or strengthen mechanisms to monitor the access of women to such positions.[41] In line with this, the Committee overseeing the International Covenant on Economic, Social and Cultural Rights (the CESCR Committee), urged States Parties to 'take appropriate steps, including through temporary special measures, to improve women's representation in the labour market, including at the upper echelons of the corporate hierarchy',[42] in General Recommendation No. 24 from 2017.

In practice, initiatives to improve the participation of women on company boards often rely on a mix of normative justifications, combining some version of the business-case with more principled equality-based considerations.[43]

3 State Obligations Under CEDAW to Ensure Women's Participation on Boards in Terms of Formal, Substantive and Transformative Equality

We now turn to the question to what extent CEDAW entails an obligation for states to ensure women's participation on company boards. In order to answer that question, we draw on the CEDAW Committee's multi-dimensional conception of

[37] UN Women and the UN Global Compact (2017), principle 1.

[38] UN (1995), para 13. Reminders of the low number of women in decision-making positions in the private sector are explicit in later documents see e.g. UN Women (2007), p. 6; UN Women (2015), p. 30.

[39] UN (1995), paras. 186, 162. (Emphasis added).

[40] Rubio-Marín (2018), p. 75.

[41] UN (1995), para. 192(a)(b), see also para. 177(b).

[42] CESCR (2017), para. 9.

[43] Lépinard and Rubio-Marín (2018b), p. 12.

equality, which informs all state obligations enumerated in the Convention.[44] The CEDAW Committee formulated three main obligations of Member States under the Convention in General Recommendation No. 25.[45] These obligations correspond to three conceptions of equality. The first is to 'ensure that there is no direct or indirect discrimination against women in their laws and that women are protected against discrimination',[46] reflecting formal equality.[47] The second obligation is to 'improve the de facto position of women through concrete and effective policies and programmes',[48] reflecting substantive equality.[49] The third obligation is to 'address prevailing gender relations and the persistence of gender-based stereotypes' that hold on to unequal gender relations 'in law, and legal and societal structures and institutions'.[50] This corresponds to transformative equality.[51] The three obligations are intertwined and each is essential in themselves to come to full gender equality.[52]

3.1 The Formal Equality Argument for Women's Participation on Boards

Formal equality prescribes that men and women receive the same treatment. In the women on boards discussion this argument has been used to point out that it is simply a matter of individual fairness to appoint women to positions of power when they have the requisite qualifications, so as to give women the same opportunities as men.[53] For this to happen, it is a prerequisite that national laws are not discriminatory. In most countries around the world, to a greater or lesser extent, women continue to face formal legal barriers in the economic sphere that do not exist for men.[54] Examples would include certain professions that are by law male-only,[55]

[44]Cusack and Pusay (2013), pp. 54, 57.

[45]CEDAW Committee (2004), paras. 6–7.

[46]CEDAW Committee (2004), para. 7.

[47]Cusack and Pusay (2013), p. 63; CEDAW Committee (2004), para. 4.

[48]CEDAW Committee (2004), para. 7.

[49]Cusack and Pusay (2013), p. 63; CEDAW Committee (2004), para. 4.

[50]CEDAW Committee (2004), para. 7.

[51]Cusack and Pusay (2013), p. 63; CEDAW Committee (2004), para. 4.

[52]CEDAW Committee (2004), para 6. The three goals are to be 'implemented in an integrated fashion [. . .]'.

[53]Senden (2014), p. 59.

[54]Raday (2019), p. 51.

[55]See e.g. CEDAW Committee (2016i), Communication No. 60/2013 (*Medvedeva v. Russia*). This case concerned the rejection of a woman's application to become helmsperson-motorist on a boat owned by a private company because of a Labour Code provision.

restrictions on women owning land, and restrictions on married women registering a business.[56]

Furthermore, formal equality is also at the basis of the state's obligation to excercise due diligence in making sure that companies do not discriminate on the basis of sex. The applicable provisions in this respect are Article 2(e) (due diligence) and Article 11 (equality in employment).[57] The due diligence obligation results from the state's responsibility to protect, and it requires states to 'react actively' so enterprises do not discriminate against women.[58] This obligation to protect women from discrimination by corporations extends to all substantive provisions in CEDAW and thus also to the field of employment that is enshrined in Article 11.[59] The state is obliged to protect women's right to receive equal pay (Article 11 (d) CEDAW), and women's right to have the same employment opportunities as men including promotion (Article 11(b) and (c)). In order to fulfil Article 2 (e) together with Article 11, the state is likely to intervene into the affairs of enterprises including in employment policy.[60]

While formal equality is crucial as a first step in the elimination of all discrimination against women, only pursuing this approach has marked limitations and is not sufficient to live up to CEDAW's goal.[61] The formal equality approach namely requires comparison and takes male-oriented social structures as the norm to which women must conform to. The underlying causes of inequality are not challenged. Rather, formal equality bolsters existing masculine structures and values, since women can only ask for those entitlements to the extent that men already enjoy them.[62]

3.2 *The Substantive Equality Argument for Women's Participation on Boards*

3.2.1 The CEDAW's Approach

For substantive equality to be attained, biological, social and cultural differences and inequalities between men and women must be taken into account, which sometimes

---

[56] Raday (2019), p. 51.

[57] Christa Tobler has argued that the adoption of gender representation rules for company boards falls under Article 2 CEDAW. Tobler (2007), pp. 854–855.

[58] Article 2(e) CEDAW; CEDAW Committee (2010), paras. 9, 10, 17.

[59] Article 11 CEDAW; CEDAW Committee (2010), paras. 13, 36; CEDAW Committee (2017h), para. 24 under b; Byrnes (2012b), p. 86.

[60] Meyersfeld (2013), p. 208; Raday (2012), p. 284.

[61] CEDAW Committee (2004), paras 8–11. In para 8 the Committee states: "In the Committee's view, a purely formal legal or programmatic approach is not sufficient to achieve women's de facto equality with men [...]".

[62] Fredman (2013), pp. 223–224; Byrnes (2012a), p. 55; CEDAW Committee (2004), paras. 8–11.

requires non-identical treatment.[63] Unlike formal equality, substantive equality is an asymetric concept; focusing on the disadvantaged group. In the CEDAW Convention, Article 3 and 4 in particular enshrine this notion of equality. Article 3 imposes a general positive duty upon States Parties to ensure the full development and advancement of women, so that they enjoy their rights equally with men.[64] Article 4(1) elaborates upon this. This article obliges States Parties to adopt where necessary *mandatory* temporary special measures to reach substantive equality.[65] In General Recommendation No. 25, which sets out the CEDAW Committee's understanding of Article 4(1) in depth, the Committee explained that substantive equality entailed both 'overcoming underrepresentation of women and a redistribution of resources and power between men and women'.[66] The Committee advises states to adopt temporary special measures whenever equal participation of women could be accelated and/or when the redistribution of power and resources could be accelerated.[67] States then 'do not have the choice to remain inactive',[68] but the Committee does not dictate what forms temporary special measures should take precisely. The Committee recognizes that such measures can come in different forms, including quotas.[69]

The CEDAW Committee has repeatedly addressed the underrepresentation of women in company boards in its Concluding Observations. The Committee is concerned about the low number of women in the private sector, by referring to women in 'managerial positions',[70] 'management positions',[71] 'leadership positions',[72] 'corporate boards',[73] 'executive positions',[74] 'decision-making

[63] CEDAW Committee (2004), para. 8.

[64] Article 3 CEDAW.

[65] CEDAW Committee (2010), para. 9; CEDAW Committee (2004), paras. 15, 18. According to the Committee Temporary special measures have a tripartite purpose. They should be invoked to (1) accelerate the improvement of the position of women to achieve substantive equality between men and women, (2) to effect the changes necessary to correct current and past (effects of) discrimination against women and to (3) provide women with compensation.

[66] CEDAW Committee (2004), para. 8.

[67] CEDAW Committee (2004), para. 39.

[68] Holtmaat (2003), p. 226.

[69] CEDAW Committee (2004), para 22.

[70] CEDAW Committee (2020b), para. 20; CEDAW Committee, 'CEDAW Committee (2017f), para. 32; CEDAW Committee (2017b), para 35; CEDAW Committee (2017a), para 22; CEDAW Committee (2016e), paras 36–37; CEDAW Committee (2016j), para 26; CEDAW Committee (2015d), paras. 28, 29; CEDAW Committee (2016a), para. 39.

[71] CEDAW Committee (2016c), para 24; CEDAW Committee (2016d), paras. 28–29; CEDAW Committee, 'Concluding observations on the combined eighth and ninth periodic reports of Sweden' (2018), 22; CEDAW Committee (2015b), paras. 23, 24; CEDAW Committee (2020c), paras. 37–38; CEDAW Committee (2017c), paras. 28–29.

[72] CEDAW Committee (2020a), paras. 28, 41, 42; CEDAW Committee (2017a), para 22.

[73] CEDAW Committee (2017d), paras 28–29; CEDAW Committee (2019), paras. 21, 22, 43.

[74] CEDAW Committee (2019), paras. 21, 22, 43; CEDAW Committee (2017e), paras. 20–21. For Norway, the Committee refers to 'executive board members'.

positions'[75] and in particular in 'private-sector boards',[76] 'the boards of private companies',[77] '[the] supervisory board',[78] '[the] boards of directors'[79] and on 'management boards'.[80] In those Concluding Observations, the Committee proposes to enforce compliance with gender quotas,[81] which can mean imposing sanctions,[82] introducing fast-track selection processes for women,[83] creating part-time positions in high company ranks[84] or flexitime arrangements[85] and, lastly, promoting women's participation within business through training on leadership skills.[86] The Committee presents most of these remarks under either a subheading titled 'temporary special measures'[87] (Article 4) or 'employment'[88] (Article 11), with few exceptions.[89]

[75]CEDAW Committee (2018a), paras. 41–42; CEDAW Committee (2018b), paras. 22, 42–43; CEDAW Committee, 'Concluding observations on the combined third to fifth periodic reports of Malaysia' (2018), paras. 37–38; CEDAW Committee (2016j), para 26; CEDAW Committee (2015a), paras. 28–29; CEDAW Committee (2015d), paras. 28, 29.

[76]CEDAW Committee (2018c), para 22.

[77]CEDAW Committee (2020c), paras. 37–38; CEDAW Committee (2017c), paras. 28–29; CEDAW Committee (2015c), paras. 28–29: instead of 'companies', 'enterprises'; CEDAW Committee (2017g), paras. 24–25.

[78]CEDAW Committee (2015a), paras. 28–29; CEDAW Committee (2015b), paras. 23, 24; CEDAW Committee (2020c), paras. 37–38; CEDAW Committee (2017c), paras. 28–29.

[79]CEDAW Committee (2015d), paras. 28, 29; CEDAW Committee (2016f), paras. 28–29; CEDAW Committee (2018b), paras. 22, 42–43.

[80]CEDAW Committee (2015e), paras. 15–16; CEDAW Committee (2016g), para. 33.

[81]CEDAW Committee (2016b), paras. 29–30; CEDAW Committee (2016a), para. 39; CEDAW Committee (2015c), paras. 28–29; CEDAW Committee (2017c), paras. 28–29; CEDAW Committee (2018c), para 22; See the following Concluding Observations on strict compliance with quotas: CEDAW Committee (2020c), paras. 37–38; CEDAW Committee (2020a), paras. 28, 41, 42; CEDAW Committee (2015d), paras. 28, 29. The Committee critiques Spanish policy because the existing legislation did not include sanctions for the non-enforcement of the required gender balance on the boards of directors of large companies.

[82]CEDAW Committee (2020b), para 20 CEDAW Committee (2020a), paras. 28, 41, 42; CEDAW Committee (2017a), para 22; CEDAW Committee (2020c), paras. 37–38.

[83]CEDAW Committee (2020a), paras. 28, 41, 42.

[84]CEDAW Committee (2017b), para 35; CEDAW Committee (2018a), paras. 41–42; CEDAW Committee (2016e), paras. 36–37. The Committee expressed its critique because Switzerland and Luxembourg had regulations that excluded part-time employment for most managerial positions.

[85]CEDAW Committee (2016h), paras. 30–31.

[86]CEDAW Committee (2017g), paras. 24–25.

[87]See e.g. CEDAW Committee (2017e), paras. 20–21; CEDAW Committee (2020a), paras. 28, 41, 42; CEDAW Committee, 'Concluding observations on the combined eighth and ninth periodic reports of Sweden' (2018), 22; CEDAW Committee (2020b), para. 20.

[88]See e.g. CEDAW Committee (2020c), paras. 37–38; CEDAW Committee (2017f), para. 32; CEDAW Committee (2016e), par. 18; CEDAW Committee (2016j), para 26; CEDAW Committee (2016d), paras. 28–29; CEDAW Committee (2016c), para 24. In the Concluding Observations of Armenia, the Committee used the almost similar subheading 'Employment and economic empowerment'.

[89]See e.g. the Concluding Observations of Slovenia, where the Committee placed the discussion under subheading 'participation in political and public life' and not under 'employment'. CEDAW Committee (2015b), para. 24;

These findings confirm that the proper implementation of CEDAW mandates States Parties to tackle the underrepresentation of women in top corporate positions, in order to achieve substantive equality. This requirement stems from Article 11 CEDAW read in conjunction with Article 4(1). While there is considerable discretion for the state to choose and give substance to the measure that they see fit for purpose, a failure to adopt any special measure without adequate justification can trigger state accountability. The Committee anticipates that some states prefer to be inactive: 'States parties should provide adequate explanations with regard to any failure to adopt temporary special measures. Such failures may not be justified simply by averring powerlessness, or by explaining inaction through predominant market or political forces, such as those inherent in the private sector'.[90] While this is a general statement of the Committee, covering all sorts of different areas, it seems a particularly apt critique of states' failure to accelerate the participation of women on company boards. The statement is also noteworthy for the Committee's insistence that the State cannot allow market forces to dictate the pace towards gender equality.

The Committee does not, however, set a specific numerical goal for the participation of women that positive action measures should strive to reach in each State Party.[91] Even so, it recommended to New Zealand in 2018 'to establish a set goal for achieving gender parity on private-sector boards.'[92] In General Recommendation No. 25 the Committee also hints that parity (50/50) is the desired outcome, which would chime with the Committee's emphasis on equality of result, rather than only equality of opportunity, which accords more with formal equality.[93] In General Recommendation No. 25 the Committee namely states: 'Equality of results is the logical corollary of de facto or substantive equality. These results may be quantitative and/or qualitative in nature; that is, women enjoying their rights in various fields in fairly equal numbers with men, enjoying the same income levels, equality in decision-making and political influence'.[94]

3.2.2 The UN Guiding Principles on Business and Human Rights

Next to CEDAW, soft law instruments on business and human rights addressing the issue of women on company boards are to a large extent also based on the substantive equality argument. The main relevant instrument is the UN Guiding Principles on Business and Human Rights (UNGPs), dating from 2011, which clarifies the obligations of states under international human rights law and the responsibilities of

[90] CEDAW Committee (2004), para 29.

[91] See also Rubio-Marín (2018), p. 80.

[92] CEDAW Committee (2018c), para 22.

[93] The distinction between equality of result and equality of opportunities is explained well in Fredman (2011), pp. 14–19.

[94] CEDAW Committee (2004), para 9.

companies regarding human rights.[95] This framework is all-encompassing: it applies to all states and all companies.[96]

The three pillars of the UNGPs—Protect, Respect, Remedy—reflect differing social roles in regulating corporate conduct.[97] The Protect pillar prescribes that the state must protect against human rights abuses by third parties.[98] The Respect pillar, which is further analysed below in Sect. 4, prescribes that each company has a responsibility to respect human rights.[99] The Remedy pillar prescribes that the state must provide for access to appropriate and effective remedies for business-related rights abuses.[100] The supplementary Gender Lens report to the UNGPs, dating from 2019, provides specific guidance and illustrations on how to integrate a gender perspective in the implementation of all principles.[101] The report builds on existing gender equality standards, involving inter alia CEDAW and the Beijing Declaration and Platform for Action.[102] The report aims for substantive equality and includes a three-step gender framework—gender responsive assessment, gender transformative measures and gender transformative remedies.[103]

The Protect Pillar elaborates on existing binding obligations to protect against abuses of enterprises and mirrors the state's due diligence obligations, such as Article 2(e) CEDAW.[104] States have to explain to business enterprises what is expected from them to respect human rights by giving concrete and specific guidance, such as to indicate expected outcomes and share best practices.[105] The underlying thought is that the state ought to take the lead in providing incentives and disincentives to induce businesses to respect human rights and remediate to adverse impact.[106] It is thus up to the state to indicate in detail how companies ought to respect women's rights and how they can contribute to achieving substantive

[95] HRC (2011) From now on this chapter will refer to the following more user-friendly report containing the principles: HR/PUB/11/04 (UNGPs).

[96] Deva (2017), pp. 62, 69.

[97] Ruggie (2020), p. 74.

[98] UNGPs, principles 1-12. The Guiding Principles are grounded in the state's tripartite responsibility to respect, protect and fulfil human rights.

[99] UNGPs. See for companies the foundational principles and principle 14. See for the corporate responsibility to respect principles 11-24. See also: OHCHR (2012).

[100] UNGPs principles 25–31.

[101] HRC (2019). See also the booklet that produces the Annex, which is the Gender Guidence for the Guiding Principles on Business and Human Rights, in a user-friendly manner: UNDP and UN Working Group on Business and Human Rights (2019); Kristiansson and Götzmann (2020), pp. 1, 38–39; Simons and Handl (2019), pp. 113, 149.

[102] HRC (2019), paras. 7, 22–35.

[103] Deva (2020), p. 20; HRC (2019), 'Introduction', 'Objectives' and referred to in different principles such as guiding principle 1(c).

[104] UNGPs, principles 1-12; Ruggie (2020), p. 64.

[105] UNGPs, principle 3(c) and commentary.

[106] Deva (2020), p. 13.

equality.[107] Amongst others, it is proposed by the Gender Lens report that states should 'encourage business enterprises to appoint a certain percentage of women to their boards and report on the gender pay gap throughout their operations'.[108] In light of substantive equality and the work of the Committee, the word choice of 'encourage' in this context surely is disappointing. On a positive note, the UNGPs together with the Gender Lens report again underline the necessary active stance of the state towards tackling the underrepresentation of women on company boards, as part of existing legal obligations.

3.3 The Transformative Equality Argument for Women's Participation on Boards: Changing Power Relations

Whether laws and policies that aim for gender balanced company boards can be considered transformative depends on whether they challenge gendered power relations. The CEDAW Committee recognized the transformative approach when it held that states must take measures 'towards a real transformation of opportunities, institutions and systems so that they are no longer grounded in historically determined male paradigms of power and life patterns.'[109] The Committee emphasises that the position of women in society will not improve if the underlying causes of inequality are not adequately addressed.[110] While measures that are grounded in formal and substantive equality are vital to eliminating all forms of discrimination against women, such efforts will, in the end, be ineffective if prevailing gender relations and gender-based stereotypes continue to exist in society and leave their mark on legal and societal structures and institutions.[111] According to the Committee, inherent to gender equality is that all human beings are free to 'develop their personal abilities, pursue their professional careers and make choices without the limitations set by stereotypes, rigid gender roles and prejudices.'[112]

Transformative equality is underpinned by Article 5 of the Convention, which focuses on modifying gender stereotypes and fixed parental gender roles.[113] States

[107] UNDP and UN Working Group on Business and Human Rights (2019), principle 1 and illustrative action c.

[108] UNDP and UN Working Group on Business and Human Rights (2019), principle 2, illustrative action b.

[109] CEDAW Committee (2004), para. 10. See also Holtmaat (2013), p. 112.

[110] CEDAW Committee (2004), para. 10.

[111] Holtmaat and Tobler (2005), p. 408; CEDAW Committee (2004), para. 7.

[112] CEDAW Committee (2010), para. 22.

[113] Article 5 CEDAW prescribes that States Parties should take all appropriate measures to '(a) To modify the social and cultural patterns of conduct of men and women, with a view to achieving the elimination of prejudices and customary and all other practices which are based on the idea of the inferiority or the superiority of either of the sexes or on stereotyped roles for men and women; (b) To ensure that family education includes a proper understanding of maternity as a social function

have an obligation to modify and transform gender stereotypes of women (and men), eliminate wrongful ones and tackle them in social and institutional structures.[114] Article 5 explicitly refers to the elimination of stereotypes that are 'based on the idea of the inferiority or the superiority of either of the sexes.'[115]

Gender stereotypes impede women's participation in company boards in various ways. To start, they create access barriers for women to enter corporate boards. The CEDAW Committee has recommended in its Concluding Observations to review social obstacles to women's access to decision-making positions in the private sector and to remove them by adopting holistic measures. An example of such a social barrier is the pressure on women to assume responsibilities at home.[116] Intersectional discriminatory stereotypes impede women from minority backgrounds and migrant women in particular to make it into corporate boardrooms and other-decision making positions.[117]

Gender stereotypes continue to disadvantage women once they have been appointed on corporate boards.[118] Women in leadership positions who show toughness are easily disliked, while women who show kindness or caring characteristics are likely viewed as lacking competitiveness.[119] Women in economic leadership positions are thus in a 'Catch-22',[120] where they cannot get it right, especially minority women. Rosenblum writes: 'Women corporate leaders face the dilemma of performing masculinity, just as minorities confront performing whiteness.'[121] What is more, there is the phenomenon of the 'glass wall', which entails that even where women have reached high-level management positions, they often do so in the 'softer' areas such as human resources, public relation and communication, and corporate social responsibility (CSR), where less economic power is wielded.[122]

Research also questions to what extent women, once appointed, have the ability to change corporate culture at the lower tiers of the corporation.[123] Carbado and Gulati, for example, challenged the idea that minority managers will help minority

---

and the recognition of the common responsibility of men and women in the upbringing and development of their children, it being understood that the interest of the children is the primordial consideration in all cases.'

[114] Articles 2(f) and 5 CEDAW; CEDAW gave notice of masculine stereotypes in CEDAW Committee (2017h), paras. 4, 30(i); Biholar (2013), p. 37.

[115] Article 5 CEDAW.

[116] CEDAW Committee, 'Concluding observations on the combined third to fifth periodic reports of Malaysia' (2018), paras. 37–38; CEDAW Committee (2015e), paras. 15–16. For Denmark, the Committee points to stereotypes concerning the traditional roles of men and women in the family and society. CEDAW Committee (2017d), paras 28–29.

[117] Carbado and Gulati (2004), p. 1645; CEDAW Committee (2015e), paras. 15–16.

[118] Boulota (2013), p. 185.

[119] Yarram and Adapa (2021), p. 3. See for more information on the social role theory and feminist ethics, Boulota (2013), p. 185.

[120] See for an early reference to this paradoxal position landmark decision of the US Supreme Court (1989) 490 U.S. 228, 44.

[121] Rosenblum (2008), p. 2888.

[122] Raday (2019), p. 56.

[123] Bertrand et al. (2019), pp. 191–239.

employees to climb upwards.[124] Some other studies, however, have included more optimistic findings.[125] The transformative power of positive measures to enhance women's participation on boards does to an important extent depend on this, because if there is no trickle down effect, than these measures only really benefit women at the top of the pyramid (i.e. empower only already relatively privileged women).

To conclude, it is questionable whether mandatory quotas or other positive measures to enhance the participation of women on company boards contribute to transformative equality. Critics argue that 'mandatory quotas result in tokenism rather than... structural change. They argue that they are not resulting in women achieving power in the boardroom.'[126] Boardroomquotas should be accompanied by other policies enabling women at all levels of the corporation to enjoy work-life balance and to progress in their careers. Moreover, the mere presence of women on boards will not necessarily bring about an improvement for all female employees as long as elements like corporate culture remain heavily founded upon 'the power of definition' of men.[127] Buikema defines the power of definition as 'the power to define who and what counts and who and what does not, what is major and what is a minor cultural or political issue'.[128] Arguably, the entire women on boards discussion presupposes the validity of the current capitalistic system; it seeks to give women a seat at the corporate table, not to get rid of that table and replace it with something else. That fundamental critique is not easy to operationalize—the capitalistic system is not likely to be overthrown anytime soon, although the efforts to create gender equality on company boards do challenge pure free market assumptions.[129] From the perspective of CEDAW's conception of transformative equality it behoves us to remain wary of an uncritical support of boardroom quotas.[130]

4 Company Obligations and Responsibilities: The Corporate Responsibility to Respect

The state-centricity of the international human rights system has hindered the development of binding direct obligations for corporations. Though this model is under pressure,[131] it is still mostly left to the state to protect individuals from harmful

[124] Carbado and Gulati (2004), p. 1645.

[125] See for example Gould et al. (2018), pp. 931–945; Biswas et al. (2021), pp. 659–680; Kirsch and Wrohlich (2020), pp. 44–49.

[126] Raday (2019), p. 55.

[127] Buikema et al. (2017), p. 4.

[128] Buikema et al. (2017), p. 4.

[129] See e.g. Bryson (1992), pp. 265–266.

[130] See in that sense also Elomäki (2018), pp. 53–68.

[131] Negotiations are held for a new internationally legally binding instrument to regulate activities of corporations. While the current draft convention gives attention to integrating a gender perspective

conduct of companies.[132] However, the Respect pillar of the UNGPs framework, introduced under Sect. 3.2.2, clarified that each company has a 'corporate responsibility to respect' human rights.[133] The standard of expected conduct for business is subject to change over time, depending on societal developments.[134] The significance of the company's responsibility to respect regarding the presence of women on boards will be the focal point of this paragraph.

The Gender Lens report to the UNGPs of 2019 acknowledges that 'the standards contained in the [CEDAW] Convention apply to all businesses as part of their responsibility to respect human rights under the Guiding Principles.'[135] Previously this was not so clear. According to the in 2011 released UNGPs, the rights that companies ought to respect at a minimum are enshrined in the International Bill of Human Rights and the ILO's Declaration on Fundamental Principles and the Rights at Work. CEDAW (and other core human rights conventions) were reduced to 'additional standards' to be considered by business enterprises.[136]

The question is whether companies are expected to act upon the underrepresentation of women on boards as part of the responsibility to respect women's rights. The corporate responsibility to respect was traditionally 'squarely'[137] based on a responsibility to do no harm, that may entail positive steps to prevent or mitigate harm.[138] Companies should avoid infringing on the rights of others and address such impacts when they occur.[139] The Gender Lens report transposes this into a responsibility to avoid infringing women's rights and to address adverse rights impacts. Companies must 'contribute to achieving substantive gender equality and avoid exacerbating or reproducing existing discrimination against women'.[140] The UNGPs, in this context, can hardly still be seen as a pure 'do no harm' framework.[141]

Under the corporate responsibility to respect, companies should take the steps that are needed to identify, prevent, mitigate and possibly remediate the human rights impacts—including impacts on their direct employees[142]—of all their business

into company policies, the draft is likely to undergo many changes until a possible adoption. Therefore, the convention is at this moment not so relevant for the discussion held here. See OEIGWG (2021). See for scholarly discussion on direct human rights obligations on the part of companies Latorre (2020) and Bilchitz (2021).

[132] See Lane (2018), pp. 6–9.

[133] UNGPs, introduction ('each company'). UNGPs, principles 14–24.

[134] López (2013), p. 68.

[135] HRC (2019), para. 24 and in Annex guiding principle 12.

[136] UNGPs, principle 12 and commentary; Deva (2017), p. 70.

[137] Wettstein (2013), p. 253.

[138] SRSG (2008), para. 55.

[139] UNGPs, principles 13, 17.

[140] HRC (2019), in Annex principle 11.

[141] See also West (2021).

[142] UNGPs, principles 13, 17; OHCHR (2012), p. 37; Meyersfeld (2013), p. 37; UN Working Group on the issue of human rights and transnational corporations and other business enterprises (2021), p. 15.

activities. This requires a continuous human rights due diligence process by corporations. Meyersfeld has described the corporate responsibility to respect as 'a standard of performance implemented through the process of due diligence.'[143] Companies should integrate a gender perspective in the due diligence process, as also explained by the Gender Lens report.[144] Companies may in that process use 'feedback loops'[145] to learn from previous findings.[146]

Concerning the underrepresentation of women on company boards, a gendered human rights due diligence process would in the first place entail that the company investigates the reasons for this underrepresentation (identify the causes of the problem) and on that basis takes measures that ultimately increases the number of women. A range of measures could be envisaged. The Gender Lens report also encourages companies to ensure 'equal representation' on boards, and mentions affirmative action measures and professional development support.[147]

Companies should also motivate their business partners to do the same.[148] The report explicitly recommends that companies aim for substantive equality as a normative principle, 'although there may also be a business case for doing so'.[149]

Based on the above, we conclude that the UNGPs expect companies to act upon the underrepresentation of women on their boards as part of the responsibility to respect women's rights. For some, this may come as an unexpected stretch of ambition for the corporate responsibility to respect. However, a voluntary adopted preferential policy, for example, is in line with the broader responsibilities of companies and in that sense follows the spirit of not only the UNGPs but also CEDAW.[150]

5 Conclusion

This chapter analyzed to what extent international human rights law mandates the use of positive measures to improve the participation of women on company boards, and what obligations this entails on the state and on companies themselves. Our analysis of the General Recommendations and Concluding Observations of the

[143] Meyersfeld (2013), p. 205.

[144] UNGPs, principle 17; HRC (2019), in Annex principle 17.

[145] The Organisation for Economic Co-operation and Development (OECD) coined the term 'feedback loops': companies must use their lessons learned from assessment, oversight and monitoring and their previously adopted measures. OECD (2018), p. 17.

[146] OHCHR (2012).

[147] HRC (2019), in Annex guiding principle 11, illustrative action (g).

[148] HRC (2019), in Annex guiding principle 11, illustrative action (g).

[149] UNGPs, principle 12, 17; HRC (2019), in Annex principle 12, illustrative action (a).

[150] As said before, the Committee strongly encourages the voluntary adoption of temporary special measures. See CEDAW Committee (2004), para. 32.

CEDAW Committee finds that the proper implementation of CEDAW indeed requires States Parties to tackle the underrepresentation of women in top corporate positions. While there is considerable discretion for the state to choose and give substance to the measure that they see fit for purpose, a failure to adopt any special measure to reduce underrepresentation without adequate justification can trigger state accountability. That means that the obligation under CEDAW is quite minimal, leans towards a due efforts commitment, and that it does not (yet) entail a concrete numerical goal, unlike for example the EU's women on boards proposal. The recommendation of the CEDAW Committee to New Zealand in 2018, to establish a set goal for gender parity on boards, provides an illustration of how States Parties could give substance to the obligation.

In our analysis of CEDAW we specifically focused on what conceptions of equality underly the CEDAW Committee's support of positive measures to create gender-balanced company boards. Our conclusion is that the Committee mainly bases itself on substantive equality in this regard. Arguably, however, transformative equality pulls into a different direction than formal and substantive equality on this issue. More women in boardrooms do not necessarily challenge the prevailing gender order, or have a trickle down effect for women lower on the corporate ladder, as long as work-life balance and corporate culture remains heavily founded upon male power of definition. It is doubtful whether measures to improve the participation of women on company boards alone are transformative.

The last part of the article discussed the responsibilities of companies in relation to the underrepresentation of women in board positions. All companies have a responsibility to avoid impacting on women's rights and to address such impacts when they do occur. We argued that companies should act upon the underrepresentation of women on boards because doing so falls under what is currently expected from companies under the responsibility to respect the UNGPs. However, to say that the expected standard on the issue is clear and convincing for all is simply a bridge too far at this moment.

Both national law and international law is developing fast when it comes both to gender equality and to business and human rights, so we do expect to see a more firm obligation to improve the participation of women in company boards in the future.

References

50/50 Women on Boards (2020). http://www.5050wob.com

Arenas Catalan E (2021) The human right to health; solidarity in the era of healthcare commercialization. Edward Elgar, Cheltenham

Bell D, Belt D, Hitchcock J (2020) New law requires diversity on boards of California-Based Companies. Harvard Law School Forum on Corporate Governance. 10 October, https://corpgov.law.harvard.edu/2020/10/10/new-law-requires-diversity-on-boards-of-california-based-companies/

Bertrand M, Black SE, Jensen S, Lleras-Muney A (2019) Breaking the glass ceiling? The effect of board quotas on female labor market outcomes in Norway. Hum Resour Manag 86:191–239

Biholar RG (2013) Transforming discriminatory sex roles and gender stereotyping. Intersentia, Cambridge

Bilchitz D (2021) Fundamental rights and the legal obligations of business. Cambridge University Press, Cambridge

Binder BCK, Dworkin TM, Nae N, Schipani CA, Averianova I (2019) The plight of women in positions of corporate leadership in the United States, the European Union, and Japan: differing laws and cultures, similar issues. Mich J Gender Law 26:279–340

Biswas PK, Roberts H, Stainback K (2021) Does women's board representation affect non-managerial gender inequality? Human Resour Manag 60:659–680

Boulota I (2013) Hidden connections: the link between board gender diversity and corporate social performance. J Bus Ethics 113:185–197

Bryson V (1992) Feminist political theory, an introduction. Palgrave Macmillan, Hampshire

Buikema R, Plate L, Thiele K (2017) Doing gender in media, art and culture: a comprehensive guide to gender studies. Routledge, Oxfordshire

Byrnes A (2012a) Article 1. In: Freeman MA, Chinkin C, Rudolf B (eds) The UN Convention on the elimination of all forms of discrimination against women: a commentary. Oxford University Press, Oxford

Byrnes A (2012b) Article 2. In: Freeman MA, Chinkin C, Rudolf B (eds) The UN Convention on the elimination of all forms of discrimination against women: a commentary. Oxford University Press, Oxford

Carbado DW, Gulati M (2004) Race to the top of the corporate ladder: what minorities do when they get there. Wash Lee Law Rev 61:1645–1693

Carbado DW, Harris CI (2019) Intersectionality at 30: mapping the margins of anti-essentialism, intersectionality, and dominance theory. Harv Law Rev 132:2193–2293

CEDAW Committee (2004) General Recommendation No. 25, on article 4, paragraph 1, of the Convention of the Elimination of All Forms of Discrimination against Women, on temporary special measures. Adopted at the Thirtieth Session of the Committee on the Elimination of Discrimination against Women

CEDAW Committee (2010) General Recommendation No. 28 on the Core Obligations of States Parties under Article 2 of the Convention on the Elimination of All Forms of Discrimination against Women. CEDAW/C/GC/28. 16 December

CEDAW Committee (2015a) Concluding observations on the combined fifth and sixth periodic reports of Slovakia. CEDAW/C/SVK/CO/5-6. 25 November

CEDAW Committee (2015b) Concluding observations on the combined fifth and sixth periodic reports of Slovenia. CEDAW/C/SVN/CO/5-6. 24 November

CEDAW Committee (2015c) Concluding observations on the combined fourth and fifth periodic reports of Croatia. CEDAW/C/HRV/CO/4-5. 28 July

CEDAW Committee (2015d) Concluding observations on the combined seventh and eighth periodic reports of Spain. CEDAW/C/WSP/CO/7-8. 29 July

CEDAW Committee (2015e) Concluding observations on the eighth periodic report of Denmark. CEDAW/C/DNK/CO/8. 11 March

CEDAW Committee (2016a) Concluding observations on the combined eight and ninth periodic reports of Canada. CEDAW/C/CAN/CO/8-9. 25 November

CEDAW Committee (2016b) Concluding observations on the combined seventh and eighth periodic reports of Iceland. CEDAW/C/ISL/CO/7-8. 10 March

CEDAW Committee (2016c) Concluding observations on the combined fifth and sixth periodic reports of Armenia. CEDAW/C/ARM/CO/5-6. 25 November

CEDAW Committee (2016d) Concluding observations on the combined fifth and sixth periodic reports of Estonia. CEDAW/C/EST/CO/5-6. 18 November

CEDAW Committee (2016e) Concluding observations on the combined fourth and fifth periodic reports of Switzerland. CEDAW/C/CHE/CO/4-5. 25 November

CEDAW Committee (2016f) Concluding observations on the combined seventh and eighth periodic reports of France. CEDAW/C/FRA/CO/7-8. 25 July

CEDAW Committee (2016g) Concluding observations on the eighth periodic report of Belarus. CEDAW/C/BLR/CO/8. 25 November
CEDAW Committee (2016h) Concluding observations on the seventh periodic report of Argentina. CEDAW/C/ARG/CO/7. 25 November
CEDAW Committee (2016i) Communication No. 60/2013 (Medvedeva v. Russia). CEDAWC/63/D/60/2013. 21 March
CEDAW Committee (2016j) Concluding observations on the sixth periodic report of the Czech Republic. CEDAW/C/CZE/CO/6. 14 March
CEDAW Committee (2017a) Concluding observations on the combined second to fourth periodic reports of the Democratic People's Republic of Korea. CEDAW/C/PRK/CO/2-4. 22 November
CEDAW Committee (2017b) Concluding observations on the combined seventh and eight periodic reports of Germany. CEDAW/C/DEU/Co/7-8. 9 March
CEDAW Committee (2017c) Concluding observations on the combined seventh and eight periodic reports of Romania. CEDAW/C/ROU/CO/7-8. 24 July
CEDAW Committee (2017d) Concluding observations on the fifth periodic report of Singapore. CEDAW/C/SGP/CO/5. 21 November
CEDAW Committee (2017e) Concluding observations on the ninth periodic report of Norway. CEDAW/C/NOR/CO/9. 22 November
CEDAW Committee (2017f) Concluding observations on the second periodic report of Montenegro. CEDAW/C/MNE/CO/2. 24 July
CEDAW Committee (2017g) Concluding observations on the seventh periodic report of Costa Rica. CEDAW/C/CRI/CO/7. 24 July
CEDAW Committee (2017h) General Recommendation No. 35 on gender-based violence against women, updating general recommendation No. 19. CEDAW/C/GC/35. 14 July
CEDAW Committee (2018a) Concluding observations on the combined sixth and seventh periodic reports of Luxembourg. CEDAW/C/LUX/CO/6-7. 14 March
CEDAW Committee (2018b) Concluding observations on the eight periodic report of Cyprus. CEDAW/C/CYP/CO/8. 25 July
CEDAW Committee (2018c) Concluding observations on the eighth periodic report of New Zealand. CEDAW/C/NZL/CO/8. 25 July
CEDAW Committee (2019) Concluding observations on the eight periodic report of the United Kingdom of Great Britain and Northern Ireland. CEDW/C/GBR/CO/8. 14 March
CEDAW Committee (2020a) Concluding observations on the fifth periodic report of Pakistan. CEDAW/C/PAK/CO/5. 10 March
CEDAW Committee (2020b) Concluding Observations on the sixth periodic report of Eritrea. CEDAW/C/ERI/CO/6. 10 March
CEDAW Committee (2020c) Concluding observations on the sixth periodic report of Zimbabwe. CEDAW/C/ZWE/CO/6. 10 March
CESCR (2017) General Comment No. 24 on State obligations under the International Covenant on Economic, Social and Cultural Rights in the context of business activities. E/C.12/GC/24. 10 August
Cusack S, Pusay L (2013) CEDAW and the rights to non-discrimination and equality. Melb J Int Law 14:54–92
Deva S (2017) Business and human rights: time to move beyond the 'Present'? In: Rodriguez-Garavito C (ed) Business and human rights: beyond the end of the beginning. Cambridge University Press, Cambridge
Deva S (2020) From 'business or human rights' to 'business and human rights': what next?'. In: Deva S, Birchall D (eds) Research handbook on Human Rights and Business. Edward Elgar, Cheltenham
Elomäki A (2018) Gender quotas for corporate boards: depoliticizing gender and the economy. Nordic J Feminist Gender Res 26:53–68
European Commission (2012) Proposal for a Directive of the European Parliament and of the Council on improving the gender balance among non-executive directors of companies listed on

stock exchanges and related measures. COM/2012/0614 final - 2012/0299 (COD). 14 November. https://eur-lex.europa.eu/legal-content/EN/TXT/?uri=celex%3A52012PC0614
European Commission (2020) A Union of Equality: Gender Equality Strategy 2020–2025. 5 March. Brussels. https://ec.europa.eu/commission/presscorner/detail/en/IP_20_358
European network of legal experts in gender equality and non-discrimination (2018) Gender-balanced company boards in Europe. European Commission. https://www.equalitylaw.eu/downloads/4537-gender-balanced-company-boards-in-europe-pdf-1-68-mb
European Parliament. Legislative Train Schedule. Area of Justice and Fundamental Rights. Gender Balance on Boards. https://www.europarl.europa.eu/legislative-train/theme-area-of-justice-and-fundamental-rights/file-gender-balance-on-boards.
EWOB (2020) European Women on Boards Gender Diversity Index 2020. https://europeanwomenonboards.eu/portfolio/gender-diversity-index-2020/
EWOB (2022). https://europeanwomenonboards.eu/portfolio/gender-diversity-index-2021/
Fisher V (2017) Overcoming challenges to gender equality in the workplace. Leadership and innovation. Int J Manag Education 15:393–394
Fredman S (2011) Discrimination law. Oxford University Press, Oxford
Fredman S (2013) Engendered socio-economic rights. In: Hellum A, Aasen HS (eds) Women's Human Rights. Cambridge University Press, Cambridge
Galbreath J (2018) Is board gender diversity linked to financial performance? The mediating mechanism of CSR. J Bus Ethics 57:853–864
Gómez Ansón, Silvia. 2012. Women on boards in Europe: past, present and future. In Women on corporate boards and in top management: Europe trends and policy, eds. Colette Fagan, Maria C. González Menéndez, Silvia Gómez Ansón. London: Palgrave Macmillan.
Gould JA, Kulik CT, Sardeshmukh SR (2018) Trickle-down effect: the impact of female board members on executive gender diversity. Hum Resour Manag 57:931–945
Grosser K (2021) Gender, business and human rights: academic activism as critical engagement in neoliberal times. Gender Work Organ 28:1624–1637
Haridasani Gupta A (2021) Surprise: women and minorities are still underrepresented in corporate boardrooms. The New York Times, June 7
Havelková B (2019) Women on company boards: equality meets subsidiarity. Camb Yearb Eur Legal Stud 21:187–216
Hirsch L (2021) The business case for boardroom diversity: when big banks see a benefit in helping companies recruit more diverse directors, it's a sign that there are not just morals at play — there is money at stake, too. The New York Times, January 23
Holtmaat R (2003) Building blocks for a general recommendation on Article 4(1) of the CEDAW Convention. In: Boerefijn I, Coomans F, Goldschmidt J, Holtmaat R, Wolleswinkel R (eds) Temporary special measures; accelerating de facto equality of women under Article 4(1) UN Convention on the Elimination of All Forms of Discrimination Against Women. Intersentia, Cambridge
Holtmaat R (2013) The CEDAW: a holistic approach to women's equality and freedom. In: Hellum A, Aasen HS (eds) Women's Human Rights. Cambridge University Press, Cambridge
Holtmaat R, Tobler C (2005) CEDAW and the European Union's Policy in the field of combating gender discrimination. Maa J Eur Comp Law 12:399–425
HRC (2011) Guiding principles on business and human rights: implementing the United Nations "Protect, Respect and Remedy" Framework. A/HRC/17/310 1 and HR/PUB/11/04. 21 March
HRC (2019) Gender Dimension of the Guiding Principles on Business and Human Rights: Report of the Working Group on the issue of human rights and transnational corporations and other business enterprises. A/HRC/41/43. 23 May
Kirsch A, Wrohlich K (2020) More women on supervisory boards: increasing indications that the effect of the gender quota extends to the executive boards. DIW Weekly Report 4–5:44–49
Kristiansson L, Götzmann N (2020) National implementation processes for the United Nations Guiding Principles on Business and Human Rights: towards gender-responsive approaches. Aust J Human Rights 26:93–109

Krook ML (2009) Quotas for women in politics: gender and candidate selection reform worldwide. Oxford University Press, Oxford

Lane L (2018) The horizontal effect of International Human Rights Law in practice: a comparative analysis of the general comments and jurisprudence selected United Nations Human Rights treaty monitoring bodies. Eur J Comp Law Governance 5:5–88

Latorre AFL (2020) In defence of direct obligations for businesses under International Human Rights Law. Bus Human Rights J 5:56–83

Legislative Train Schedule: Area of Justice and Fundamental Rights. https://www.europarl.europa.eu/legislative-train/theme-area-of-justice-and-fundamental-rights/file-gender-balance-on-boards

Lépinard É, Rubio-Marín R (2018a) Conclusion. In: Lépinard É, Rubio-Marín R (eds) Transforming gender citizenship: the irresistible rise of gender quotas in Europe. Cambridge University Press, Cambridge

Lépinard É, Rubio-Marín R (2018b) Introduction. In: Lépinard É, Rubio-Marín R (eds) Transforming gender citizenship: the irresistible rise of gender quotas in Europe. Cambridge University Press, Cambridge

López C (2013) The 'Ruggie process': from legal obligations to corporate social responsibility? In: Deva S (ed) Human Rights obligations: beyond the corporate responsibilty to respect? Cambridge University Press, Cambridge

Machold, Silke, Morten Huse, Katrin Hansen and Marina Brogi. 2013. Getting women on to corporate boards: a snowball starting in Norway. 2013. Cheltenham: Edward Elgar.

Meyersfeld B (2013) Business, human rights and gender: a legal approach to external and internal considerations. In: Deva S (ed) Human Rights Obligations of business: beyond the corporate responsibility to respect? Cambridge University Press, Cambridge

Morehead Dworkin T, Shipani CA (2018) The role of gender diversity in corporate Governance. Univ Pa J Bus Law 21:105–141

Moyn S (2018) Not enough: human rights in an unequal world. Harvard University Press, Cambridge

OECD (2018) OECD due diligence guidance for responsible conduct. https://www.oecd.org/investment/due-diligence-guidance-for-responsible-business-conduct.htm

OECD (2020) What big data can tell us about women on boards. March. https://www.oecd.org/gender/data/what-big-data-can-tell-us-about-women-on-boards.htm

OEIGWG (2021) Chairmanship Third Revised Draft: Legally Binding Instrument to Regulate, in International Human Rights Law, the Activities of Transnational Corporations and Other Business Enterprises. 17 August. https://www.ohchr.org/sites/default/files/Documents/HRBodies/HRCouncil/WGTransCorp/Session6/LBI3rdDRAFT.pdf

OHCHR (2012) The corporate responsibility to respect Human Rights: An Interpretive Guide. HR/PUB/12/02. https://www.ohchr.org/sites/default/files/Documents/Publications/HR.PUB.12.2_En.pdf

Oppenheimer D (2019) The ubiquity of positive measures for addressing systemic discrimination and inequality: a comparative global perspective. Brill, Leiden

Raday F (2012) Article 11. In: Freeman MA, Chinkin C, Rudolf B (eds) The UN Convention on the elimination of all forms of discrimination against women: a commentary. Oxford University Press, Oxford

Raday F (2019) Economic woman: gender economic inequality in the age of capital. Routledge, London

Ramasastry A (2015) Corporate social responsibility versus business and human rights: bridging the gap between responsibility and accountability. J Human Rights 14:237–259

Roberts A (2015) The political economy of 'Transnational Business Feminism': problematizing the corporate-led gender equality agenda. Int Feminist J Politics 17:209–231

Rosenblum D (2008) Loving gender balance: reframing identity-based inequality remedies. Fordham Law Rev 76:2873–2893

Roux T (2014) Judging the quality of legal research: a qualified response for the demand for greater methodological rigour. Legal Educational Rev 24:173–200
Rubio-Marín R (2018) Women's participation in the public domain under human rights law: towards a participatory equality paradigm shift. In: Rubio-Marín R, Kymlicka W (eds) Gender parity and multicultural feminism: towards a new synthesis. Oxford University Press, Oxford
Ruggie JG (2020) The social construction of the UN Guiding principles on Business and Human Rights. In: Deva S, Birchall D (eds) Research handbook on Human Rights and Business. Edward Elgar Publishing, Cheltenham
Seierstad C, Gabaldon P, Mensi-Klarbach H (2017) Gender diversity in the boardroom volume 1: the use of different quota regulations. Palgrave Macmillan, London
Senden L (2014) The multiplicity of regulatory responses to remedy the gender imbalance on company boards. Utrecht Law Rev 10:51–66
Senden L (2016) Getting women on company boards in the EU: a tale of power-balancing in three acts. In: Bodiroga-Vukobrat N, Rodin S, Gerald SG (eds) New Europe - old values? Springer International, Cham
Simons P, Handl M (2019) Relations of ruling: a feminist critique of the United Nations guiding principles on Business and Human Rights and Violence against women in the context of resource extraction. Can J Women Law 31:113–150
SRSG (2008) Protect, respect and remedy: a framework for Business and Human Rights. A/HRC/8/5. 7 April
Szydlo M (2015) Gender equality on boards of EU companies: between economic efficiency, fundamental rights and democratic legitimisation of economic Governance. Eur Law J 21:97–115
Tobler, Christa. 2007. Going global in sex equality law: the case of gender representation rules for company boards. In Economic law and justice in terms of globalisation, eds. Mario Monti, Prinz Nikolaus von und zu Liechtenstein, Bo Vesterdorp, Jay Westbrook, Luzius Wildhaber. Baden-Baden: Nomos.
UN (1995) The Bejing Declaration and Platform for Action adopted by the Fourth World Conference on Women: Action for Equality, Development and Peace. September
UN General Assembly (2015) Transforming our world: the 2030 Agenda for Sustainable Development. A/RES/70/1. 21 October
UN Women (2007) Bejing at Ten and Beyond. Women in power and decision-making. https://www.un.org/womenwatch/daw/beijing/beijingat10/index.html
UN Women (2015) The Bejing declaration and platform for action turns 20. summary report of E/CN.6/2015/3. March. https://sustainabledevelopment.un.org/index.php?page=view&type=400&nr=1776&menu=1515
UN Women and the UN Global Compact (2017) Women's Empowerment Principles (WEPs) Implementation Guide: Equality Means Business. ISBN: 978-1-63214-069-2. https://eca.unwomen.org/en/digital-library/publications/2017/01/weps-implementation-guide
UN Working Group on the issue of human rights and transnational corporations and other business enterprises (2021) Guiding Principles on Business And Human Rights at 10: taking stock of the first decade. A/HRC/7/39. June, https://www.ohchr.org/Documents/Issues/Business/UNGPs10/Stocktaking-reader-friendly.pdf
UNDP and UN Working Group on Business and Human Rights. 2019. Gender dimensions of the guiding principles on business and human rights (Booklet). 22 November. https://www.undp.org/library/gender-dimensions-guiding-principles-business-and-human-rights
US Supreme Court (1989) Price Waterhouse, Petitioner v. Ann B. Hopkins. 490 U.S. 228
West F (2021) The quiet radicalism of the responsibility to respect. Shift. June. http://shiftproject.org/ungps-radicalism/
Wettstein F (2013) Making noise about silent complicity: the moral inconsistency of the protect, respect and remedy framework. In: Deva S (ed) Human Rights obligations: beyond the corporate responsibility to respect? Cambridge Univesity Press, Cambridge

Wettstein F (2020) The history of 'business and human rights' and its relationship with corporate social responsibility. In: Deva S, Birchall D (eds) Research Handbook on Human Rights and Business. Edward Elgar, Cheltenham

Whyte J (2019) The morals of the market: human rights and the rise of neoliberalism. Verso Books, New York

World Bank (2011) World Development Report 2012: gender equality and development. Washington, DC. doi: https://doi.org/10.1596/978-0-8213-8810-5. https://web.worldbank.org/archive/website01250/WEB/IMAGES/COMPLETE.PDF

Yarram SR, Adapa S (2021) Board gender diversity and corporate social responsibility: Is there a case for critical mass? J Cleaner Production 278:1–11

Linde Verhoeven is student of the Legal Research Master at Utrecht University. She specializes in international human rights law. The current chapter is based on research that she conducted under the supervision of dr. mr. Alexandra Timmer as part of the masters' programme. During her studies she, amongst others, interned in human rights law firm Prakken d'Oliveira and in the human rights section of the Dutch Ministry of Justice and Security.

Alexandra Timmer is associate professor of human rights law at the Netherlands Institute of Human Rights (SIM) at Utrecht University. Her research focuses on equality and non-discrimination, in particular in relation to EU law, the ECHR and international human rights treaties. In addition, she is co-coordinator gender equality of the European network of legal experts in gender equality and non-discrimination (www.equalitylaw.eu). In 2017 she was awarded a prestigious Veni grant by the Dutch Scientific Organization for her project on gender justice in European human rights law, which funded her research for this paper (NWO: 451-17-029 4130).

Promoting Gender Equality in International Trade Agreements: Pioneering or Pipe Dream?

Mareike Fröhlich

Contents

Abstract Recently, new deep and comprehensive trade agreements started to deal with gender issues whereas old ones were mainly gender-blind.

In 2021, the first gender-only Global Trade and Gender Arrangement between Canada, Chile and New Zealand was signed, but there are various other agreements which included gender provisions or gender-related provisions. The main actors in this field are Chile, Canada, the EU and its member states as well as others. It will be analysed how and why these countries and the EU took action. This will be put also in a broader context of their international engagement in other international organisations or trade agreements.

M. Fröhlich (✉)
Saarland University, Faculty of Law, Europa-Institut, Saarbrucken, Germany
e-mail: froehlich@europainstitut.de

I. Krstić et al. (eds.), *Legal Issues of International Law from a Gender Perspective*, Gender Perspectives in Law 3, https://doi.org/10.1007/978-3-031-13459-3_9

This contribution will deal with four different aspects: types of agreements and main actors, types of regulations, enforcement of regulations and impact of gender provisions in trade agreements. Gender provisions can be found in different parts of the agreements, starting with general references to gender equality and its importance in the preamble, following the obligation to take gender equality into account while implementing the agreement as well as specific gender-related provisions in special gender chapters. After the explanation of the nexus of trade and gender, the different provisions will be analysed, categorized and compared. Finally, the contribution critically assesses the provisions and gives recommendations for improvement.

1 Introduction

Gender also plays a role in the economic sector and requires closer examination and consideration in this context in order to better understand the impact of gender equity on the welfare of a state and its society. The economic empowerment of women and their representation in company boards has been analyzed extensively in the last decade but until now trade policy was not on the main agenda as a tool for gender promotion. Although there is no general pattern how trade liberalization affects and reduces gender inequalities, the causal link between trade liberalization in form of tariff reductions or other measures and positive effects on gender inequalities which women observe as consumers, workers and producers cannot be ignored. In principle, it can be assumed that countries that are open to trade liberalization also have higher levels of gender equality.[1] Recent developments—like the servicification of the economy, the diversification in global value chains and new digital technologies—lead to increased trading opportunities and allow a higher employability rate of women across the globe.[2]

Open trade does however not only have positive effects on women's empowerment. The determining factor is often whether the industry is male-intensive or female-intensive.[3] For example, fewer women than men work in export-dependent companies or are more often found in the public sector, such as education, health care and administration,[4] and can therefore only benefit to a limited extent from any trade liberalization which has to be taken into account when negotiating a new trade agreement.

Moreover, despite all developments and a higher employment rate than previously, women still face various constraints that are also facilitated by trade policies and measures. Women remain predominantly the main care-taker in families, which

[1] World Bank Group/World Trade Organization (2020), pp. 4, 23, 27.

[2] World Bank Group/World Trade Organization (2020), p.7 et seq

[3] Pieters (2018), p. 6; Fontana (2016), p. 18.

[4] Korinek et al. (2021), p. 11 et seq.; Brodsky et al. (2021), p. 8.

shortens their time for work, further education and networking. Combined with and due to limited education possibilities, they are more often employed in low-to-middle skilled jobs, or even worse, in the informal sector (grey economy) compared to men. Women experience as workers and producers higher trading costs at the border, such as tariffs, non-tariff measures and discrimination since they are employed to a bigger extent than men in sectors which face higher trade barriers. The competitive pressure, especially also in the global value chains, leads to low wages and discriminatory working conditions for women.[5] They are also impacted as consumers by import tariffs due to the fact that higher tariffs are applied to female products than to similar male products, like clothing,[6] or they are over proportionally compared to men buy products with high tariffs, like agricultural goods for the family supply.[7] In addition, women entrepreneurs have limited access to financial services, which means in some countries already basic financial services, like a bank account, or the opportunity to receive a credit or a credit to the same conditions as male-owned companies, are not available for most of the female entrepreneurs.[8] Finally, the legal protection of women varies drastically across the countries and puts additional barriers, as the possibilities to own property or to set up their own business.[9] The reduction of the above mentioned trade barriers for women would enhance the participation of women in trade.

The trade barriers for women all lead to unused potential regarding the economic development of countries. In 2015, women only contributed to 37% of the global gross domestic product, even though they make up more than half of the world's population.[10] If women unleashed the same economic potential as men, the global GDP could be increased by $28 trillion, or 26%, which corresponds to the size of the U.S. and Chinese economies. However, these impressive numbers in a best-practice scenario are put into perspective when one looks at the latest figures on the global gender pay gap.[11] In its latest report, the World Economic Forum estimates that it will take 151 years to close the gap in terms of economic participation.[12]

In this context, the last 10 years have seen a greater focus on gender equality and combating the disadvantages of women. Therefore, also the World Trade Organization (WTO) took action and at the 11th Ministerial Conference the Buenos Aires in 2017 endorsed Declaration on Trade and Women's Economic Empowerment,[13]

---

[5] World Bank Group/World Trade Organization (2020), pp. 84 et seq., 161 et seq.

[6] Korinek et al. (2021), p. 32.

[7] World Bank Group/World Trade Organization (2020), p. 62.

[8] World Bank Group/World Trade Organization (2020), p. 95 et seq.

[9] World Bank Group/World Trade Organization (2020), p. 83 et seq.; Brodsky et al. (2021), p. 7 et seq.

[10] Examining 95 countries, McKinsey Global Institute (2015), pp. 2, 25.

[11] McKinsey Global Institute (2015), p. 8.

[12] World Economic Forum (2022), p. 5.

[13] WTO (2017), Joint Declaration on Trade and Women's Economic Empowerment. https://www.wto.org/english/thewto_e/minist_e/mc11_e/genderdeclarationmc11_e.pdf.

which supports the exchange of experiences and best practices as well as initiates discussions. In the aftermath, the 127 WTO members, who support the declaration, established in 2020 the WTO Informal Working Group on Trade and Gender, which initiated the Joint Ministerial Declaration on Gender Equality and Women's Economic Empowerment within Trade.[14] The declaration of 2017 aims to include a gender-responsive perspective into trade and investment policies since they acknowledge that gender equality and women's economic empowerment can be enhanced by inclusive trade policies and that economic growth is boosted by international trade and investment for all countries. This can lead to better access of women to various opportunities and reduced trade barriers for their participation in economies worldwide.[15] Besides a regular monitoring and reporting to the Informal Working Group, the members are asked "to review, develop and improve national and/or regional collection of gender-disaggregated data", "utilize research initiatives to inform trade policy instruments and programmes to support women's empowerment", "explore and analyse a gender perspective [. . .] in the work of the WTO" and "promote and highlight the collaboration on trade and gender between international and regional organisations".[16] This action plan sets out clear goals and could serve as a basis for future activities and reforms but only the future will show if the "political impetus" will be used or if the consensus-based system of the WTO hinders any progress, as happened with most developments and reforms since the Ministerial Conference in Doha in 2001. Since then, a more far-reaching tariff-based trade liberalization and the reform of so-called WTO+ issues, such as anti-dumping, public procurement or GATS, but also the inclusion of WTO-x areas, i.e. those for which the WTO currently has no mandate, such as human rights, administration, social issues, taxes, has not been successful due to different interests of the member states.

Therefore, in the last 20 years, free trade agreements have become increasingly popular, not only bilaterally but also plurilaterally and regionally since cross-border trade relations are crucial for the international competitiveness of states. The EU, too, is shifting its efforts towards concluding deep and comprehensive free trade agreements, which, however, go far beyond the multilateral world trade arrangements of the WTO. In addition to tariff issues, the canon of regulations is expanding to include important topics such as labor standards, discrimination issues, ecological issues, modern investment protection or sustainability, among others. Consequently, more and more countries introduce in their free trade agreements either stand-alone chapters on gender and/or they try to gender mainstream throughout the whole agreement. As the Office of the Special Advisor on Gender to the United Nations puts it, "[Gender] [m]ainstreaming is not an end in itself but a strategy, an approach,

[14]WTO (2021), Joint Ministerial Declaration on the Advancement of Gender Equality and Women's Empowerment within Trade. WT/MIN(21)/4/Rev. 1.

[15]WTO (2017), Joint Declaration on Trade and Women's Economic Empowerment. https://www.wto.org/english/thewto_e/minist_e/mc11_e/genderdeclarationmc11_e.pdf.

[16]WTO (2021), 2.

a means to achieve the goal of gender equality. Mainstreaming involves ensuring that gender perspectives and attention to the goal of gender equality are central to all activities," including activities associated with the development, implementation and monitoring of government policies, programs and projects.[17] These considerations drive countries, such as Chile, Canada, Israel, and others to take action and to set up the most modern agreements in the area of gender empowerment. The included gender provisions in FTAs can be categorized in four parts: (1) reaffirmation clauses regarding existing commitments to gender equality in international treaties, (2) "safeguarding" principles that ensure that the trade provisions do not undermine gender equality, (3) cooperation provisions that promote and empower women's economic participation and (4) procedural rules on consultation and dispute settlement.[18]

Keeping this in mind, this chapter first analyses the content of different regulations by examining a number of free trade agreements (FTAs). Thereafter, the results are compared with the recently adopted Global Trade and Gender Arrangement. Finally, the chapter concludes by answering the questions of whether there is a positive impact of FTAs on gender empowerment and how FTAs need to be designed to have such effects.

2 Gender Provisions in Free Trade Agreements

The number of gender or gender-related provisions has increased in bilateral or regional trade agreements in the last decades, so that 353 agreements are currently in force and notified to the WTO. At the end of 2020, although only 305 agreements were in force, 83 of them already contained explicit gender provisions, and if also implicit provisions are included the number is even higher—257 agreements support the protection of gender equality in different ways and on different levels.[19] The most important players are Canada and Chile, as they have the largest number of agreements with explicit gender provisions—they include specific gender standalone chapters into their FTAs. In the second place are Israel, Japan, the United Kingdom, Argentina, Brazil, Uruguay, and the European Union, who also include different gender provisions.[20] This shows that the main actors are found among high- and middle-income countries and reflects the fact that of the mentioned 83 agreements around 70% were concluded between developing and developed countries, so-called North-South agreements.[21] In contrast only 16% between developing countries (South-South FTAs) and 14% between developed countries

[17] See https://www.un.org/womenwatch/osagi/gendermainstreaming.htm.

[18] The first three are also mentioned by Korinek et al. (2021), p. 40.

[19] Monteiro (2021), p. 2.

[20] Listing according to Monteiro (2021), p. 9.

[21] Monteiro (2021), pp. 2, 4 et seq.

(North-North-FTAs) include gender provisions. It can be concluded from this that especially in North-South trade agreements, regulations should be used to develop and ensure gender equality. This seems to be taken for granted in agreements only among industrialised countries or they are already bound by other agreements, such as the European Convention on Human Rights. Among developing countries, this issue does not enjoy much attention at the moment, as other problems are much more urgent to deal with.

This is also underpinned by the fact that countries which, according to the Human Development Index, have a high level of human development, especially in the field of education, life expectancy and per capita income, have included more gender provisions than others and these provisions are characterised by a higher comprehensiveness.[22] In addition, it is interesting that most customs unions get engaged in the field of gender empowerment. Examples are MERCOSUR (Mercado Común del Sur/ Southern Common Market), Andean Community (Community Andina), CARICOM (Caribbean Community), COMESA (Common Market for Eastern and Southern Africa) and SADC (Southern African Development Community).[23] This is because most of those member states have a low participation of women in the labour market and trade flows or/and their economic outcome of their participation is low.

2.1 Main Players for Gender Chapters in Free Trade Agreements

In the following parts, the most recent agreements with a special chapter with gender or gender-related provisions will be analysed with a special focus on Chile and Canada as the most successful negotiators in case of gender mainstreaming of their FTAs. To top this up, the engagement of the EU will be examined to see how a regional organisation could effectively influence this topic.

2.1.1 Chile

The main player for the inclusion of gender or gender-related provisions is Chile. Gender equality was placed on the government's agenda in the second presidency by then-President Michelle Bachelet as part of Chile's trade policy. This policy option could have been due to the fact that Chile had a relatively poor gender inequality score in human development indexes[24] at that time. Another factor might have been Bachelet's previous position as executive director of the UN organization UN

[22] Monteiro (2021), pp. 9 et seq., 13.

[23] Monteiro (2021), p. 16.

[24] Frohmann (2017), p. 12.

Women. In 2016, the Ministry of Women and Gender Equality and other institutions were established, and several studies were conducted on women's economic participation. Chile was found to be below average in this regard. Since then and in light of this, all future Chilean FTAs have included gender chapters.

Chile concluded an agreement with Uruguay in 2016 that included various gender provisions in Chapter 14.[25] Uruguay had been seeking a partner outside of the MERCOSUR countries at the time. This agreement was intended to serve as a blueprint for future agreements, as is common in free trade negotiations. This was the case with the FTAs with Argentina,[26] Brazil and Canada. The latter repeatedly emphasize their progressive trade agenda, which also includes gender equality. This shows that trade is not liberalized at any price, but that domestic policy objectives are equally pursued. The new Chile-Canada Agreement is a reformed version of the 1997 agreement, and Chile has also concluded FTAs with Brazil in 2018[27] and with Ecuador in 2020[28] that include a gender chapter. The wording of all agreements is either identical or very similar and includes the reaffirmation of international commitments, the recognition and possibilities of cooperation as well as the establishment of a trade and gender committee and national contact points. Differences arise in particular from the fact that the individual contracting parties have entered into various international commitments in international organizations, such as the International Labour Organization, or that the respective international treaties to which the FTAs refer had not yet been concluded at the time of the negotiations.[29] Only the agreement between Chile and Ecuador includes a detailed article on consultations whereas the others just have a general consultation clause. The strategy of Chile to conclude with neighbouring countries FTAs with gender provisions led to a South American approach since also those countries started to implement the provisions in their FTAs with other countries.

2.1.2 Canada

Another player is Canada, which follows a more inclusive approach to trade. As explained earlier, part of the progressive trade agenda is the inclusion of gender issues, as gender equality and the fight against gender discrimination has been one of

[25] Chile – Uruguay Free Trade Agreement. 2016. https://edit.wti.org/document/show/d1cba00f-4306-48a6-843d-c9a4bdcf7a93.

[26] Trade Agreement between the Argentine Republic and the Republic of Chile. 2017. https://edit.wti.org/document/show/bf9aa665-cb2a-472f-849d-090e28b096fb?textBlockId=1626fde6-14f9-4cd9-bbb0-050b1b012b0c&page=1.

[27] Free Trade Agreement between the Republic of Chile and the Federative Republic of Brazil. 2018. https://edit.wti.org/document/show/e62cfb4c-abbf-43d9-ae34-a15c7d057ab4.

[28] Economic Complementation Agreement N° 75 between the Republic of Chile and the Republic of Ecuador. 2020. https://edit.wti.org/document/show/0283d464-5b81-46ab-8080-e093534b34d9?textBlockId=4cf4eefc-ac24-4896-bad2-b209bb751477&page=1.

[29] Dorota López et al. (2019), p. 11 et seq.

the priorities in the negotiations of labour cooperation agreements and labour chapters in FTAs. The Canadian government attaches a crucial role to gender equality and empowerment in the long-term and sustainable development of the state, not only in economic terms, as well as for social progress. For this reason, the Canadian government is taking a two-pronged approach to mainstreaming gender issues in FTAs. On the one hand, stand-alone chapters on trade and gender are to be included, on the other hand, FTAs are to be mainstreamed, i.e. gender-related provisions are to be included in various parts of the FTA. In the case of a stand-alone chapter, great emphasis will be placed on cooperation and a common platform. If such a chapter is not possible, then by way of mainstreaming, in addition to including the topic in the preamble, gender-specific regulations would be included in the labour chapter, discrimination on the basis of gender would be prohibited in the area of services, and a right to further regulation for reasons of public interest would be made possible. Furthermore, it is proposed that gender-responsive regulations be enacted in the area of investments regarding senior management, board members and arbitrators. In addition, gender equity is to be strengthened in the context of corporate social responsibility and also taken into account in the context of procurement guidelines for small and medium-sized enterprises (SME).[30]

The FTA concluded with Chile in 2017 contains such an initial chapter and is based in terms of content on the agreement previously concluded by Chile with Uruguay (CCFTA).[31] Subsequently, Canada also incorporated an exclusive trade and gender chapter into the FTA with Israel in 2018 (CIFTA).[32] This also mirrors the wording of the Chilean agreements, but with one special feature. Article 13.6 of CIFTA does not preclude recourse to the agreement's dispute settlement mechanism from the outset in the event of violations but makes this dependent on the consent of the parties to the agreement. This is considered a major milestone, making the agreement the most modern treaty in the field of gender to come into force. Unfortunately, Canada failed to include a gender chapter in the United States-Mexico-Canada Agreement (USMCA), which replaced the former NAFTA.

[30] Government of Canada. Trade and gender in free trade agreements: The Canadian approach. https://www.international.gc.ca/trade-commerce/gender_equality-egalite_genres/trade_gender_fta-ale-commerce_genre.aspx?lang=eng.

[31] Appendix II, Canada-Chile Free Trade Agreement. 2019. https://www.international.gc.ca/trade-commerce/trade-agreements-accords-commerciaux/agr-acc/chile-chili/fta-ale/2017_Amend_Modif-App2-Chap-N.aspx?lang=eng&_ga=2.72837781.702618115.1644942043-1306034251.1644165122.

[32] Canada-Israel Free Trade Agreement. 2019. https://www.international.gc.ca/trade-commerce/trade-agreements-accords-commerciaux/agr-acc/israel/fta-ale/text-texte/13.aspx?lang=eng&_ga=2.6685492.702618115.1644942043-1306034251.1644165122.

2.1.3 European Union

The European Union was in its latest FTAs reluctant to include gender chapters to FTAs. In the last agreements with Singapore, Korea, Australia, Mexico, Mercosur, Vietnam and UK, Gender equality is only included in the parts about trade and sustainable development or labour standards.

Interestingly, the Comprehensive Economic and Trade Agreement (CETA) between Canada and the EU does not include a stand-alone chapter on gender issues despite the fact that Canada considers gender mainstreaming as one of its top priorities. The only explicit mentioning of gender equality in the main text is in the chapter about investment protection in Article 8.10, which states that any gender discrimination will be considered as a violation of the fair and equitable treatment principle.[33] Nevertheless, the CETA Joint Committee adopted in September 2018 a recommendation on trade and gender, which in parts reflects the provisions set in the other Canadian FTAs. They reaffirm to implement their commitments under international agreements and highlight the importance of cooperation, especially in the context of the impact of trade on gender equality and the participation of women in the economy. Moreover, several regular meetings took place and a workplan for 2020-2021 was developed.[34]

Although the present activities are not convincing, the EU started in 2017 to renegotiate the existing FTA with Chile of 2002.[35] It seems that Chile could successfully implement its approach to include a gender chapter here as well, because the proposed text includes a draft of such a chapter. And unlike the previous Chilean chapters in FTAs, as well as all other existing chapters on trade and gender, this one goes beyond the previous regulations. It already differs in the structure and wording of certain parts. The main achievements are Article 3, which details the parties' obligations against discrimination and includes an explicit derogation clause in paragraph 6. The main differences are the diversified provisions for government consultations and in case of their failure the possibility to request a panel of experts to resolve the matter. Since this is a draft version that is still under negotiations, there could be substantive changes. It will be interesting to see if the parties are able to successfully come to a solution without making any particular changes. In this case, this chapter would be the most modern and detailed one and could act as a model for future EU free trade negotiations, as suggested by the European Parliament already back in 2016.[36]

---

[33] Comprehensive Economic and Trade Agreement (CETA) between Canada, of the one part, and the European Union and its Member States, of the other part. 2017. OJL L 11. 14 January 2017, 23.

[34] Recommendation 002/2018 of 26 September 2018 of the CETA Joint Committee on Trade and Gender. 2018. https://www.international.gc.ca/trade-commerce/trade-agreements-accords-commerciaux/agr-acc/ceta-aecg/rec-002.aspx?lang=eng.

[35] Draft provisions on Trade and Gender Equality in the context of the Modernisation of the EU-Chile Association Agreement. Published on 22 June 2018. https://trade.ec.europa.eu/doclib/docs/2018/june/tradoc_156962.pdf.

[36] Fontana (2016), p. 36.

2.2 *Content of Gender and Gender-Related Provisions*

In general, the content on gender issues which can be found in FTAs is heterogeneous as well as the place where it can be found. Mostly, the provisions are included in the main text but then a specific structure is not prominently used since the majority of gender or gender-related provisions are not included in a special article or chapter.[37] In the main text, gender-related issues are mostly mentioned in the parts about economic or development cooperation, labour and sustainable development, social cooperation and in the preamble, as explained for most EU FTAs in force.[38] Further gender-related provisions can be found in chapters or regulations that deal with government procurement, corporate social responsibility, gender balance in boards, trade in service (prohibition of gender-based discrimination related to licensing and qualification requirements), technical barriers (development of gender-responsive norms and standards) and sanitary and phytosanitary measures (promotion of capacity building). These chapters have significant similarities. In the following, the examination is focussed on the content of specific gender chapters.

2.2.1 General Provisions

All chapters have as a common objective the recognition of the importance of "gender mainstreaming in promoting inclusive economic growth" or "incorporating a gender perspective into the promotion of inclusive growth" and refer to the "key role gender policies can play in achieving greater sustainable development". Only the wording of the draft proposal of the EU-Chile FTA goes further and is more detailed. It emphasises the participation of women in economic activities and the removal of barriers for this purpose. They name women's economic empowerment and equality between men and women as crucial for economic growth. In addition, the different roles as workers, producers, traders or consumers are pointed out.

Moreover, all agreements refer to the commitment of the parties regarding the UN 2030 Agenda for Sustainable Development and in particular to the Sustainable Development Goal 5, "which seeks to achieve gender equality and the empowerment of all women and girls."

Furthermore, all agreements include declaratory provisions, which reaffirm existing commitments under international or multilateral agreements, such as the Convention of the International Labour Organization, the 1979 UN Convention on the Elimination of all Forms of Discrimination against Women (CEDAW), the Joint Declaration on Trade and Women's Economic Empowerment on the occasion of the WTO Ministerial Conference in Buenos Aires in 2017, the 1995 Beijing Declaration and Platform for Action, the OECD Guidelines for Multinational Enterprises, the UN Universal Declaration of Human Rights and the UN Covenant on Social and

---

[37] Monteiro (2021), p. 14.

[38] Monteiro (2021), p. 17.

Economic Rights, the Addis Ababa Action Agenda as well as the Inter-American Convention on the Prevention, Punishment and Eradication of Violence against Women. The references differ depending on whether the parties are also parties to those agreements, but all agreements include a general clause, which gives the parties the freedom to implement obligations under other international agreements addressing gender equality or women's rights.

2.2.2 Cooperation Activities

Analysing the agreements of the main actors, in all agreements, the articles on cooperation are the heart of the chapters and describe in detail the different activities, objectives, and participants. The main principle is the exchange of experiences by various means and the intention to set up programmes of cooperation activities. The underlying objective is to enhance and improve the capacities and conditions for women so that they can benefit the most from the opportunities developed by the FTAs. For this purpose, the parties should involve their governments, businesses, and other stakeholders.[39]

The parties identified as areas for cooperation capacity-building and skills enhancement of women, a better access to education with a focus on STEM disciplines, the advancement of women's leadership and the development of women's networks, the access to financial services and training, raising awareness of the importance of gender equality, the participation of women in decision-making, the promotion of women's entrepreneurship, the exchange of information about experiences with the implementation of policies and programs, the exchange of best practices and the exchange on methods and procedures for the collection and analysis of trade-related sex-disaggregated data as well as various other areas empowering the economic participation of women.[40] In all activities, which are exemplary listed,[41] the agreements encourage the invitation of third parties, like international donor organisations or non-governmental organisations.[42]

These provisions are in most agreements very comprehensive and point out to the parties the various possibilities to exchange experiences and cooperate in certain areas. It is important that all agreements oblige the parties to increase the available sex-disaggregated data in the field of trade activities and provisions to evaluate their impact on gender equality and the empowerment of women.

[39] Compare Art. N *bis*-03 para. 1-2 of the Appendix II of the FTA Canada-Chile.

[40] Most of the FTAs have an non-exhaustive list of areas included, compare Art. N *bis*-03 para. 4 of the FTA Canada-Chile.

[41] Compare Art. N *bis*-03 para. 5 of the FTA Canada-Chile.

[42] Compare Art. N *bis*-03 para. 3. of the FTA Canada-Chile.

2.2.3 Trade and Gender Committee

All chapters establish a joint trade and gender committee, which organises the cooperation activities by setting up a work plan, monitoring the progress of implementation of the provisions and making recommendations to improve this implementation. The committee should meet, in most cases, annually which in the case of Chile has not happened.[43] The committee is asked to work together with and encourage committees or other groups established under the agreements. Finally, all chapters oblige the parties to establish a point of contact for a proper communication.

The establishment of committees and national contact points are necessary to create special institutions with experts to discuss and monitor the implementation of the provisions as well as to open an opportunity for the parties and others to complain about problems and failed implementation

2.2.4 Domestic Policies

Most of the chapters include some "safeguard provisions", which guarantee that the FTA does not affect gender equality activities on the national level. Therefore, the parties allow in a general clause "to adopt, maintain and effectively implement their laws, regulations, policies and good practices on gender equality." The newer agreements of Chile with Argentina und Ecuador additionally point out that the parties have the "right to establish, modify and monitor compliance with its laws, regulations and policies on gender issues, in accordance with its priorities" for the purpose to improve their existing legislation.

The EU-Chile draft proposal follows a different approach. The chapter also contains similar wording in spirit, but here it is made clear that each party may pursue its own scope and standard of protection. The minimum level here is considered to be the commitments of the parties under the international agreements mentioned in the chapter. Moreover, it is stated in Article 3.6 that "the parties shall not waive or otherwise derogate from their respective laws that protect the equality of opportunities for men and women in order to encourage trade or investment." It also permits in Article 3.7 that "the parties shall not, through a sustained or recurring course of action or inaction, fail to effectively enforce their respective laws that protect the equality of opportunities for men and women in order to encourage trade or investments."

These formulations have not been used by any other agreement before so that the negotiations will show if the explicit non-derogation clause remains. The clause prohibits a derogation of existing legislation only in the context of trade and investment and not for any other purposes. The parties are still free, in their legal framework, to change their existing level of protection in other areas. For the EU, the

[43] Cohen (2021), p. 86.

risk of a reduction of the level of protection is relatively low because gender equality is anchored in the legal framework of the EU since the Rome treaties in 1957. Nowadays, gender equality can be found in the values and tasks of the Treaty of the European Union and Article 8 TFEU obliges the EU "to eliminate inequalities, and to promote equality, between men and women." This is rounded up in Article 21 and other articles of the Charter of Fundamental Rights, which prohibit discrimination on grounds of sex. Various acts of secondary legislation were enacted in the last decades and also implemented in national law. Nevertheless, such non-derogation clauses give a clear statement that also for the implementation of the main objectives (here: encouragement of trade and investment) of the agreement in question a derogation or waiver is not acceptable. This is promising for the future implementation of negotiated trade measures since this safeguards the obligations of the parties regarding the promotion of gender equality.

2.2.5 Consultations and Dispute Settlement

One of the main criticisms of the gender chapters is that most of them exclude the dispute settlement mechanism of the agreement to be applied to the gender chapter.[44] This mechanism is implemented in most FTAs and can be used in case that one party violates an obligation of the FTA or the parties disagree about the interpretation of one provision. Nevertheless, sensitive or important issues are often excluded from the dispute settlement and also applies to the gender chapters. It ives the contracting parties the freedom to implement the regulations and to react on national societal changes and protests. This leads to a restricted enforceability of the different provisions in the gender chapter.

However, all agreements provide the possibility of dialogue, consultations and cooperation for the interpretation and application of the different provisions. This is stated mostly in one sentence without further details about the procedure. The Chile-Ecuador FTA and the EU-Chile FTA draft proposal include more detailed rules. For consultations, a written request stating the main reasons for the complaint needs to be submitted to the established contact point of the other party. The consultations should start within a certain timeframe (between 30 and 90 days) after receipt of the request. The parties are allowed to involve independent experts and other international organisations. They can also achieve a solution in a procedure based on mediation principles. In case a resolution cannot be reached the Chile-Ecuador FTA allows filing a request to the trade and gender committee and in case of failure the requesting party can forward the matter to the ministerial level to find a political decision while the EU-Chile FTA draft proposal establishes upon request a panel of experts which is developed by the trade and gender committee and the parties. Article 7.3-7.5 gives further details on the expertise of the experts and the composition of the panel. The terms of references and the way of interpretation are also

[44] International Trade Center (2020a, b), 19.

mentioned. Article 7.9 explicitly explains the timeframe for a decision as well as the minimum requirements for the final report and recommendations of the panel. Finally, appropriate measures shall be discussed by the parties and their progress is monitored by the Committee on Trade and Gender. There is no other enforcement mechanism or sanctioning possibility foreseen as in the case of the regular dispute settlement mechanism of the agreement. In this context, the EU-Chile FTA draft proposal goes beyond the consultation procedures in all other agreements but still cannot be as successful as the regular dispute settlement mechanisms.

This might be the reason why Canada and Israel allowed in their gender chapter in CIFTA that in case the consultations fail, the parties can submit the case to the dispute settlement mechanism laid down in Article 19. The only pre-condition is that the parties express their consent, so that there is no obligatory way to the dispute settlement mechanism. This inclusion was often praised to be particularly modern and it achieved more as all other agreements before but the future will show if the parties will consent to the dispute settlement matters in different matters. If not, then it is just a testimonial without function and the way which is proposed by the EU could be more effective.

3 Global Trade and Gender Arrangement

The Global Trade and Gender Arrangement (GTAGA) is the first multilateral agreement exclusively on gender matters. Since 2018, Chile, Canada and New Zealand worked together in the Inclusive Trade Action Group (ITAG), which was established at the Asia-Pacific Economic Cooperation (APEC) Leaders' Summit in the same year in the context of the signing of the Comprehensive and Progressive Agreement for Trans-Pacific Partnership (CPTPP) by the three countries. The main objective of the ITAG is the cooperation "to help make international trade policies more progressive and inclusive in order to ensure that the benefits of trade and investment are more broadly shared, which can have a positive impact on economic growth and helps to reduce inequality and poverty."[45] They outline the importance of a sustainable development in the field of trade and gender equality. One major step was the development and signing of the GTAGA in 2020. For the period of 2020–2022, the ITAG wants to enquire if other members to the CPTPP and APEC or WTO could get involved and convince them to sign the GTAGA as well.[46] In one part they already have been successful, since Mexico joined in 2021 as the fourth member state the ITAG and GTAGA.

[45] CPTPP, Joint Declaration on Fostering Progressive and Inclusive Trade. 2018. https://www.mfat.govt.nz/assets/Trade-agreements/CPTPP/CPTPP-Joint-Declaration-Progressive-and-Inclusive-Trade-Final.pdf.

[46] ITAG. 2020. Work Programme 2020-2022. https://www.mfat.govt.nz/assets/Trade-General/Trade-policy/ITAG-Inclusive-Trade-Action-Group/ITAG-work-programme-2020-2022.pdf.

Moreover, they want to implement further cooperation activities in the framework of the arrangement, which resembles in most articles the existing gender chapter in FTA but differs when it comes to the naming of the objectives. This is done not only at the beginning of the arrangement but also throughout the text with a more special approach. The GTAGA clearly states in Article 4 that measures addressed to services should not discriminate based on gender. This is not explicitly included in other chapters. A differential treatment is justified or exempted on grounds of public policy. In addition, the arrangement also makes clear that not only the parties themselves implement all standards, guidelines and principles of international agreements addressing gender equality but that these also need to be incorporated by companies which have to be encouraged by the parties. The parties give special emphasize to any discrimination in the workplace as they provide for an article focusing solely on this topic. The list of areas for cooperation is long and includes topics addressing economic participation, education and skill enhancement, access to financial services, entrepreneurship and leadership. These can be found in all chapters as well as other topics addressing SMEs, trade missions, rural and indigenous women and diverse suppliers. Article 13 gives the parties the mandate to reach out for further members which are accepted by the decision of the Trade and Gender Working Group established by the GTAGA.[47] All countries who want to be engaged in the field of gender equality could become a new member. It will be interesting to see, if Canada and Australia who are one of the key players in the field of women's economic participation and gender equality as well as members to CPTPP and APEC will become the next members.

4 Evaluation and Recommendations

Based on the above analysis, there are several issues that need to be critically considered and that require some improvement in the gender-responsiveness of FTAs.

4.1 Gender-Related Assessments

One main problem is the limited availability of gender- and sex-aggregated data. This has been repeatedly urged by scholars and organizations and has led all chapters of gender issues to seek a commitment to collaborate and share in the collection and

[47] Global Trade and Gender Arrangement. 2020. https://www.mfat.govt.nz/assets/Trade-General/Trade-policy/ITAG-Inclusive-Trade-Action-Group/ITAG_Global-Trade-and-Gender-Arrangement-Text-for-signed-Arrangement.pdf.

analysis of data.[48] Such data are necessary to better understand the relationship between trade and gender and to draw conclusions about the impacts of progressive trade liberalization, meaning the reduction or removal of tariffs or any other trade barriers. In this regard, sector- and country-specific studies must be undertaken in addition to general impacts.

Impact assessments are carried out in other areas, such as in the EU on sustainability (sustainability impact assessment), but gender is rarely considered. This need to be changed in order that decisionmakers and legislators are able to make decisions based on facts. Here, ex-ante and ex-post considerations would have to be carried out. Before concluding an agreement, it should be examined how the various trade concessions will affect the contracting countries and their societies, in particular, of course, the economic participation of women. At regular intervals, agreements should be reviewed with regard to their gender responsiveness. A poor assessment should be taken into account when reforming the regulations.

It would be useful to develop uniform criteria for the intended gender impact assessments. For this purpose, uniform indicators, categories and units of measurement as well as classification criteria would have to be defined.[49] The ITAG could play an important role here, as it probably has the largest number of members.

4.2 Enforceability

Even if an increasing number of FTAs include gender equity provisions, most have limited enforceability and are therefore often considered relatively ineffective when recourse to an agreement's dispute settlement mechanisms is excluded. In principle, other issues are also often excluded, such as competition policy issues, but this diminishes the importance and progress made by including gender issues in the first place.

The CIFTA and the EU-Chile FTA chapters show that the parties are aware of this and are attempting to give greater weight to the provisions either through detailed consultation procedures with multiple hearing bodies or through voluntary recourse to dispute settlement. In this context, two further problems need to be discussed. First, the implementation of gender equity often entails far-reaching social changes. While this will also depend on the level of development of individual countries, such an approach as a top-down approach might not be sustainable to the same extent as fundamental social change.[50] Second, the provisions in the respective regulations must also be designed in such a way that they are justiciable and implementable or could give rise to a claim at all. Most agreements rely on aspirational formulations, but these contain numerous indeterminate variables. Furthermore, in most cases only

[48] Korinek et al. (2021), p. 50 et seq.

[49] E.g. Brodsky et al. (2021), p. 11 et seq.; International Trade Center (2020a, b), p. 4 et seq.

[50] International Trade Center 2020a, b), p. 19.

few enforcement actions or remedies are foreseen and they have only a limited scope. Especially in the consultation procedures, a failure of the negotiations is not sanctioned.

4.3 *Specific Rules and Regulations*

When analyzing gender chapters, it is noticeable that they are very similar in their formulations and differ only to a limited extent that they address specific peculiarities. For the most FTAs, a difference only exists when reference is made to obligations from other international agreements and different memberships result from this. In order to achieve better enforceability of the regulations, both specific formulations of obligations of the contracting parties and specific regulations for the respective sectors or countries would be helpful.

A major point of criticism of the gender chapters is the wording, which is mostly rather general or refers to existing agreements. Neither indicators nor legal minimum standards are specified, so that these are soft law regulations that are both quantitatively and qualitatively or legally verifiable. One prominent example is the requirement on equal pay for equal work which is stated in several agreements but without further requirements for the domestic legislator.[51]

Besides a more country-specific approach of the gender chapters, which take into account specific obligations and particularities of the country in question, the agreements also have to differentiate among the different sectors. In this regard, the existing gender chapters already point out several action fields, but future gender chapters should go beyond that and put a focus especially on trade in services and gender-based discrimination in relation to licensing and qualification requirements. The same applies regarding gender-specific standards as technical barriers to trade, which could increase product standards and safety.[52] Moreover, two important sectors, which should also be addressed are public government procurement and investment provisions since they impact directly the market access and trade barriers for women.[53]

5 Conclusion

The times that trade agreements focus only on trade topics are over, already the topics of sustainability and environmental protection found their way to trade agreements due to their societal impact. The urgency of those topics requires a

[51] International Trade Center (2020a, b), p. 16; Cohen (2021), p. 86.
[52] Korinek et al. (2021), p. 46 et seq.
[53] International Trade Center (2020b), p. 10 et seq.

multi-faceted approach which asks that those topics, and this also applies to gender equity, to be included in all regulations, laws and agreements of countries and other organisations to force all actors to implement the obligations. In this regard, free trade agreements set the ground and the level playing field for future trade of the parties. Moreover, they initiate a discussion and are able to raise the awareness about gender aspects of trade barriers which are addressed in FTAs.

There is no doubt that trade facilitation has both a positive and a negative effect on women's economic activity and on gender equality. Nevertheless, the above stated explanations and analysis show that it is necessary to take the gender perspective of trade liberalization into account since the impact of the different trade barriers can make a notable change for gender equality and women's economic empowerment. The reduction or even better removal of trade barriers, especially in female-dominated trade sectors, could achieve higher wages and better working conditions. Moreover, gender chapters in FTAs point out that a better access to education and finances allow a better inclusion of women in male-dominated sectors and as entrepreneurs. Although this will bring prosperity to societies and countries, it is not only an economic necessity for the development of countries and market economies but also a legal obligation of countries to prohibit and stop the discrimination of women. Trade liberalization should support and develop the welfare of all people, which over the past decades was achieved in a successful way in a lot of parts in the world, especially in Europe.

To support these developments a better understanding of the impact of trade barriers and policies is needed. Therefore gender-related assessments have to become a global standard in the ex-ante and ex-post evaluation of all trade negotiations. The lack of data reinforces the fact that women are not perceived as an independent factor in economic life and are therefore not addressed or promoted separately. However, a globalised economy cannot afford this in the long run.

Even though there is still a long way to go for gender-responsive trade policies, considerable progress has been made in the last 5 years. Within this time, several countries, but also regional groupings, such as the EU or APEC, have dealt with the matter in greater depth and have recognised the importance of gender equality in economic activities. Among those countries are also G7 countries, like Canada, Japan, and the EU member states Germany, France and Italy. The WTO has put the issue on its agenda and supports various initiatives. Based on this, a first multilateral agreement on trade and gender—GTAGA—was adopted in a very short time, which includes an invitation to other countries to join it. Keeping this in mind, it can be stated that good progress was achieved so far but that the road is still long since other countries and regions ignore the gender topic completely.

In conclusion, the engagement of various countries needs to be seen as pioneering and offering new perspectives on gender equality and women's economic participation in trade to other countries. The future will show if this will end as a pipe dream or if those FTAs will find copycats which set gender-responsive trade agreements as well as trade measures and policies as a global standard.

References

Brodsky A, Lim J, Reinsch W (2021) Women and trade – how trade agreements can level the gender playing field. Center for Stragic & International Studies. https://csis-website-prod.s3.amazonaws.com/s3fs-public/publication/210527_Brodsky_Women_and_Trade_1.pdf?L5StVPbcLYxaN49VusatkUMAlI3g42yG

Cohen MS (2021) The Pink Trojan Horse: inserting gender issues into free trade agreements. Int Public Aff 5:75–91

Dorota López G, Felipe Munoz N, Javiera Cáceres B (2019) Gender inclusion in Chilean Free Trade Agreements

Fontana M (2016) Gender equality in Trade Agreements. Study for the FEMM Committee. European Parliament. https://www.europarl.europa.eu/RegData/etudes/STUD/2016/571388/IPOL_STU(2016)571388_EN.pdf

Frohmann A (2017) Gender equality and trade policy. SECO/WTI Academic Cooperation Project Working Paper Series 2017/24. https://www.wti.org/media/filer_public/8b/a8/8ba88d03-1a2b-4311-af6a-629d9997c54c/working_paper_no_24_2017_frohmann.pdf

International Trade Center (2020a) Mainstreaming gender in free trade agreements. https://intracen.org/media/file/2411

International Trade Center (2020b) Delivering on the Buenos Aires declaration on trade and women's economic empowerment

Korinek J, Moise E, Tange J (2021) Trade and gender – a framework of analysis. OECD Trade Policy Papers No. 246. OECD Publishing, Paris. https://doi.org/10.1787/6db59d80-en

McKinsey Global Institute (2015) The power of parity: how advancing women's equality can add $12 Trillion to Global Growth. https://www.mckinsey.com/~/media/mckinsey/industries/public%20and%20social%20sector/our%20insights/how%20advancing%20womens%20equality%20can%20add%2012%20trillion%20to%20global%20growth/mgi%20power%20of%20parity_full%20report_september%202015.pdf

Monteiro JA (2021) The evolution of gender-related provisions in Regional Trade Agreements. *WTO Staff Working Paper* ERSD-2021-8

Pieters J (2018) Trade liberalization and gender inequality. *IZA World of Labor*. https://wol.iza.org/articles/trade-liberalization-and-gender-inequality

World Bank Group/World Trade Organization (2020) Women and Trade. the role of trade in promoting gender equality

World Economic Forum (2022) Global Gender Gap Report 2022. https://www3.weforum.org/docs/WEF_GGGR_2022.pdf

Mareike Fröhlich is a research associate at the Europa-Institut of Saarland University and specialized in European and International Economic Law. She studied law at the Rhenish Friedrich Wilhelm University of Bonn (German: Rheinische Friedrich-Wilhelms-Universität Bonn) and graduated in 2005. She holds a LL.M. in European and International Law of the Europa-Institut of Saarland University. She did her legal clerkship at the Land Rheinland-Pfalz and is a fully qualified lawyer. In 2021, she defended her doctoral thesis at Saarland University in the field of European and International Competition Law. She coordinates several European and international projects.

Standing Alone but Standing Tall: A Female Perspective of International Law from the Interwar Yugoslavia

Sanja Djajić

Contents

Abstract The interwar period was the best of times and was the worst of times. Following changes to the institutional and political landscape of Europe and beyond in the aftermath of the World War I, the new international legal order enthused the oppressed and unprivileged with the nascent liberal aspirations of a democratic world. International law was reinvented and reinforced with the sense of possibility and progress, while internationalism and universalism were upped to a new level of global governance in the form of the League of Nations. Those times witnessed some extraordinary individuals who personally experienced all illusions and realities of these changes, and how internationalism turned hostile and universalism failed to become egalitarian. Anka Godjevac Subbotić (Anka Godyevatz Soubbotitch, Анка Гођевац Субботић), the first and only female international lawyer of the interwar Yugoslavia, was one of these exceptional personalities. As an international lawyer, scholar, activist, feminist, journalist and novelist, active both in Yugoslavia and abroad, she was the pioneer of combining feminism and international law in the Balkans. This contribution aims to be the story about international law told both from her national and gender perspectives, set in different interwar contexts: of women in Serbia and Yugoslavia, of women in international law, and of the Balkans in international law and society. This will be the tale of international law told from

S. Djajić (✉)
University of Novi Sad, Faculty of Law, Novi Sad, Serbia
e-mail: sdjajic@pf.uns.ac.rs

I. Krstić et al. (eds.), *Legal Issues of International Law from a Gender Perspective*, Gender Perspectives in Law 3, https://doi.org/10.1007/978-3-031-13459-3_10

different peripheries that only a woman in the interwar Yugoslavia and the Balkans could inhabit and experience.

1 Introduction

Footprints of feminist and female international legal scholarship in Serbia are small and fairly recent. They can be traced back to Belgrade between the two World Wars and belonged to one lady only—Anka Godjevac Subbotić. These small footprints were important, original and revolutionary for a variety of reasons, and her choices made literally despite all odds. In a country which was not a champion of gender equality, which itself struggled for the place in the family of nations, the choice of international law discipline, which per se was exclusionary towards women, prompts questions on perceptions and expectations a woman in the Balkans might have had of international law. Was international law perceived as a powerful instrument for emancipatory struggles of all sorts, gender and national?[1] Was it the fact that international law was so dramatically and radically changed and reinvented following the Great War that it inevitably infatuated many and drew in new followers? Was there a sense of promise or entitlement that was not to be found within national boundaries, or was it just this overwhelmingly universal post-war enthusiasm and spirit that equally inspired disadvantaged groups of all sorts, including women and Balkan nations?

For these reasons this will be the tale of international law told from different peripheries that only a woman in the interwar Yugoslavia and the Balkans could inhabit and experience. In order to reconstruct and tell her personal story of international law, I will situate documentary evidence in different interwar contexts: of women in Serbia and Yugoslavia, of women in international law, and of the Balkans in international law and society. Public and private personal accounts of events, scholarly work and social engagements, read from a contemporary perspective could potentially tell us more about periphery-centre gaps of the time, and to what extent the periphery was and remained the destiny of women international lawyers in the Balkans. The idea behind this contribution is to give voice to those who were silenced then, but equally to challenge the silence of today.

[1] "Though fascinating in hindsight, these peripheral European histories were local but showed that lawyers from less powerful states found it important to present their national grievances in the new language of international law while giving their state a role in a historical European narrative." Obregon (2019), p. 440.

2 Personal History of Women in Serbia and the Kingdom of Yugoslavia

Much of this history, its dynamics and general trends, can be traced through the personal biography of Anka Godjevac Subbotić (1890–1983). She was born on the periphery of the family of nations, in the Kingdom of Serbia during its early years of independence and struggle for its position in the international community. Serbia was on the edge of modernity both in terms of territory and culture, and national liberation was, and would be, the prime political goal for a long time. The position of Serbia was difficult due to its underdevelopment and the Balkans' "hybrid position between East and West"[2] but also because of the outer perceptions of the Balkans in general.[3] In political terms, the Balkans "were synonymous with struggle, inter-ethnic rivalry, disorder, and danger",[4] unable to fully embrace modernity,[5] which kept the Balkans languishing on the periphery. The Balkans was a myth, narrative, political destiny, and international legal problem.

Despite all the disadvantages of being born and raised in Serbia at the end of the nineteenth century, Anka Godjevac did lead a privileged life by any measure. Brought up in a well-off and cultured family, she received schooling in Austria, Germany and Serbia. Her social background and family fortunes provided exceptional educational opportunities generally unavailable to girls in Serbia of that time. The belief in, or rather devotion to education as a form of emancipation must have been instilled in her early as she returned to school and entered university immediately after she had divorced her first husband. She was married at the age of 19 and was seemingly set on the path of having the typical life of a married woman in Serbia at that time, restricted solely to being a wife and mother. However, the legal position of married women in Serbia was quite disadvantageous under the 1844 Serbian Civil Code. A woman would lose her legal standing upon marriage.[6] A married woman could not own or inherit property, gain employment, enter contracts, or conduct any other transaction without the consent of her husband.[7] She could act on her own in an

[2] "It was partly due to this liminality – this hybrid position between East and West – that made the Balkans not only too 'advanced' for direct colonial rule but also unfit for independence, and this was also at the root of the legal innovation and experimentation in regard to the region." Tzouvala (2019), p. 1153.

[3] The collective image of the Balkans as such, or of particular Balkan nations, created a specific discourse, which Maria Todorova terms 'balkanism': "'[B]alkanism' expresses the idea that explanatory approaches to phenomena in the Balkans often rest upon a discourse or a stable system of stereotypes that place the Balkans in a cognitive straightjacket." Todorova (2009), p. 193.

[4] Crampton (2007), p. 237.

[5] Norris (1999).

[6] "It was particularly difficult to guarantee the protection of women when they had no legal stature as individuals. (...) Marriage, in fact, took important rights away from women." Emmert (1999), p. 37.

[7] Perić (1928), pp. 6–31.

extremely limited number of cases.[8] Her legal standing was only equal to those of minors and the insane,[9] and her capacity to act was consumed by the husband's authority over her[10] and was based on her legal duty to be obedient to her husband (Article 110 of the 1844 Serbian Civil Code). This nearly slave-like status of women ("A man is a noble, a woman is a serf."[11]) was clearly the result of the long patriarchal tradition and would not be changed until after the Second World War, despite the liberal influences of the modern Europe to which Serbia strived to belong.

When Anka divorced in 1921 she became fully emancipated in the original meaning of the word. The change of her life path coincided with the end of the First World War and emancipation of nations under the Hapsburg rule, the creation of the new state in the Balkans (Kingdom of Serbs, Croats and Slovenes to be renamed to the Kingdom of Yugoslavia in 1929), the emergence of the new Versailles system, and changed international law with liberal and universal aspirations. This was the period of breaking with tradition and the end of the First World War marked a huge leap towards modernity. These tumultuous years and grandiose events did shape personal choices of many. Anka fully embraced her regained legal capacity and continued her education, found employment, began her career as a novelist and became involved with feminist movements. The new age seemed promising for the empowerment of the disadvantaged, to women and liberated nations alike.

While in Serbia and Yugoslavia the *ancien regime des hommes* was still in place, some progress was being made. For example, following the war and her divorce, Anka entered university at the age of 33 and graduated with honours in 1927 at the age of 37. During her doctoral studies she attended the 1930 session of the Hague Academy for International Law.[12] In 1932 she received her doctoral degree in public international law at the Belgrade University Faculty of Law with the thesis "Principles and rules of international law as derived from the jurisprudence of the Permanent Court of International Justice."[13] This dissertation was referenced in several bibliographies, reviewed in academic journals[14] and hailed by feminists.[15] She was the first woman to receive a doctorate in law at the Belgrade University and it was the

---

[8] Draškić and Popović-Obradović (1998), pp. 16–17.

[9] Article 920 of the 1844 Serbian Civil Code provided that minors and certain categories of adults could not own or dispose with property. These categories included insane, persons deprived by the court of their capacity to own property due to their overspending, homeless, those heavily in debt, and married women while their husbands were still alive.

[10] Perić (1928), p. 9.

[11] Perić (1928), p. 9.

[12] Godjevac (1931c), pp. 167–171.

[13] Dissertation was published as a monograph the following year. Godjevac (1933).

[14] Katičić (1937), pp. 269–272.

[15] Special report on the public defense of Anka Godjevac's dissertation, that was "attended by lawyers, diplomats and feminists", was given in the feminist journal *Women's Movement. – Ženski pokret* (Godjevac 1932c), p. 32.

first doctorate in public international law ever awarded at the Belgrade Faculty of Law.

Higher education in Serbia was conceived in the second half of the nineteenth century but was not formally raised to the level of university until 1905. Although it became open to men and women equally, the number of female students before the First World War was miniscule, [16] due to several reasons, but mostly due to the lack of sufficient or accessible undergraduate education for women and cultural prejudices against education for girls.[17] Despite some possibilities for women to start law education, it seems that the law school was the last university institution to welcome female students.[18] The reasons for withholding law studies from women could well be the role that lawyers play in the power-sharing game within a state structure. Therefore, this exclusionary tendency manifested by law schools in general is more concerned with deeply rooted societal prejudices[19] than with education as such. As Ulrike Schulz explained: "Ever since antiquity, individual female members of social elites had occasionally been allowed to perform legal functions, but in principle law and administration were seen to be central to state power and a male prerogative."[20]

The first woman received her law degree from the Belgrade University in 1911.[21] The number of female students would increase following the war but would still be small: only 10–20% of the student population in the interwar period were women[22] and only 468 women received a law degree in Yugoslavia from 1919 to 1938 (at four law schools that existed at the time: Belgrade, Subotica, Zagreb and Ljubljana).[23] However, even though law studies were now open to women, impediments loomed.

---

[16] Trgovčević (2011).

[17] Stojanović (2013), pp. 236–241.

[18] Magazinović (2000), p. 175.

[19] Persuasive argument on rationales and consequences of women's muteness in public sphere, from antiquity to modern times, was made by Mary Beard: "This 'muteness' is not just a reflection of women's general disempowerment throughout the classical world: no voting rights, limited legal and economic independence and so on. It was partly that. Ancient women were obviously not likely to raise their voices in a political sphere in which they had no formal stake. But we are dealing with a much more active and loaded exclusion of women from public speech – and one with a much greater impact than we usually acknowledge on our own traditions, conventions and assumptions about the voice of women. What I mean is that public speaking and oratory were not merely things that ancient women *didn't do*: they were exclusive practices and skills that defined masculinity as a gender. As we saw with Telemachus, to become a man (or at least an elite man) was to claim the right to speak. Public speech was a – if not *the* – defining attribute of maleness. Or, to quote a well-known Roman slogan, the elite male citizen could be summed up as *vir bonus dicendi peritus*, 'a good man, skilled in speaking'. A woman speaking in public was, in most circumstances, by definition not a woman." Beard (2017), p. 13.

[20] Schulz (2003), p. xxxii.

[21] Lebl-Albala (1928), pp. 17–28.

[22] Vučetić (2007), p. 135. Lebl-Albala offers different figures which show participation of over 20% of women in university studies: in school year 1926/27 there were 4688 male and 1235 female students at the Belgrade university. (n 21,25).

[23] Knežević (1967), p. 239.

Paradoxically, it was the law which denied them the right to practice law, to practice what they were legally allowed to train for. For example, while women were allowed to be employed as court's administrators or trainees, they were directly and openly forbidden to become judges or public prosecutors. Article 2(2) of the 1928 Law on Judges provided that: "Women may not be judges." The same gender exclusion was reproduced in Article 7 of the 1928 Law on Public Prosecutors. These openly discriminatory provisions were justified before the Legislative Committee of the National Assembly as necessary because women allegedly were not apt for adjudication as a fundamental State function, that population would resist female judges, or that a woman's physiology, her "nervousness", morality and sensitivity make her incapable for performing a judicial function.[24] The first reason echoes the already heard arguments about the woman's innate inability to perform state functions.[25]

On the other hand, the 1929 Law on Advocacy expressly allowed women to be advocates and members of the bar[26] (Anka Godjevac shortly trained at a law office following her graduation though she would never practice law as an attorney). However, the glass ceiling was in place: only 15 women, as opposed to 3000 men, practiced as attorneys in the period 1929–1939.[27] Women with a law degree could work in state administration and as public notaries but while only a handful of women would get the position of a clerk in administration with rare or no promotions (as Anka's personal experience would vividly illustrate), no woman ever got the position of a public notary.[28] Law schools were overwhelmingly dominated by men. No woman held any academic positions in law during the interwar period despite the absence of formal impediments. Anka Godjevac Subbotić was most likely the only female candidate who applied for the position of the university law professor during the interwar period. Her application for the position of professor for public international law at the Belgrade Faculty of Law in 1933 was rejected,[29] without even having been shortlisted. This could not have been a surprise to anyone—perhaps it was an act of wilful spite rather than merely the formal job application process.

These ambivalent statutory provisions on women in the law profession demonstrate a general incoherence in removing legal obstacles for obtaining full equality between men and women. Such an incoherent legal framework led to certain paradoxes as exemplified by Ida Knežević, one of the rare interwar female attorneys: "As a female attorney I had capacity to draft a will, but I had to ask a doorman to act as a testamentary witness!"[30]

---

[24] Vlajić (1928), pp. 1–2.

[25] Beard (2017) and Schulz (2003).

[26] For general overview of female lawyers and attorneys in the interwar Yugoslavia, see Stojaković (2017), pp. 174–197.

[27] Knežević (1967), p. 240.

[28] Knežević (1967), p. 240.

[29] Kandić (2002), p. 110.

[30] Knežević (1967), p. 239.

While still a law student Anka gained employment with the Ministry of Foreign Affairs as a clerk (1925–1927). This short episode did not end well—she was involved in litigation in which her employment contract was challenged, and she was denied promotion unlike her male peers. This triggered her fierce resignation.[31] The Ministry of Foreign Affairs must have been a tough battleground for women of that time as they were markedly absent from diplomatic service and any other foreign affairs matter. For some Serbian legal scholars this was understandable given the legal status of a married woman: she was primarily subjected to the authority of her husband, so it was difficult for any married woman to be unconditionally loyal to the interests of the State.[32] However, Anka decided not to be denied. Despite this bitter experience, and only after she excelled academically and proved herself as a scholar, in 1930 she was appointed as the first female representative of the official Yugoslav delegation to the Hague Codification Conference, as a "technical adviser"[33] and expert on women's rights. Eventually she succeeded and was the first woman to step into the male dominated territory of foreign affairs.

Women's rights in the newly created Kingdom of the Serbs, Croats and Slovenes were slowly and unsystematically improved. The creation of the new country was not followed by radical legal reforms in all areas and it fell short of the Constitutional promise on equality before the law for all of its citizens.[34] There existed six different legal systems of private law as prior to the creation of the new state.[35] In terms of rules on the position of women in relation to their legal status and rights under private law (family status, inheritance, property, contracts, delicts, etc.) it meant an unequal position of women of the same nationality depending on the applicable law that was determined on the basis of their residence. Such unequal and differentiated treatment of women amounted to discriminatory practice and systematic disadvantage. All these detriments were even more harsh for women living in the territory of the former kingdoms of Serbia and Montenegro[36] especially for married women[37] and their position in private law would not be changed for the whole interwar period.

[31]"Despite all the efforts I invested and despite all capabilities I demonstrated, as confirmed by the positive review of my two years here at the Ministry by my superiors, I was degraded to the lower position, which I find humiliating. This is why I submit my unconditional resignation." Yugoslav Archive, Ministry of Foreign Affairs of the Kingdom of Yugoslavia, 334-146-438.

[32]Ćirković (1928), p. 27.

[33]"Convention on Certain Questions Relating to the Conflict of Nationality Laws", *League of Nations Official Journal* 11, no. 7 (July 1930): 847–928, at 911.

[34]"All citizens are equal before the law" - Article 4 of the 1921 Vidovdan Constitution.

[35]For a comparative overview of differential women's rights under the private law in the newly created Kingdom of Serbs, Croats and Slovenes, see Krkljuš (1990), pp. 97–103.

[36]Draškić and Popović-Obradović (1998), p. 18.

[37]Emmert (1999), p. 37.

However, such "balkanism" existed in other parts of Europe as well.[38] It seems that admission of women to legal professions was a daunting task in many European countries and at the same time the cause for action for many feminist movements in the quest for emancipation.[39]

As one of the rare female lawyers, coming with a strong academic background, and as the only woman in interwar Yugoslavia engaged in international law, with personal experience of systematic disadvantages, Anka was naturally drawn to women's rights and feminist movements. In her analysis of the position of women within the Yugoslav legal system, she extensively analysed six different systems of private law applicable in the then Yugoslavia.[40] Such differential treatment of women of the same nationality was discriminatory per se and in terms of the principle of gender equality these legal systems were categorized by Anka as "progressive, less progressive and quite regressive."[41] She found that the status of women in Serbia was particularly difficult due to the "most regressive provisions" of the Serbian Civil Code in practically all matters of private law. In contrast, several new pieces of uniform legislation enabled women to have a profession and contained the equality clause. This constituted progress for working women provided that a married woman subject to the Serbian Civil Code had the consent of her husband to be employed (due to her legal incapacity). Anka considered that employment was a crucial instrument for economic emancipation of women: "A woman's right to work and right to have profession need to be understood as a legacy and benefit of the progress of humanity".[42] As she noted: "Depriving a woman of employment just because she is a mother, is horrible!"[43] She argued that, contrary to popular belief, employment had beneficial effect on marriages and families, as the empowerment which comes with employment brings about equality between partners and healthy relationships. Equal partners, rather than enslaved women, secure good marriages.

---

[38] In her account of the personal biographies of Gezina Van der Molen and Kanter-van Hettinga Tromp, Anka's Dutch counterparts and contemporaries, Janne E. Nijman wrote about the legal position of women in the interwar Netherlands:

"At the time [in 1923], the 1838 Civil Code was still in place, which considered married women *de jure* incapable of *any* legal act. They were *personae miserabilis*, and during the interwar period the legal position of married women deteriorated even further. From 1924 onwards, women who worked as civil servants were fired the day they married and married women were unemployable. After 1935, the law was extended to married female teachers at primary and secondary schools. They, too, were dismissed and would not be re-hired. Even while women had full suffrage, it would take until the mid-1950s for this discriminatory law to be abolished. This legislation had direct implications for young female international lawyers. Leiden, for example, was a state university. The law barred married women outright from any formal or recognized academic position, depriving them of a context for their scientific and professional ambitions. They had to choose between marriage or professional life." Nijman (2020), pp. 1036–1037.

[39] Mossman (2014), pp. 231–252.

[40] Godjevac (1934a), pp. 164–181.

[41] Godjevac (1934a), p. 165.

[42] Crnjanski (1931), p. 3.

[43] Crnjanski (1931), p. 3.

Stereotypes about women and their alleged inferiority are just the consequence of the centuries long slavery.[44]

The disadvantaged position of women in law in the interwar period was beyond any doubt. The problem was difficult to solve not only because the legislature was impenetrable for ideas of equality before the law or for political participation of women (the right to vote was not granted to women in Yugoslavia despite the promise made in the 1921 Constitution)[45] but also because culture and tradition stood in the way. Indeed, the law was the mirror of the society's understanding of women. How then to approach the problem and where to begin? In her article "On the battle of sexes" she asked: "How to calculate the equation involving a woman in public – is she a man plus or a man minus?" but concluded that "a man must abandon prejudices on his superiority and woman's inferiority, abandon his Balkan nature and recognize a woman for a *human being*."[46]

Therefore, the law of Yugoslavia in the interwar period was Anka's best companion and worst enemy. Although she had received the doctorate in public international law and published around 20 scholarly articles and the monograph on the Permanent Court of International Justice, in the course of only ten years, with some experience in foreign affairs and in international organisations, the question still remains whether she could call herself an international lawyer. Was it ever to be a profession of any women in Yugoslavia before the Second World War? She was devoted to the discipline as her profession although it certainly did not pay the bills.

In 1938 Anka married for the second time, at the age of 48, to Ivan Subbotić, international lawyer and diplomat, who received his doctorate in international law from the University of Lausanne in 1926 and who spent the whole interwar period in the diplomatic service of the Kingdom of Yugoslavia. He was a permanent delegate of the Kingdom of Yugoslavia in the League of Nations (1935–1939) and ambassador in London (1939–1941). In this marriage there did not seem to be problems for Anka's emancipation if for nothing else than for the fact that Ivan Subbotić was the grandson of Savka Subbotić, the first Serbian feminist. During the war this international law power couple moved to the United States where they effectively became refugees and in 1952 they both became U.S. citizens. Therefore, at the age of 54 she found for herself a new periphery: exile. She spent the last four decades of her life in New York. While in her new life she was still involved in women's rights, participating in organisations and associations, publishing and giving lectures, this was certainly done much less than before the war. Although effectively expelled from Yugoslavia, where her property was nationalized, she and her husband bequeathed valuable paintings and personal belongings to national institutions for culture in Serbia. Anka passed away at the age of 93 in New York of which she said "Once something is gone, nobody turns around or remembers. This is the city where dead

[44] Crnjanski (1931), p. 3.

[45] Article 70 of the 1921 Constitution delegated the issue of women's right to vote to ordinary legislation which then granted political rights solely to men.

[46] Godjevac (1928c), p. 3 (emphasis original).

do not disturb the living. Those who died once were and now are gone. No one wears a black mourning dress.”.[47]

3 Personal History of Women in International Law: Gender Exclusion and Feminist Solidarity

After the Great War feminist movements diversified, intensified and internationalised, so they quite early and easily formed transnational groups which tried to gain political leverage on both national and international level for their causes.[48] Although these movements had been heterogenous and scattered in different countries and gathered around different causes, the similar problems shared across the borders led to initiatives to collaborate on transnational and international levels. Therefore, women’s organisations naturally gravitated towards international law and the international legal sphere became an important site of activity for women[49] engaged in activism, journalism, culture or academia. As these interests generally included the problem of equality before the law and the right to vote, as well as interests in pacifism,[50] the interwar period of feminism is indeed best described as liberal feminism, and Yugoslavia was no exception in this respect.[51]

The involvement of women in war efforts, and casualties suffered by women and children in warfare unseen before, gave certain impetus to women’s rights and the legitimacy to their claims. These changes, within national borders, were strongly felt on the international stage, due to the change of the international landscape with the introduction of the Versailles system and the creation of the League of Nations.[52] Although international women’s organisations failed to secure participation at the Paris Peace Conference for which they fiercely lobbied (which demonstrates the silencing of female voices even in the renewed liberal settings), they still managed to acquire the right to submit proposals to certain committees.[53] This effort resulted in several provisions of the Covenant of the League of Nations addressing the status of women, this time in an international legal instrument. Article 23 requested the Member States endeavour to secure human labour conditions for men, women and children. The same provision entrusted the League with the right to supervise “the

[47] Godjevac-Subbotić (1961), p. 109.

[48] Rupp (1997), pp. 13–44.

[49] De la Rasilla (2020), p. 239.

[50] Vellacott (2001), pp. 375–94.

[51] Grubački (2020).

[52] “In 1919, with the war over and formal peace-making discussions among the victorious Entente powers in progress, feminist women brought renewed bravado to their internationalist agenda: a League of Nations that would stand up for women’s rights as well as maintain world peace.” Sluga (2016), p. 66.

[53] Macfayden et al. (2019) and Stienstra (1994), p. 73.

execution of agreements with regard to the traffic in women and children". Article 7(3) imposed gender equality as an obligation for the League itself: "All positions under or in connection with the League, including the Secretariat, shall be open equally to men and women." Universalism and internationalism announced by the creation of the League of Nations provided a new and promising platform for feminist movements and women's rights,[54] which must have been a success not only because general gender equality clauses were absent from national legal systems but also because the League of Nations rejected the insertion of the racial equality clause in the text of its Covenant.[55]

Although international feminist organisations managed to make the status of women an international question,[56] gender equality would never become a major international issue during the interwar period. Nevertheless, certain women's rights made their way on to the international law agenda and gained support of the League of Nations.[57] Immediately after the war certain women's organisations gained a small foothold at the League of Nations, most prominently the International Council of Women. This organization initiated the Joint Standing Committee of Women's International Organisations, later transformed to the Liaison Committee of Women's International Organisations, which worked to enable the participation of women in the League of Nations.[58] The initial plan of women's organisations was to procure the Equality Treaty, as a general gender equality instrument, but this attempt failed.

Women's rights and feminism movements had gained ground in Serbia and other territories of the future Yugoslavia back in the nineteenth century, but their expansion and development correspond to the interwar period.[59] This is of no coincidence as the women's movements in the Balkans generally followed the development of feminism worldwide. Within the Kingdom of Yugoslavia numerous women's organisations revived their activities and many new that were set up engaged in feminist activism. Anka Godjevac was a member of several women's and feminist organizations in the country (Women's Movement, Association of University Women,[60] Women's League for Peace, Yugoslav's Women Union, Women Lawyers Group of Yugoslavia) but also a prominent member of several international associations (International Alliance of Women for Suffrage and Equal Citizenship, L'Association des femmes diplomées aux Universités, World Woman's Party). She published in journals on feminism (Ženski pokret—Women's Movement) and extensively

[54] Lake (2001), p. 254.

[55] MacFayden et al. (2019), pp. 121, 241.

[56] Lake (2001), p. 254.

[57] Pietilä (2007), p. 8.

[58] De Haan (2020), https://ehne.fr/en/node/21305.

[59] Božinović (1996), pp. 2–5.

[60] This association was founded in 1927 and became member of the International Federation of University Women, itself established in 1919 as part of the trend of promotion of women's rights. The latter still exists today as Graduate Women International, https://graduatewomen.org/.

lectured mostly on the rights of women under private law in Yugoslavia, on nationality of married women, and on the legal issues relating to women that were raised within the League of Nations. She spoke and wrote about international feminism and pacifism.[61] As a writer herself she wrote extensively about feminist literature and women writers such as Grazia Deledda and Karin Michaëlis,[62] activity very common with interwar Yugoslav feminists. After all, activism for women's rights was commonplace for female intellectuals of that time, not only in Yugoslavia.

Anka Godjevac was appointed as an international law expert for nationality of married women, within the national delegation for the Hague Codification Conference in 1930,[63] which was the success credited to feminist organisations.[64] Nationality of married women was high on the feminist agenda of that time[65] and the Hague Codification Conference agenda on nationality was an important battlefield for the feminist groups as they lobbied the States to adopt the equal rights principle regarding the nationality of married women and their right to choose nationality upon marriage if their national law excluded the possibility of dual nationality. The Hague Codification Conference was a disappointment for feminists as the Convention upheld the so-called principle of family unity which favoured automatic acquisition of the husband's nationality upon marriage thereby confirming the gender inequality between spouses. According to feminists at the Conference, the deprivation of nationality upon marriage amounted to the deprivation of the most fundamental political right, the right to citizenship.[66] In addition, the Conference refused to insert the equality clause in the text of the convention.[67]

Many national women's organisations formed international alliances and federations, made closely knitted networks and collaborated on different levels.[68] This in itself was an act of solidarity and evidence of the universal problems of gender inequality in different national settings. Initiatives were coming from international and transnational networks to national level and the other way round. An example of how the transnational network influenced feminist organizing in Yugoslavia is the Association of University Women that was established in Yugoslavia in 1927 following the initiative and support of the International Federation of University Women and its president Ellen Gleditsch.[69] Intergovernmental initiatives also gave impetus to feminist transnational organizations. The Little Entente of Women was

[61] Godjevac (1937), pp. 442–443. Within the organisation of the Women's League for Peace she lectured about the pacifism of Bertha von Suttner, *Vreme* (1932, April 9).

[62] Godjevac (1927); Godjevac (1928a), pp. 189–202; Godjevac (1928b).

[63] Convention on Certain Questions Relating to the Conflict of Nationality Laws, League of Nations Official Journal 11, no. 7 (July 1930), 847-928, at 911); Godjevac (1930).

[64] Atanacković (1930), pp. 2–3.

[65] Sluga (2000), pp. 495–521.

[66] Miller (1994), p. 227.

[67] Stienstra (1994), p. 68; Godjevac (1931a).

[68] Rupp (1997), pp. 13–44; Stienstra (1994), pp. 65–66; Ludi (2019), p. 13.

[69] Obradović (1998), pp. 254–255.

modelled in line with the Little Entente of Czechoslovakia, Romania and Yugoslavia.[70] Also, feminist organisations of the Balkan states undertook concerted action to participate in the Balkan Conferences in Athens (1930), Istanbul (1931) and Bucharest (1932).[71] Anka participated in the third Balkan Conference where several Yugoslav feminists took roles in different working bodies and commissions, while Anka Godjevac acted as the president of all women's societies at the conference[72] Such feminist organizing along the lines of different state initiatives (Little Entente—Little Entente of Women; initiative for the Balkan alliance—Balkan conferences; League of Nations—Women for the League of Nations) was a general trend of interwar liberal feminism[73] and partly explains the lenient attitude of women toward the foreign policies of their own governments. The goal of feminists was to use the international stage and existing infrastructure to set international standards that could potentially effectuate changes on national levels.

Following the successful participation at the conferences in the Hague and Bucharest, Anka was invited by the Joint Standing Committee of Women's International Organizations to attend as an expert at the session of the League of Nations in the autumn of 1931.[74] In 1935 she attended the 12th congress of the International Alliance of Women for Suffrage and Equal Citizenship held in Istanbul, as a part of the national delegation.[75] The support of international feminist organisations continued and Anka subsequently was appointed as one of seven members of the Committee of Experts for Legal Status of Women, set up by the League of Nations in 1937.[76] The Committee had four female members: Anka Godjevac, Susanne Bastide (France, professor of international law), Dorothy Kenyon (U.S., lawyer and activist), and Kerstin Hesselgren (Sweden, rapporteur on the status of women to the First Committee of the Assembly).[77] The Committee was set up with the task to provide a comparative survey of the legal status of women in different countries and legal systems. Anka seemed to have been the candidate proposed by the equalitarian fraction of international women's organizations:[78] "The equalitarians

---

[70] Grubački (2020).

[71] Davaz (2020), pp. 1–11.

[72] Lebl-Albala (1939), pp. 28–29; Godjevac (1931b).

[73] Grubački (2020).

[74] Obradović (1998), p. 258.

[75] *Report of the Twelfth Congress, Istanbul, 18-24 April, 1935*, p. 210. London, England: International Alliance of Women Records, 1906-2009 (Box 2, Folder 6, 217pp.), Sophia Smith Collection. Women's History Archive. Wadsworth and Company.

[76] League of Nations 1937. V. 49–50.

[77] League Committee of Experts on Status of Women (1937), International Documents on Status of Women, Bulletin of the Woman's Bureau No. 217, 11-12.

[78] Equal Rights International (ERI) proposed Betty Archdale (Great Britain) and Anka Godjevac (Yugoslavia) - *Council Meeting Minutes of the Equal Rights International, January 6th, 1938,* p. 1 para. 3. National Woman's Party Records, 1850-1975 (Folder 6, Box IV:15). United States. Library of Congress. Manuscript Division. Retrieved from Women and Social Movements, International database.

were represented by the Yugoslav Anna Godjevac."[79] unlike some others, such as Dorothy Kenyon, who was perceived as advocating so-called protectionist policies.[80] However, one should not disregard the fact that the Secretariat of the League shortlisting the candidates gave precedence to those who had the approval of their governments,[81] which means that Anka must have also had support and possibly close connections with the Yugoslav political establishment.

While setting up the committee to provide a comparative overview of the legal status of women fell short of the ambitions of feminists pursuing something grander, such as the Equal Rights Treaty,[82] there still was hope that this study could end up with propositions to improve gender equality by adopting such a treaty.[83] It was still a success because, as Regula Ludi observes, the Committee of Experts was the first intergovernmental agency that addressed the disadvantages that women suffered worldwide as a matter of international concern, and the first and only League's body constituted on the basis of gender parity.[84] There was a close link between the Hague Conference and the Committee as the latter was established due to the League's agenda on Equal Nationality Treaty[85] so the activities on equal rights which failed in the Hague, were continued within the League of Nations, and Anka's involvement in the work of the Hague Codification Conference partly explains her candidacy for the Committee and the support she gained from international women's organisations. The Committee was empowered[86] to work closely with international women's organizations.[87] Despite all accolades for the Committee and its female fighters for equality, it needs to be noted, as Regula Ludi puts it that "[h]ardly any of the vociferous defenders of sex equality represented countries with outstanding records of improving women's status."[88]

---

[79] Eisenberg (2013), p. 13.

[80] Eisenberg (2013), p. 139. Protectionists generally strived to gradual and gender-sensitive improvement of women's rights, while equalitarians fought for the full equality of women with men.

[81] Ludi (2019), pp. 20–21.

[82] Miller (1994), pp. 236–237.

[83] Pfeffer (1985), p. 467.

[84] Ludi (2019), p. 13.

[85] Eisenberg (2013), pp. 11–13.

[86] "Considering that this committee should have power to consult women's international organizations and invite their cooperation in any form which it thinks advisable." – Resolution Creating Committee of Experts on Legal Status of Women, Adopted by League of Nations Assembly, 1937, League of Nations, Official No. A. 64. 1937. V, para. 10.

[87] "Although it was emphasized that the Experts' recommendations would be entirely 'objective', eight international women's organizations – Equal Rights International, the International Alliance of Women for Suffrage and Equal Citizenship, the International Council of Women, the International Federation of Women Magistrates and members of the Legal Profession, St Joan's Social and Political Alliance, the Women's International League for Peace and Freedom, the World Union of Women for International Concord and the World Woman's Christian Temperance Union – were permitted to make representations to the Committee of Experts" – Lake (2001), p. 262.

[88] Ludi (2019), p. 23.

Anka's connections with organisations which fought for full gender equality, most notably her personal friendship with Alice Paul, legendary feminist and leader of the National Women's Party, are evidenced in their personal correspondence. Alice Paul was a fierce feminist and tireless lobbyist who was behind the 19th amendment of the U.S. Constitution on women's right to vote, but who was also behind ERA (Equal Rights Amendment proposal for the U.S. Constitution), ERI (Equal Rights International), and initiatives to make gender equality a condition for membership in the League of Nations. She was further the author of the draft of the Equal Rights Treaty[89] and "was instrumental in having a reference to sex equality included in the preamble to the United Nations charter".[90] Alice Paul launched a similar campaign for equal rights with respect to the jurisdiction of the Permanent Court of International Justice under the optional clause by proposing the equality reservation to be inserted in the potential declaration of the Unites States accepting jurisdiction. Anka Godjevac supported the initiative and proposed amendments for the equality reservation.[91] Her involvement with the National Woman's Party and friendship with Alice Paul continued following the interwar period, after Anka had found refuge in the United States. Anka became the honorary secretary and member of the World Council of the World Woman's Party, established in 1938 to fight for the equality clause in all international agreements, which provided shelter to many feminists during the war.[92] The World Woman's Party was pivotal for securing the equality clause in the UN Charter and UN Declaration on Human Rights.[93] In her 1947 report "Progress for Women in the United States" Anka described the efforts behind the adoption of the first UN GA resolution on political rights of women in 1946,[94] the adoption of which was attended by Alice Paul, Anka Soubbotitch and other members of the World Woman's Party who were "present in the gallery to witness the historic victory".[95]

Feminist engagement with international law and the League of Nations fell short of initial hopes and plans. While women were given the right to make certain proposals, the concessions made were still minimal and strictly limited to 'women's issues'.[96] Limiting women's engagement to interests based on gender perceptions is a step away from stereotyping. Full equality for which international feminists fought

---

[89] Stienstra (1994), p. 73.

[90] Frost-Knappman and Cullen-DuPont (2005), p. 445.

[91] National Women's Party (1932), p. 4-4.

[92] Stienstra (1994), p. 76.

[93] Harvard Radcliffe Institute. https://www.radcliffe.harvard.edu/schlesinger-library/collections/alice-paul

[94] Political Rights of Women, A/RES/56(I), Adopted at the 55th plenary meeting, 11 Dec. 1946.

[95] Soubbotitch (1947), *Progress for Women in the United States*, National Woman's Party Records, 1850-1975 (Series VII, Reel 175), United States. Library of Congress. Manuscript Division. Retrieved from Women and Social Movements, International database, 5-6.

[96] "Finally the League gave international women's groups observer status to those committees that addressed 'women's issues'. Women's groups were not given access to committees that discussed political or financial matters, nor did they challenge their limited access."—Stienstra (n 53) 154.

exceeded roles traditionally attributed to women. While any breakthrough on the international stage must have been seen as progress during the interwar period, in terms of winning the right to voice opinion even if only on matters directly affecting women, it still falls short of substantive equality.[97] As contemporary studies persuasively demonstrate the presence of women in international courts proves that women judges "discharged the duties expected of any person holding a judicial office" but also "that women have made a particularly distinct contribution to the understanding and development of international human rights and criminal law in so far as it takes into account women's rights and perspectives."[98] There is no justification for limiting the role of international female lawyers or for preserving the glass ceiling.

The history of women's rights in the League of Nations puts some of its results into a different perspective today and what could originally be termed as championing women's rights might have easily turned into reinforcing stereotypes and ghettoization. As noted by Grossman in 2016: "UN human rights treaty bodies show ghettoization of women on the Committee on the Elimination of Discrimination Against Women, where women made up 22 of 23 members, and on the Committee on the Rights of the Child, where they accounted for 11 of 18 members. Yet women made up only 10% of the UN Committee on Enforced Disappearances, 22% of the UN Human Rights Committee, the Committee on Economic, Social and Cultural Rights, and the Committee on the Elimination of Racial Discrimination."[99] These developments demonstrate the perplexing persistence of a 'gendered persona',[100] even a paradox, because claims to equality and inclusion have had the opposite effect in inequality and exclusion. Such segregation of women, on one hand, and underrepresentation, on the other, fall short of the idea that women's rights are human rights and represents rather an awkward method of remedying the systemic disadvantage of women and of attaining the substantive, as opposed to formal equality.

This is, of course, part of the wider debate on why and how women should be represented in international decision-making bodies. The 'why' question might seem easy to answer. It is the history of marginalization and bias that have plagued decision-making, and that representativeness of women could ensure legitimacy of

[97] "[T]he history of the engagement of women's rights advocates with human rights law highlights a conundrum; feminist inclusion strategies have reproduced unequal relations of gender power in their efforts to make women's gender-specific human rights violations legally cognizable and achieve women's full inclusion in a universal discourse. The method of making the 'gendered human rights facts' of women's lives legally actionable repeats the hierarchical gender scripts that produce the gendered violations in the first place. Unless feminist strategies can be re-scripted to disrupt the circular restaging of women's marginalization, the most that will be achieved will be some uncertain improvements in the conditions of that marginalization, which will always be vulnerable to reversal because the underpinnings of women's inequality will not have been disrupted." Otto (2006), p. 351.

[98] Powderly and Chylinski (2017), p. 179.

[99] Grossman (2016), p. 341.

[100] Otto (2006), pp. 320–321.

institutions and their decisions because of the underlying assumption that interests of certain groups are protected by the inclusion of a member of that group in the decision-making process. While this assumption is not to be refuted too easily or too hastily, there are plausible arguments that gender equality may not necessarily be achieved by a mere inclusion of women in a decision-making process as they themselves might inherit gender stereotypes but also inhabit different identities and backgrounds, from nationality and race to social class. These other identities may pervade their gender sensitivities in decision-making, or women may easily wish to adapt to new environment of male peers and adjust their judicial or other preferences to them.[101]

These insights shed light on some appointments for the League of Nations Committee on the Status of Women. For example, the obvious candidate from the United States for the place on the Committee was Alice Paul, but her government decided to appoint Dorothy Kenyon who was considered a protectionist and more moderate and who opposed the equal rights approach.[102] We do not know much about how Anka's gender and national background affected her equal rights approach and participation within the Committee: was it driven by her marginalized position in terms of her activism, nationality and gender, or was it more complacent towards the role of the League of Nations in minimising gender issues? The second question is how women should be represented in order to instigate change within international decision-making. Føllesdal identifies four levels of inequality discussed in the literature and in the arguments supporting different levels of participation of women in international courts: a token representation of at least one member of the two prevalent sexes, a critical mass of 15–25%, a parity zone of at least 40% of each, or complete parity of sex representation.[103] All these considerations demonstrate that attaining substantive gender equality includes not only the delicate issue of representation, which is prone to the risks of both under- and over- representation, but also the ability for gendering agendas of international decision-making. The short episode of the League of Nations Committee on the Status of Women illustrates the illusion of victory as women's representation did not bring about the change hoped for.

4 Personal History of the Inter-War Period: From Peace Treaties to Peace Collapse

The newly formed Kingdom of Serbs, Croats and Slovenes (Yugoslavia) was a latecomer to modern development, a peripheral country in the new world. The history and destiny of Serbia and Yugoslavia are closely intertwined with the

---

[101] Hunter (2015), pp. 119–141.
[102] Pfeffer (1985), p. 467.
[103] Føllesdal (2021), pp. 1–23.

Great War and its aftermath. Already exhausted by the Balkan wars (1912–1913) Serbia suffered devastating human casualties and huge material losses, arguably the worst of any other country: one million or one fourth of its pre-war population died and one half of the pre-war wealth was destroyed during the war.[104] However, it emerged from the war victorious as part of the Allied and Associated Powers, which further led to the creation of a new country, the Kingdom of Serbs, Croats and Slovenes, which was renamed to the Kingdom of Yugoslavia in 1929. As a member of the victors' bloc, the new country shared the spirit of internationalism of the new era. After all, the creation of the Kingdom of Yugoslavia was ratified by Peace Treaties and international law seemed to be an ally of the new country. The benefits of the new international legal system were not only in the aggrandisement of the territory and emancipation of its peoples, but also in the entitlement to war reparations and to participation in the newly established League of Nations. However, the proclaimed sovereign equality was less equal for some: the newcomers received additional obligations in minority treaties[105] and there was difference in distribution of war reparations[106] so the distinction between the Allied and Associated countries became the one between the centre and periphery. This was but one confirmation of the perception of the Balkans preceding and following the Great War: "The Balkans were always, and have perhaps remained, second-class states in the European polity."[107]

Set out on task to modernize society, with international legal system on its side, it followed naturally for Yugoslavia and its elite to turn to international law. Therefore, the interest of Anka Godjevac in international law was strongly rooted in both her citizenship and feminism. There was yet another feature of the new international law: strong support for the principle of peaceful settlement of international disputes resulting in the creation of the Permanent Court of International Justice, which fitted well with the politics of pacifism pursued by feminist organizations. Her doctoral dissertation "Principles and rules of international law as derived from the jurisprudence of the Permanent Court of International Justice" represents a detailed analysis of the case law of the PCIJ and a meticulous exercise in legal positivism. Her approach was as close to the scientific analysis of law as possible, a laboratory exercise in collecting and organizing international legal rules. In an attempt to be scientifically objective, she openly declared that "the purpose and goal of this research is to induce and systematize all rules of international law which were expressly or tacitly affirmed by the PCIJ during the first nine years of its work. (. . .) Therefore, no critical evaluation of the Court's judgments and opinions will be

[104] Aldcroft (2006), pp. 77–78.

[105] "[M]inorities regime, a system through which the League Council, guided by Secretariat officials, sought to hold a dozen new or reconstituted East European or Balkan states to promises of minority rights they had made as the price of sovereignty." Pedersen (2015), p. 9.

[106] Glasgow (1930), p. 233; Steiner (2005), pp. 58, 92; Tyler (1930), p. 113; Vučo (1968), pp. 5–8.

[107] Crampton (2007), p. 269.

present in this work."[108] Anka even counted the number of rules extrapolated from the jurisprudence of the PCIJ – she found "over 120 of international rules" identified as such and applied by the PCIJ.[109]

Her focus on peaceful settlement of international disputes as an international law discipline was natural and nearly instinctive. It combined well her interest in the new international law epitomised in the creation of the first permanent international court and her pacifism. Although she argued that "among all means for peaceful settlement of international disputes available today, the PCIJ is certainly the most perfect institution",[110] she would write critically of the PCIJ. For example, in her analysis of the *Serbian Loans* case[111] she criticized the PCIJ decision on jurisdiction arguing against the finding of the Court that the dispute between private French creditors and the Kingdom of Serbs, Croats and Slovenes was of international law character as there was no international obligation of the Kingdom in relation to French creditors.[112] Consequently, she argues, there was no jurisdiction *ratione materiae* and the fact that there were negotiations between the two governments did not turn the dispute into an international law dispute which is a prerequisite for the Court to take the case. Will this be an exceptional case, or will it set the path for new rules on jurisdiction *ratione materiae*? If the latter is the case than "practically any private law dispute can come under the jurisdiction of the PCIJ." Her sense of the novelty of the issue was later confirmed as subsequent commentaries qualified this judgment as a precedent for investment treaty protection of foreign debt.[113]

Concerns regarding the creation of international obligations that could adversely affect certain countries, which might had not even participated in their creation, came also to the forefront in her analysis of the Hague Codification Conference in 1930. One of the questions on the agenda was the responsibility of states for damage done in their territory to the person or property of foreigners. The context was the idea to set the clear rules on state responsibility for injuries to aliens, most particularly with respect to Soviet Russia and China. She noted the following: "The problems occurred at the very beginning with the definition of international obligation that was to be the ground for state responsibility for these matters. While certain states argued that only international agreements could create such an obligation, Great Powers tried to incorporate all obligations including those arising under customary international law. Small states, especially those with a substantial number of aliens with business and profit-making purposes, opposed this interpretation as this could vest aliens with more rights and privileges than their own nationals. These questions split the committee into two groups: minority comprised of Great Powers

[108] Godjevac (1933), p. 3.

[109] Godjevac (1932b), p. 84.

[110] Godjevac (1935, March 28).

[111] Payment of Various Serbian Loans Issued in France (France v Kingdom of the Serbs, Croats, and Slovenes), Judgment of 12 July 1929, PCIJ Series A no 20.

[112] Godjevac (1934b), pp. 208–214.

[113] Wälde (2004).

and countries whose nationals travel abroad for profit-making purposes, on one hand, and another, but larger minority, comprised of states to which aliens come to make profit, on the other hand. The question of legal position of aliens in relation to nationals was the thorny issue at both the autumn International Paris Conference (1929) and the Hague Conference (1930)."[114] This initiative failed as did several earlier drafts and resolutions.[115] In 2018 Chimni illustrated the perception of the customary international law by countries of the third world which demonstrates the long-lasting anxieties of underdeveloped countries and mistrust in the very concept of customary law. As Chimni argues, customary international law has served for the benefits of colonial, imperial and postcolonial projects, while third world countries were caught in the concept without any real possibility to participate in the creation of either practice or *opinion juris*.[116] The same mistrust was plainly demonstrated much earlier and Anka's view of the 1930 Hague Conference is yet another example.

International legal scholarship in Yugoslavia thrived during the interwar period but was overly dominated by men. Anka Godjevac was the only female member of the Yugoslav Association of International Law during that time and the only woman who authored texts on international law.[117] Her texts on the Permanent Court of International Justice published in legal journals belong to the mainstream scholarship and there was little which could differentiate her from her male colleagues in terms of originality or criticism.[118] However, the mere presence of a woman in the gentlemen's club was what really mattered for the emancipation of legal scholarship and was a genuine claim for gender equality.

There was another periphery that was available where she settled herself comfortably. That was her national identity and her patriotism which seemed complementary to her feminism[119] and internationalism. When she was asked to comment on her participation in the national delegation at the Hague Codification Conference on nationality of married women, she was proud of both her role and a new piece of progressive Yugoslav legislation which provided the right of choice of nationality of a married woman. The right to retain nationality equalled women with men. Her position demonstrates her feminist patriotism but also the sense of marginalisation, different identities she inhabited: "As a feminist I was delighted to be with my female friends in the Hague regardless of the fact that only few of us were there. (. . .) I felt so small in that world of great lawyers but at the same time I was very happy I

[114]Godjevac (1985), pp. 21–22.

[115]The similar assessment of the failed initiatives at the 1930 Hague Conference can be found in the work of the International Law Commission. – First Report on State Responsibility by Roberto Ago, Yearbook of International Law Commission 1969, Vol. II, 132.

[116]Chimni (2018), pp. 1–46.

[117]Bibliography of international law texts written by Yugoslav authors in the interwar period (1920-1936) contains around 2000 bibliographical units. Anka Godjevac is the only female international lawyer referenced in the bibliography. Pržić (1931), pp. 351–393; Pržić (1937), pp. 351–424.

[118]Godjevac (1926, 1929, 1932b, 1933, 1934b, 1934c, 1935).

[119]Just like Svetlana Tomić described another Serbian feminist, Jelena Dimitrijević. Tomić (2014), p. 120.

could present our progressive legislation on nationality of married women, and I have to notice that a mere fact that our country sent a female delegate was wonderfully received in that world that does not know us well. (...) Our laws which defend women left some impression. You know how the West still perceives the Balkans."[120] Indeed, who would think that the request to place the question of the status of women on the agenda of the Assembly of the League of Nations in 1937 came from the periphery, from Albania, Bolivia, Bulgaria, China, Columbia, Cuba, Czechoslovakia, Ecuador, Haiti, Latvia, Turkey, and Yugoslavia?[121]

Anka Godjevac Subbotić was a staunch proponent of cooperation of the Balkan countries. Her participation at the third Balkan conference and writings on cooperation in the Balkans imply the idea of emancipation of the region and the strong feeling of identity of not only countries but also of peoples of the region of Balkans. As part of her unwavering support for cooperation and alliance of Balkan countries, she made a remark on the cultural chauvinism of the day: "Romanian Minister of Foreign Affairs, Mr. Titulescu, was so right when he remarked in his opening speech that it was high time for the Western Europe and the world to cease treating us as the hotbed of turmoil and chaos."[122] In the turmoil and chaos to come, Yugoslavia and the Balkans were rather the victims than villains. In her essay "Agony of the Balkans" she described the eruption of the war in the Balkans,[123] the war which made her a refugee: "we who lost everything of any importance, we who lost our country and our names."[124]

5 Conclusion

Following the First World War international law seemed promising for disadvantaged groups including women and Balkan nations. New international law projected a sense of progress and new possibilities, the air of universalism and pacifism. These new ideas attracted many to international law which was perceived as a powerful instrument for emancipatory struggles. These ideas were embraced by women in their quest for equality and by new nations to claim their rightful position in the family of nations. The League of Nations seemed as a new champion of international law and edifice for peace in the new legal order. However, despite some progress made the new system ultimately betrayed its followers—gender equality was never

[120] Crnjanski (1931), p. 3.

[121] "We consider that, in the present crisis in human affairs, it is important that the League of Nations should encourage the co-operation of all elements not now fully represented among us, and we therefore deem it wise for the League to consider the wishes of international groups of women as of all other groups." League of Nations 1937, pp. 45–46.

[122] Godjevac (1932c), p. 160.

[123] Godjevac-Subbotić (1966).

[124] Godjevac-Subbotić (1961), p. 122.

fully attained on either national and international level and states in the Balkans soon found that their position in the periphery was their political reality. International law failed to deliver peace, progress and universalism once promised. The collapse of interwar international law, the League of Nations, and Yugoslavia marked the end of the era.

The personal history of Anka Godjevac Subbotić follows the trajectory of the history of Yugoslavia and the development of interwar international law. Given that she was the first and only woman engaged in international law during the interwar Yugoslavia, her personal and professional background, her activism and feminism, provide us with unique perspectives on the era, of both the centre and the periphery. Her story is the story of women in Yugoslavia and in international law, of local and international feminist movements, and of the rise and fall of interwar international law and Yugoslavia. Breaking the silence surrounding her life could be empowering for all Ankas of the new age so that her tall figure does not stand alone anymore.

References

Aldcroft DH (2006) Europe's Third World: the European periphery in the interwar years. Ashgate, Aldershot

Atanacković M (1930) G-đa Anka Gođevac: ekspert pri delegaciji naše države na konferenciji u Hagu. Ženski pokret 11(5/6):2–3

Beard M (2017) Women and power: a manifesto. Profile Books, London

Božinović N (1996) Žensko pitanje u Srbiji u XIX i XX veku. Devedesetčetvrta – Žene u crnom, Belgrade

Chimni BS (2018) Customary international law: a third world perspective. Am J Int Law 112:1–46

Ćirković S (1928) Žena i diplomacija – Treba li ženama dopustiti stupanje u diplomatsku službu? Dom maloletnika, Belgrade

Crampton RJ (2007) The Balkans. In: Gerwarth R (ed) Twisted paths: Europe 1914–1945. Oxford University Press, New York, pp 237–270

Crnjanski M (1931) Gde živi najsrećnija žena Jugoslavije – Razgovor sa gospođom Ankom Gođevac. Vreme, January 31

Davaz A (2020) An annotated archive of entangled European feminist history: The Union of Turkish Women, the Second Balkan Conference and Cécile Brunschvicg's Visit to Balkan Feminists (1923-1935). Feminist Encounters J Critical Stud Culture Politics 4(2):28

De Haan F (2020) European Women and the Main International Women's Organizations. Encyclopédie d'histoire numérique de l'Europe. https://ehne.fr/en/node/21305

De la Rasilla I (2020) Concepción Arenal and the place of women in modern international law. Tijdschrift voor Rechtsgeschiedenis 88:211–253

Draškić M, Popović-Obradović O (1998) Pravni položaj žene prema Srpskom građanskom zakoniku (1844-1946). In: Perović L (ed) Srbija u modernizacijskim procesima 19. i 20. veka - Položaj žene kao merilo modernizacije. Institut za noviju istoriju Srbije, Belgrade, pp 11–25

Eisenberg J (2013) The status of women: a bridge from the League of Nations to the United Nations. J Int Organ Stud 4:8–24

Emmert T (1999) Ženski pokret: the feminist movement in Serbia in the 1920s. In: Ramet SP (ed) Gender politics in the Western Balkans: women and society in Yugoslavia and the Yugoslav successor states. The Pennsylvania State University Press, University Park Pennsylvania, pp 33–49

Føllesdal A (2021) How many women judges are enough on international courts? J Soc Philos

Frost-Knappman E, Cullen-DuPont K (2005) Women's suffrage in America. Facts on File, New York
Glasgow G (1930) The Hague conference and Non-German reparations. J Royal Institute Int Aff 9: 232–235
Godjevac A (1926) Liga naroda i medjunarodni problemi. Arhiv za pravne i društvene nauke 22: 327–331
Godjevac A (1927) Karin Mihaelis. Misao 23:327–333
Godjevac A (1928a) Poslednja Nobelova nagrada za književnost i italijanska spisateljka Gracija Deleda. Letopis Matice srpske 102:189–202
Godjevac A (1928b) G-đa Karin Mihaelis, čuvena danska spisateljka doputovala je juče u Beograd. Vreme, February 7
Godjevac A (1928c) O borbi polova. Ženski pokret 9:3
Godjevac A (1929) La composition du Conseil de la Société des Nations. Srpski književni glasnik 28:25–26
Godjevac A (1930) Rad i rezultati Konferencije za kodifikaciju medjunarodnog prava. In: Pereplotčkov R (ed) Dr Anka Godjevac: Pravni članci i rasprave, 1980. Katarina Perić, Ružica Pereplotčikov, Belgrade, pp 15–22
Godjevac A (1931a) Pitanje državljanstva žene pred Savetom Društva naroda. Vreme, August 24
Godjevac A (1931b) Međunarodni biro za mir i Balkanska konferencija. Letopis Matice srpske 327: 133–136
Godjevac A (1931c) Letošnji kursevi na Haškoj akademiji za međunarodno pravo. Arhiv za pravne i društvene nauke 41:167–171
Godjevac A (1932a) Pitanje državljanstva udate žene pred Ligom naroda. Letopis Matice srpske 334:69–79
Godjevac A (1932b) Osnovna pravna načela na kojima počiva jurisprudencija Stalnog suda međunarodne pravde. Arhiv za pravne i društvene nauke 42:83–95
Godjevac A (1932c) O radu III Balkanske konferencije u Bukureštu. Ženski pokret 13:160–161
Godjevac A (1933) Principles and rules of international law as derived from the jurisprudence of the Permanent Court of International Justice. Geca Kon, Belgrade
Godjevac A (1934a) Položaj žene u Jugoslaviji prema građanskom pravu i prema specijalnim zakonima. In: Djurdjević Č, Veljić J (eds) Treća balkanska konferencija – Rad jugoslovenske nacionalne grupe. Jugoslovenska nacionalna grupa za Balkansku konferenciju, Belgrade, pp 164–181
Godjevac A (1934b) Compétence de la Cour Permanente de Justice Internationale ratione personae et ratione materiae par rapport au différend concertant les emprunts Serbes. Annuaire de l'Association Yougoslave de Droit International 2:208–214
Godjevac A (1934c) Medjunarodno pravosudje današnjice. Arhiv za pravne i društvene nauke 46(2):397–405
Godjevac A (1935) Permanent Court of International Justice in light of interesting interstate disputes. Pravda, March 28
Godjevac A (1937) Activité pacifiste des femmes en Yougoslavie. Annuaire de l'Association Yougoslave de Droit Internatonal 3:442–443
Godjevac-Subbotić A (1961) Sa tri kontinenta: sabrani putopisi. Srpska misao, Melburn
Godjevac-Subbotić A (1966) Agonija Balkana – ispisi iz mog ratnog dnevnika. Srpska Misao 1956-1966. Srpska misao, Melbourne
Godjevac A (1985) Pravni članci i rasprave. Katarina Perić i Ružica Pereplotčkov, Beograd
Grossman N (2016) Shattering the glass ceiling in International adjudication. Va J Int Law 56:339–406
Grubački I (2020) The Emergence of the Yugoslav Interwar Liberal Feminist Movement and the Little Entente of Women: An Entangled History Approach (1919–1924). Feminist Encounters: A Journal of Critical Studies in Culture and Politics
Hunter R (2015) More than just a different face? Judicial diversity and decision-making. Curr Legal Prob 68:119–141

Kandić L (2002) Istorija Pravnog fakulteta u Beogradu 1905-1941, vol II(2). University of Belgrade Faculty of Law, Belgrade
Katičić N (1937) Principes et règles de droit international qui se dégagent de la jurisprudence de la Cour permanente de Justice Internatioanle de La Haye. Thèse de doctorat de Mme Anka Godyevatz. Annuaire de l'Association Yougoslave de Droit International 3:269–272
Knežević I (1967) Stručni problem žena pravnika u staroj Jugoslaviji. Odvjetnik 7:237–242
Krkljuš L (1990) Pravni položaj žene u Vojvodini pre Drugog svetskog rata. Zbornik Matice srpske za društvene nauke 88:93–104
Lake M (2001) From self-determination via protection to equality via non- discrimination: defining women's rights at the league of Nations. In: Grimshaw P, Holmes K, Lake M (eds) Women's Rights and Human Rights: International Historical Perspectives. Palgrave, New York, pp 254–275
League of Nations (1937) Status of Women - Communication from Fifteen Delegations Regarding the Placing of the Above Matter on the Assembly's Agenda. League Nations Official J Special Supplement 170:42–53
Lebl-Albala P (1928) Razvoj univerzitetskog obrazovanja naših žena. Letopis Matice srpske 316: 17–28
Lebl-Albala P (1939) Deset godina rada Udruženja univerzitetski obrazovanih žena u Jugoslaviji: 1928-1938. Udruženje univerzitetski obrazovanih žena: Sloboda, Beograd
Ludi R (2019) Setting new standards: International feminism and the league of nation's inquiry into the status of women. J Women's History 31:12–36
Macfayden D, Davies MDV, Carr MN, Burley J (2019) Eric Drummond and his legacies the league of Nations and the beginnings of Global Governance. Palgrave Macmillan, Geneva
Magazinović M (2000) In: Šantić J (ed) Moj život. Clio, Belgrade
Miller C (1994) "Geneva – the key to equality": inter-war feminists and the league of nations. Women's History Rev 3:219–245
Mossman MJ (2014) Women lawyers and women's equality movements at the turn of the twentieth century: paradoxical relationships? In: Schandevyl E (ed) Women in law and lawmaking in nineteenth and twentieth-century Europe. Ashgate, Burlington, pp 231–252
National Women's Party (1932) Anna Godyevatz supports equality reservation. Equal Rights 18:4–4
Nijman JE (2020) Marked absences: locating gender and race in International Legal History. Eur J Int Law 31:1025–1050
Norris D (1999) In the wake of the Balkan myth. MacMillan Press Ltd, London
Obradović M (1998) Udruženje univerzitetski obrazovanih žena u Jugoslaviji 1927-1941. godine. In: Perović L (ed) Srbija u modernizacijskim procesima 19. i 20. veka - Položaj žene kao merilo modernizacije. Institut za noviju istoriju Srbije, Belgrade, pp 252–222
Obregon L (2019) Peripheral histories of International Law. Ann Rev Law Soc Sci 15:437–451. https://www.annualreviews.org/doi/10.1146/annurev-lawsocsci-110316-113348
Otto D (2006) Lost in translation: re-scripting the sexed subjects of international human rights law. In: Orford A (ed) International Law and Its Others. Cambridge University Press, Cambridge, pp 318–356
Pedersen S (2015) The guardians: the league of nations and the crisis of Empire. Oxford University Press, Oxford
Perić Ž (1928) Položaj žene u Srpskom građanskom zakoniku. Arhiv za pravne i društvene nauke 16:6–31
Pfeffer P (1985) 'A Whisper in the Assembly of Nations;' United States' Participation in the International Movement for Women's Rights from the League of Nations to the United Nations. Women's Stud Int Forum 8:459–471
Pietilä H (2007) The unfinished story of women and the United Nations. United Nations, New York
Powderly J, Chylinski J (2017) The women judges: leading the line in the development of international law. In: Schabas W, Murphy S (eds) Research Handbook on International Courts and Tribunals. Edgar Elgar Publishing, Cheltenham, pp 143–180

Pržić, Ilija. 1931. Bibliography. Annuaire de l'Association Yougoslave de Droit International, 351–393. Belgrade–Paris
Pržić I (1937) Bibliography. Annuaire de l'Association Yougoslave de Droit International, troisième volume, 351–424. Belgrade-Paris
Rupp LJ (1997) Worlds of Women: the making of an International Women's Movement. Princeton University Press, Princeton
Schulz U (2003) Introduction: women in the World's Legal Professions: overview and synthesis. In: Schulz U, Shaw G (eds) Women in the World's Legal Professions. Hart Publishing, Oxford, pp xxv–lxii
Sluga G (2000) Female and national self-determination, a gender re-reading of 'The Apogee of Nationalism'. Nations Nationalism 6:495–521
Sluga G (2016) Women, feminisms and twentieth-century internationalisms. In: Sluga G, Clavin P (eds) Internationalisms: a twentieth-century history. Cambridge University Press, Cambridge, pp 61–84
Soubbotitch A (1947) Progress for Women in the United States. National Woman's Party Records, 1850-1975 (Series VII, Reel 175), United States. Library of Congress. Manuscript Division. Retrieved from Women and Social Movements, International database
Steiner Z (2005) The lights that failed: European International History 1919–1933. Oxford University Press, Oxford
Stienstra D (1994) Women's movements and international organizations. Macmillan Press Ltd, London
Stojaković G (2017) The First lawyers and attorneys: the struggle for professional recognition of women's rights in Yugoslavia (1918–1953). In: Kimble SL, Röwenkamp M (eds) New perspectives on European's Women Legal History. Routledge, New York, pp 174–197
Stojanović D (2013) Iza zavese: ogledi iz društvene istorije Srbije 1890-2013. Udruženje za društvenu istoriju, Belgrade
Todorova M (2009) Imagining the Balkans. Oxford University Press, New York
Tomić S (2014) The travel writings of Jelena J. Dimitrijević: Feminist Politics and Privileged Intellectual Identity. In: Bogdanović J, Robinson LF, Marjanović I (eds) On the very edge: modernism and modernity in the arts and architecture of interwar Serbia. Leuven University Press, Leuven, pp 115–133
Trgovčević L (2011) The professional emancipation of women in 19th-century Serbia. Serbian Studies. https://www.thefreelibrary.com/The+professional+emancipation+of+women+in+19th-century+Serbia.-a0357472010
Tyler R (1930) The Eastern reparations settlement. Foreign Aff 9:106–117
Tzouvala N (2019) 'These Ancient Arenas of Racial Struggles': International Law and the Balkans, 1878–1949. Eur J Int Law 29:1149–1171
Vellacott J (2001) Feminism as if all people mattered: working to remove the causes of war, 1919–1929. Contemp Eur History 10:375–394
Vlajić M (1928) Žene sudije. Ženski pokret, June 1
Vučetić R (2007) Žena u gradu – između rezervata privatnog i osvajanja mesta u javnom životu (1918-1941). In: Ristović M (ed) Privatni život kod Srba u 20. veku. Clio, Belgrade, pp 131–164
Vučo N (1968) Agrarna kriza u Jugoslaviji 1930-1934. Prosveta, Belgrade
Wälde T (2004) The Serbian loans case - a precedent for investment treaty protection of foreign debt? Transnational Dispute Management. URL: www.transnational-dispute-management.com/article.asp?key=316

Sanja Djajić is tenured Professor of Public International Law at the University of Novi Sad School of Law. She studied at law schools in Serbia (Belgrade, Novi Sad), United States (UCONN School of Law) and United Kingdom (LSE) and was a visiting fellow at several universities such as LSE, K.U. Leuven and Vienna. Ron Brown and Chevening scholar. While her original and main professional focus is public international law, she has come to combine a variety of legal disciplines both academically and in practice, such as human rights, international investment law, history and theory of international law, and application of international law within national legal systems. She has acted as counsel and a member of legal teams in several international investment proceedings under UNCITRAL and ICSID arbitration rules, before the European Court for Human Rights, and before the International Court of Justice. She has served as arbitrator with the Permanent Arbitration of the Chamber of Commerce of Serbia. Professor Sanja Djajić is author of publications on international dispute settlement, international investment law, and human rights law. Current research projects and interests include the history of international law, freedom of expression, human right to water, investment arbitration and countries in transition, and the national application of the European Convention on Human Rights.

www.ingramcontent.com/pod-product-compliance
Ingram Content Group UK Ltd.
Pitfield, Milton Keynes, MK11 3LW, UK
UKHW020808290926
15470UKWH00003B/1033
* 9 7 8 3 0 3 1 1 3 4 5 8 6 *